CHRISTOPHER AND COLUMBUS

By

ELIZABETH VON ARNIM

Double 9
BOOKS

CHRISTOPHER AND COLUMBUS
by ELIZABETH VON ARNIM

ISBN: 978-93-59955-80-3
Published by

DOUBLE 9 BOOKS

2/13-B, Ansari Road
Daryaganj, New Delhi – 110002
info@double9books.com
www.double9books.com
Tel. 011-40042856

ABOUT THE AUTHOR

Elizabeth von Arnim (31 August 1866 – 9 February 1941) was an English novelist born Mary Annette Beauchamp. She was born in Australia, married a German aristocrat, and her early works take place in Germany. Her first marriage elevated her to the title of Countess von Arnim-Schlagenthin, and her second marriage elevated her to the title of Countess Russell. Following the death of her first husband, she had a three-year affair with novelist H. G. Wells, and then married Frank Russell, the elder brother of Nobel laureate and philosopher Bertrand Russell. Katherine Mansfield, a New Zealand-born novelist, was her cousin. Though she was born May, her debut novel introduced her to readers as Elizabeth, which she later became to friends and family. Elizabeth von Arnim is credited with her writings. She wrote only one novel under the pen name Alice Cholmondeley, Christine, in 1917. She was born on Kirribilli Point in Sydney, Australia, to rich shipping entrepreneur Henry Herron Beauchamp (1825-1907) and Elizabeth (nicknamed Louey) Weiss Lassetter (1836-1919). Her family referred to her as May. She was the youngest of five siblings. Kathleen Beauchamp, who was born in New Zealand and wrote under the pen name Katherine Mansfield, was one of her cousins. The family went to England when she was three years old, where they lived in London but also spent several years in Switzerland.

CONTENTS

CHAPTER I 7

CHAPTER II..15

CHAPTER III...24

CHAPTER IV...33

CHAPTER V 37

CHAPTER VI...44

CHAPTER VII 51

CHAPTER VIII...61

CHAPTER IX...70

CHAPTER X 83

CHAPTER XI...89

CHAPTER XII 96

CHAPTER XIII 100

CHAPTER XIV 107

CHAPTER XV 116

CHAPTER XVI...124

CHAPTER XVII..131

CHAPTER XVIII 134

CHAPTER XIX 143

CHAPTER XX 151

CHAPTER XXI 160

CHAPTER XXII..166

CHAPTER XXIII 174

CHAPTER XXIV 180

CHAPTER XXV..192

CHAPTER XXVI 201

CHAPTER XXVII...207

CHAPTER XXVIII..217

CHAPTER XXIX...224

CHAPTER XXX..232

CHAPTER XXXI...238

CHAPTER XXXII 247

CHAPTER XXXIII..254

CHAPTER XXXIV...262

CHAPTER XXXV 268

CHAPTER XXXVI...275

CHAPTER XXXVII 283

CHAPTER XXXVIII...291

CHAPTER I

Their names were really Anna-Rose and Anna-Felicitas; but they decided, as they sat huddled together in a corner of the second-class deck of the American liner *St. Luke*, and watched the dirty water of the Mersey slipping past and the Liverpool landing-stage disappearing into mist, and felt that it was comfortless and cold, and knew they hadn't got a father or a mother, and remembered that they were aliens, and realized that in front of them lay a great deal of gray, uneasy, dreadfully wet sea, endless stretches of it, days and days of it, with waves on top of it to make them sick and submarines beneath it to kill them if they could, and knew that they hadn't the remotest idea, not the very remotest, what was before them when and if they did get across to the other side, and knew that they were refugees, castaways, derelicts, two wretched little Germans who were neither really Germans nor really English because they so unfortunately, so complicatedly were both,—they decided, looking very calm and determined and sitting very close together beneath the rug their English aunt had given them to put round their miserable alien legs, that what they really were, were Christopher and Columbus, because they were setting out to discover a New World.

"It's very pleasant," said Anna-Rose. "It's very pleasant to go and discover America. All for ourselves."

It was Anna-Rosa who suggested their being Christopher and Columbus. She was the elder by twenty minutes. Both had had their seventeenth birthday—and what a birthday: no cake, no candles, no kisses and wreaths and home-made poems; but then, as Anna-Felicitas pointed out, to comfort Anna-Rose who was taking it hard, you can't get blood out of an aunt—only a month before. Both were very German outside and very English inside. Both had fair hair, and the sorts of chins Germans have, and eyes the colour of the sky in August along the shores of the Baltic. Their noses were brief, and had been objected to in Germany, where, if you are a Junker's daughter, you are expected to show it in your nose. Anna-Rose had a tight little body, inclined to the round. Anna-Felicitas, in spite of being a twin, seemed to have made the most of her twenty extra minutes to grow more in; anyhow she was tall and thin, and she drooped; and having perhaps grown quicker made her eyes more dreamy, and her thoughts more slow. And both held their heads up with a great air of calm whenever anybody on the ship looked at them, as who should say serenely, "We're *thoroughly* happy, and having the time of our lives."

For worlds they wouldn't have admitted to each other that they were even aware of such a thing as being anxious or wanting to cry. Like other persons of English blood, they never were so cheerful nor pretended to be so much amused as when they were right down on the very bottom of their luck. Like other persons of German blood, they had the squashiest corners deep in their hearts, where they secretly clung to cakes and Christmas trees, and fought a tendency to celebrate every possible anniversary, both dead and alive.

The gulls, circling white against the gloomy sky over the rubbish that floated on the Mersey, made them feel extraordinarily forlorn. Empty boxes, bits of straw, orange-peel, a variety of dismal dirtiness lay about on the sullen water; England was slipping away, England, their mother's country, the country of their dreams ever since they could remember—and the *St. Luke* with a loud screech had suddenly stopped.

Neither of them could help jumping a little at that and getting an inch closer together beneath the rug. Surely it wasn't a submarine already?

"We're Christopher and Columbus," said Anna-Rose quickly, changing as it were the unspoken conversation.

As the eldest she had a great sense of her responsibility toward her twin, and considered it one of her first duties to cheer and encourage her. Their mother had always cheered and encouraged them, and hadn't seemed to mind anything, however awful it was, that happened to her,—such as, for instance, when the war began and they three, their father having died some years before, left their home up by the Baltic, just as there was the most heavenly weather going on, and the garden was a dream, and the blue Chinchilla cat had produced four perfect kittens that very day,—all of whom had to be left to what Anna-Felicitas, whose thoughts if slow were picturesque once she had got them, called the tender mercies of a savage and licentious soldiery,—and came by slow and difficult stages to England; or such as when their mother began catching cold and didn't seem at last ever able to leave off catching cold, and though she tried to pretend she didn't mind colds and that they didn't matter, it was plain that these colds did at last matter very much, for between them they killed her.

Their mother had always been cheerful and full of hope. Now that she was dead, it was clearly Anna-Rose's duty, as the next eldest in the family, to carry on the tradition and discountenance too much drooping in Anna-

Felicitas. Anna-Felicitas was staring much too thoughtfully at the deepening gloom of the late afternoon sky and the rubbish brooding on the face of the waters, and she had jumped rather excessively when the *St. Luke* stopped so suddenly, just as if it were putting on the brake hard, and emitted that agonized whistle.

"We're Christopher and Columbus," said Anna-Rose quickly, "and we're going to discover America."

"Very well," said Anna-Felicitas. "I'll be Christopher."

"No. I'll be Christopher," said Anna-Rose.

"Very well," said Anna-Felicitas, who was the most amiable, acquiescent person in the world. "Then I suppose I'll have to be Columbus. But I think Christopher sounds prettier."

Both rolled their r's incurably. It was evidently in their blood, for nothing, no amount of teaching and admonishment, could get them out of it. Before they were able to talk at all, in those happy days when parents make astounding assertions to other parents about the intelligence and certain future brilliancy of their offspring, and the other parents, however much they may pity such self-deception, can't contradict, because after all it just possibly may be so, the most foolish people occasionally producing geniuses,—in those happy days of undisturbed bright castle-building, the mother, who was English, of the two derelicts now huddled on the dank deck of the *St. Luke*, said to the father, who was German, "At any rate these two blessed little bundles of deliciousness"—she had one on each arm and was tickling their noses alternately with her eyelashes, and they were screaming for joy—"won't have to learn either German or English. They'll just *know* them."

"Perhaps," said the father, who was a cautious man.

"They're born bi-lingual," said the mother; and the twins wheezed and choked with laughter, for she was tickling them beneath their chins, softly fluttering her eyelashes along the creases of fat she thought so adorable.

"Perhaps," said the father.

"It gives them a tremendous start," said the mother; and the twins squirmed in a dreadful ecstasy, for she had now got to their ears.

"Perhaps," said the father.

But what happened was that they didn't speak either language. Not, that is, as a native should. Their German bristled with mistakes. They spoke it with a foreign accent. It was copious, but incorrect. Almost the last thing their father, an accurate man, said to them as he lay dying, had to do with a misplaced dative. And when they talked English it rolled about uncontrollably on its r's, and had a great many long words in it got from Milton, and Dr. Johnson, and people like that, whom their mother had particularly loved, but as they talked far more to their mother than to their father, who was a man of much briefness in words though not in temper, they were better on the whole at English than German.

Their mother, who loved England more the longer she lived away from it,—"As one does; and the same principle," Anna-Rose explained to Anna-Felicitas when they had lived some time with their aunt and uncle, "applies to relations, aunts' husbands, and the clergy,"—never tired of telling her children about it, and its poetry, and its spirit, and the greatness and glory of its points of view. They drank it all in and believed every word of it, for so did their mother; and as they grew up they flung themselves on all the English books they could lay hands upon, and they read with their mother and learned by heart most of the obviously beautiful things; and because she glowed with enthusiasm they glowed too—Anna-Rose in a flare and a flash, Anna-Felicitas slow and steadily. They adored their mother. Whatever she loved they loved blindly. It was a pity she died. She died soon after the war began. They had been so happy, so *dreadfully* happy....

"You can't be Christopher," said Anna-Rose, giving herself a shake, for here she was thinking of her mother, and it didn't do to think of one's mother, she found; at least, not when one is off to a new life and everything is all promise because it isn't anything else, and not if one's mother happened to have been so—well, so fearfully sweet. "You can't be Christopher, because, you see, I'm the eldest."

Anna-Felicitas didn't see what being the eldest had to do with it, but she only said, "Very well," in her soft voice, and expressed a hope that Anna-Rose would see her way not to call her Col for short. "I'm afraid you will, though," she added, "and then I shall feel so like Onkel Nicolas."

This was their German uncle, known during his life-time, which had abruptly left off when the twins were ten, as Onkel Col; a very ancient person, older by far even than their father, who had seemed so very old. But Onkel Col had been older than anybody at all, except the pictures of the *liebe Gott* in Blake's illustrations to the Book of Job. He came to a bad end. Neither their father nor their mother told them anything except that Onkel Col was dead; and their father put a black band round the left sleeve of his tweed country suit and was more good-tempered than ever, and their mother, when they questioned her, just said that poor Onkel Col had gone to heaven, and that in future they would speak of him as Onkel Nicolas, because it was more respectful.

"But why does mummy call him poor, when he's gone to heaven?" Anna-Felicitas asked Anna-Rose privately, in the recesses of the garden.

"First of all," said Anna-Rose, who, being the eldest, as she so often explained to her sister, naturally knew more about everything, "because the angels won't like him. Nobody *could* like Onkel Col. Even if they're angels. And though they're obliged to have him there because he was such a very good man, they won't talk to him much or notice him much when God isn't looking. And second of all, because you *are* poor when you get to heaven. Everybody is poor in heaven. Nobody takes their things with them, and all Onkel Col's money is still on earth. He couldn't even take his clothes with him."

"Then is he quite—did Onkel Col go there quite—"

Anna-Felicitas stopped. The word seemed too awful in connection with Onkel Col, that terrifying old gentleman who had roared at them from the folds of so many wonderful wadded garments whenever they were led in, trembling, to see him, for he had gout and was very terrible; and it seemed particularly awful when one thought of Onkel Col going to heaven, which was surely of all places the most *endimanché*.

"Of course," nodded Anna-Rose; but even she dropped her voice a little. She peeped about among the bushes a moment, then put her mouth close to Anna-Felicitas's ear, and whispered, "Stark."

They stared at one another for a space with awe and horror in their eyes.

"You see," then went on Anna-Rose rather quickly, hurrying away from the awful vision, "one knows one doesn't have clothes in heaven because they don't have the moth there. It says so in the Bible. And you can't have the moth without having anything for it to go into."

"Then they don't have to have naphthalin either," said Anna-Felicitas, "and don't all have to smell horrid in the autumn when they take their furs out."

"No. And thieves don't break in and steal either in heaven," continued Anna-Rose, "and the reason why is that there *isn't* anything to steal."

"There's angels," suggested Anna-Felicitas after a pause, for she didn't like to think there was nothing really valuable in heaven.

"Oh, nobody ever steals *them*," said Anna-Rose.

Anna-Felicitas's slow thoughts revolved round this new uncomfortable view of heaven. It seemed, if Anna-Rose were right, and she always was right for she said so herself, that heaven couldn't be such a safe place after all, nor such a kind place. Thieves could break in and steal if they wanted to.

She had a proper horror of thieves. She was sure the night would certainly come when they would break into her father's *Schloss*, or, as her English nurse called it, her dear Papa's slosh; and she was worried that poor Onkel Col should be being snubbed up there, and without anything to put on, which would make being snubbed so much worse, for clothes did somehow comfort one.

She took her worries to the nursemaid, and choosing a moment when she knew Anna-Rose wished to be unnoticed, it being her hour for inconspicuously eating unripe apples at the bottom of the orchard, an exercise Anna-Felicitas only didn't indulge in because she had learned through affliction that her inside, fond and proud of it as she was, was yet not of that superior and blessed kind that suffers green apples gladly—she sought out the nursemaid, whose name, too, confusingly, was Anna, and led the conversation up to heaven and the possible conditions prevailing in it by asking her to tell her, in strict confidence and as woman to woman, what she thought Onkel Col exactly looked like at that moment.

"Unrecognizable," said the nursemaid promptly.

"Unrecognizable?" echoed Anna-Felicitas.

And the nursemaid, after glancing over her shoulder to see if the governess were nowhere in sight, told Anna-Felicitas the true story of Onkel Col's end: which is so bad that it isn't fit to be put in any book except one with an appendix.

A stewardess passed just as Anna-Felicitas was asking Anna-Rose not to remind her of these grim portions of the past by calling her Col, a stewardess in such a very clean white cap that she looked both reliable and benevolent, while secretly she was neither.

"Can you please tell us why we're stopping?" Anna-Rose inquired of her politely, leaning forward to catch her attention as she hurried by.

The stewardess allowed her roving eye to alight for a moment on the two objects beneath the rug. Their chairs were close together, and the rug covered them both up to their chins. Over the top of it their heads appeared, exactly alike as far as she could see in the dusk; round heads, each with a blue knitted cap pulled well over its ears, and round eyes staring at her with what anybody except the stewardess would have recognized as a passionate desire for some sort of reassurance. They might have been seven instead of seventeen for all the stewardess could tell. They looked younger than anything she had yet seen sitting alone on a deck and asking questions. But she was an exasperated widow, who had never had children and wasn't to be touched by anything except a tip, besides despising, because she was herself a second-class stewardess, all second-class passengers,—"As one does," Anna-Rose explained later on to Anna-Felicitas, "and the same principle applies to Jews." So she said with an acidity completely at variance with the promise of her cap, "Ask the Captain," and disappeared.

The twins looked at each other. They knew very well that captains on ships were mighty beings who were not asked questions.

"She's trifling with us," murmured Anna-Felicitas.

"Yes," Anna-Rose was obliged to admit, though the thought was repugnant to her that they should look like people a stewardess would dare trifle with.

"Perhaps she thinks we're younger than we are," she said after a silence.

"Yes. She couldn't see how long our dresses are, because of the rug."

"No. And it's only that end of us that really shows we're grown up."

"Yes. She ought to have seen us six months ago."

Indeed she ought. Even the stewardess would have been surprised at the activities and complete appearance of the two pupæ now rolled motionless in the rug. For, six months ago, they had both been probationers in a children's hospital in Worcestershire, arrayed, even as the stewardess, in spotless caps, hurrying hither and thither with trays of food, sweeping and washing up, learning to make beds in a given time, and be deft, and quick, and never tired, and always punctual.

This place had been got them by the efforts and influence of their Aunt Alice, that aunt who had given them the rug on their departure and who had omitted to celebrate their birthday. She was an amiable aunt, but she didn't understand about birthdays. It was the first one they had had since they were complete orphans, and so they were rather sensitive about it. But they hadn't cried, because since their mother's death they had done with crying. What could there ever again be in the world bad enough to cry about after that? And besides, just before she dropped away from them into the unconsciousness out of which she never came back, but instead just dropped a little further into death, she had opened her eyes unexpectedly and caught them sitting together in a row by her bed, two images of agony, with tears rolling down their swollen faces and their noses in a hopeless state, and after looking at them a moment as if she had slowly come up from some vast depth and distance and were gradually recognizing them, she had whispered with a flicker of the old encouraging smile that had comforted every hurt and bruise they had ever had, "*Don't cry* ... little darlings, *don't cry*...."

But on that first birthday after her death they had got more and more solemn as time passed, and breakfast was cleared away, and there were no sounds, prick up their ears as they might, of subdued preparations in the next room, no stealthy going up and down stairs to fetch the presents, and at last no hope at all of the final glorious flinging open of the door and the vision inside of two cakes all glittering with candles, each on a table covered with flowers and all the things one has most wanted.

Their aunt didn't know. How should she? England was a great and beloved country, but it didn't have proper birthdays.

"Every country has one drawback," Anna-Rose explained to Anna-Felicitas when the morning was finally over, in case she should by any chance be thinking badly of the dear country that had produced their mother as well as Shakespeare, "and not knowing about birthdays is England's."

"There's Uncle Arthur," said Anna-Felicitas, whose honest mind groped continually after accuracy.

"Yes," Anna-Rose admitted after a pause. "Yes. There's Uncle Arthur."

CHAPTER II

Uncle Arthur was the husband of Aunt Alice. He didn't like foreigners, and said so. He never had liked them and had always said so. It wasn't the war at all, it was the foreigners. But as the war went on, and these German nieces of his wife became more and more, as he told her, a blighted nuisance, so did he become more and more pointed, and said he didn't mind French foreigners, nor Russian foreigners; and a few weeks later, that it wasn't Italian foreigners either that he minded; and still later, that nor was it foreigners indigenous to the soil of countries called neutral. These things he said aloud at meals in a general way. To his wife when alone he said much more.

Anna-Rose, who was nothing if not intrepid, at first tried to soften his heart by offering to read aloud to him in the evenings when he came home weary from his daily avocations, which were golf. Her own suggestion instantly projected a touching picture on her impressionable imagination of youth, grateful for a roof over its head, in return alleviating the tedium of crabbed age by introducing its uncle, who from his remarks was evidently unacquainted with them, to the best productions of the great masters of English literature.

But Uncle Arthur merely stared at her with a lacklustre eye when she proposed it, from his wide-legged position on the hearthrug, where he was moving money about in trouser-pockets of the best material. And later on she discovered that he had always supposed the "Faery Queen," and "Adonais," and "In Memoriam," names he had heard at intervals during his life, for he was fifty and such things do sometimes get mentioned were well-known racehorses.

Uncle Arthur, like Onkel Col, was a very good man, and though he said things about foreigners he did stick to these unfortunate alien nieces longer than one would have supposed possible if one had overheard what he said to Aunt Alice in the seclusion of their bed. His ordered existence, shaken enough by the war, Heaven knew, was shaken in its innermost parts, in its very marrow, by the arrival of the two Germans. Other people round about had Belgians in their homes, and groaned; but who but he, the most immensely British of anybody, had Germans? And he couldn't groan, because they were, besides being motherless creatures, his own wife's flesh and blood. Not openly at least could he groan; but he could and did do it in bed. Why on earth that silly mother of theirs couldn't have stayed quietly on her Pomeranian sand-heap where she belonged, instead of coming gallivanting over to England, and then when she had got there not even decently staying alive and seeing to her children herself, he at frequent intervals told Aunt Alice in bed that he would like to know.

Aunt Alice, who after twenty years of life with Uncle Arthur was both silent and sleek (for he fed her well), sighed and said nothing. She herself was quietly going through very much on behalf of her nieces. Jessup didn't like handing dishes to Germans. The tradespeople twitted the cook with having to cook for them and were facetious about sausages and asked how one made sauerkraut. Her acquaintances told her they were very sorry for her, and said they supposed she knew what she was doing and that it was all right about spies, but really one heard such strange things, one never could possibly tell even with children; and regularly the local policeman bicycled over to see if the aliens, who were registered at the county-town police-station, were still safe. And then they looked so very German, Aunt Alice felt. There was no mistaking them. And every time they opened their mouths there were all those r's rolling about. She hardly liked callers to find her nieces in her drawing-room at tea-time, they were so difficult to explain; yet they were too old to shut up in a nursery.

After three months of them, Uncle Arthur suggested sending them back to Germany; but their consternation had been so great and their entreaties to be kept where they were so desperate that he said no more about that. Besides, they told him that if they went back there they would be sure to be shot as spies, for over there nobody would believe they were German, just as over here nobody would believe they were English; and besides, this was in those days of the war when England was still regarding Germany as more mistaken than vicious, and was as full as ever of the tradition of great and elaborate indulgence and generosity toward a foe, and Uncle Arthur, whatever he might say, was not going to be behind his country in generosity.

Yet as time passed, and feeling tightened, and the hideous necklace of war grew more and more frightful with each fresh bead of horror strung upon it, Uncle Arthur, though still in principle remaining good, in practice found himself vindictive. He was saddled; that's what he was. Saddled with this monstrous unmerited burden. He, the most patriotic of Britons, looked at askance by his best friends, being given notice by his old servants, having particular attention paid his house at night by the police, getting anonymous letters about lights seen in his upper windows the nights; the Zeppelins came, which were the windows of the floor those blighted twins slept on, and all because he had married Aunt Alice.

At this period Aunt Alice went to bed with reluctance. It was not a place she had ever gone to very willingly since she married Uncle Arthur, for he was the kind of husband who rebukes in bed; but now she was downright reluctant. It was painful to her to be told that she had brought this disturbance into Uncle Arthur's life by having let him marry her. Inquiring backwards into her recollections it appeared to her that she had had no say at all about being married, but that Uncle Arthur had told her she was going to be, and then that she had been. Which was what had indeed happened; for Aunt Alice was a round little woman even in those days, nicely though not obtrusively padded with agreeable fat at the corners, and her skin, just as now, had the moist delicacy that comes from eating a great many chickens. Also she suggested, just as now, most of the things most men want to come home to,—slippers, and drawn curtains, and a blazing fire, and peace within one's borders, and even, as Anna-Rose pointed out privately to Anna-Felicitas after they had come across them for the first time, she suggested muffins; and so, being in these varied fashions succulent, she was doomed to make some good man happy. But she did find it real hard work.

It grew plain to Aunt Alice after another month of them that Uncle Arthur would not much longer endure his nieces, and that even if he did she would not be able to endure Uncle Arthur. The thought was very dreadful to her that she was being forced to choose between two duties, and that she could not fulfil both. It came to this at last, that she must either stand by her nieces, her dead sister's fatherless children, and face all the difficulties and discomforts of such a standing by, go away with them, take care of them, till the war was over; or she must stand by Arthur.

She chose Arthur.

How could she, for nieces she had hardly seen, abandon her husband? Besides, he had scolded her so steadily during the whole of their married life that she was now unalterably attached to him. Sometimes a wild thought did for a moment illuminate the soothing dusk of her mind, the thought of doing the heroic thing, leaving him for them, and helping and protecting the two poor aliens till happier days should return. If there were any good stuff in Arthur would he not recognize, however angry he might be, that she was doing at least a Christian thing? But this illumination would soon die out. Her comforts choked it. She was too well-fed. After twenty years of it, she no longer had the figure for lean and dangerous enterprises.

And having definitely chosen Arthur, she concentrated what she had of determination in finding an employment for her nieces that would remove them beyond the range of his growing wrath. She found it in a children's hospital as far away as Worcestershire, a hospital subscribed to very largely by Arthur, for being a good man he subscribed to hospitals. The matron objected, but Aunt Alice overrode the matron; and from January to April Uncle Arthur's house was pure from Germans.

Then they came back again.

It had been impossible to keep them. The nurses wouldn't work with them. The sick children had relapses when they discovered who it was who brought them their food, and cried for their mothers. It had been arranged between Aunt Alice and the matron that the unfortunate nationality of her nieces should not be mentioned. They were just to be Aunt Alice's nieces, the Miss Twinklers,—("We will leave out the von," said Aunt Alice, full of unnatural cunning. "They have a von, you know, poor things—such a very labelling thing to have. But Twinkler without it might quite well be English. Who can possibly tell? It isn't as though they had had some shocking name like Bismarck.")

Nothing, however, availed against the damning evidence of the rolled r's. Combined with the silvery fair hair and the determined little mouths and chins, it was irresistible. Clearly they were foreigners, and equally clearly they were not Italians, or Russians, or French. Within a week the nurses spoke of them in private as Fritz and Franz. Within a fortnight a deputation of staff sisters went to the matron and asked, on patriotic grounds, for the removal of the Misses Twinkler. The matron, with the fear of Uncle Arthur in her heart, for he was altogether the biggest subscriber, sharply sent the deputation about its business; and being a matron of great competence and courage she would probably have continued to be able to force the new probationers upon the nurses if it had not been for the inability, which was conspicuous, of the younger Miss Twinkler to acquire efficiency.

In vain did Anna-Rose try to make up for Anna-Felicitas's shortcomings by a double zeal, a double willingness and cheerfulness. Anna-Felicitas was a born dreamer, a born bungler with her hands and feet. She not only never from first to last succeeded in filling the thirty hot-water bottles, which were her care, in thirty minutes, which was her duty, but every time she met a pail standing about she knocked against it and it fell over. Patients and nurses watched her approach with apprehension. Her ward was in a constant condition of flood.

"It's because she's thinking of something else," Anna-Rose tried eagerly to explain to the indignant sister-in-charge.

"Thinking of something else!" echoed the sister.

"She reads, you see, a lot—whenever she gets the chance she reads—"

"Reads!" echoed the sister.

"And then, you see, she gets thinking—"

"Thinking! Reading doesn't make *me* think."

"With much regret," wrote the matron to Aunt Alice, "I am obliged to dismiss your younger niece, Nurse Twinkler II. She has no vocation for nursing. On the other hand, your elder niece is shaping well and I shall be pleased to keep her on."

"But I can't stop on," Anna-Rose said to the matron when she announced these decisions to her. "I can't be separated from my sister. I'd like very much to know what would become of that poor child without me to look after her. You forget I'm the eldest."

The matron put down her pen,—she was a woman who made many notes—and stared at Nurse Twinkler. Not in this fashion did her nurses speak to her. But Anna-Rose, having been brought up in a spot remote from everything except love and laughter, had all the fearlessness of ignorance; and in her extreme youth and smallness, with her eyes shining and her face heated she appeared to the matron rather like an indignant kitten.

"Very well," said the matron gravely, suppressing a smile. "One should always do what one considers one's first duty."

So the Twinklers went back to Uncle Arthur, and the matron was greatly relieved, for she certainly didn't want them, and Uncle Arthur said Damn.

"Arthur," gently reproved his wife.

"I say Damn and I mean Damn," said Uncle Arthur. "What the hell can we—"

"Arthur," said his wife.

"I say, what the hell can we do with a couple of Germans? If people wouldn't swallow them last winter are they going to swallow them any better now? God, what troubles a man lets himself in for when he marries!"

"I do beg you, Arthur, not to use those coarse words," said Aunt Alice, tears in her gentle eyes.

There followed a period of desperate exertion on the part of Aunt Alice. She answered advertisements and offered the twins as nursery governesses, as cheerful companions, as mothers' helps, even as orphans willing to be adopted. She relinquished every claim on salaries, she offered them for nothing, and at last she offered them accompanied by a bonus. "Their mother was English. They are quite English," wrote Aunt Alice innumerable times in innumerable letters. "I feel bound, however, to tell you that they once had a German father, but of course it was through no fault of their own," etc., etc. Aunt Alice's hand ached with writing letters; and any solution of the problem that might possibly have been arrived at came to nothing because Anna-Rose would not be separated from Anna-Felicitas, and if it was difficult to find anybody who would take on one German nobody at all could be found to take on two.

Meanwhile Uncle Arthur grew nightly more dreadful in bed. Aunt Alice was at her wits' end, and took to crying helplessly. The twins racked their brains to find a way out, quite as anxious to relieve Uncle Arthur of their presence as he was to be relieved. If only they could be independent, do something, work, go as housemaids,—anything.

They concocted an anonymous-advertisement and secretly sent it to *The Times*, clubbing their pocket-money together to pay for it. The advertisement was:

> Energetic Sisters of belligerent ancestry but unimpeachable sympathies wish for any sort of work consistent with respectability. No objection to being demeaned.

Anna-Felicitas inquired what that last word meant for it was Anna-Rose's word, and Anna-Rose explained that it meant not minding things like being housemaids. "Which we don't," said Anna-Rose. "Upper and Under. I'll be Upper, of course, because I'm the eldest."

Anna-Felicitas suggested putting in what it meant then, for she regarded it with some doubt, but Anna-Rose, it being her word, liked it, and explained that it Put a whole sentence into a nut-shell, and wouldn't change it.

No one answered this advertisement except a society in London for helping alien enemies in distress.

"Charity," said Anna-Rose, turning up her nose.

"And fancy thinking *us* enemies," said Anna-Felicitas, "Us. While mummy—" Her eyes filled with tears. She kept them back, however, behind convenient long eye-lashes.

Then they saw an advertisement in the front page of *The Times* that they instantly answered without saying a word to Aunt Alice. The advertisement was:

> Slightly wounded Officer would be glad to find intelligent
> and interesting companion who can drive a 14 h.p.
> Humber. Emoluments
> by arrangement.

"We'll *tell* him we're intelligent and interesting," said Anna-Rose, eagerly.

"Yes—who knows if we wouldn't be really, if we were given a chance?" said Anna-Felicitas, quite flushed with excitement.

"And if he engages us we'll take him on in turns, so that the emoluments won't have to be doubled."

"Yes—because he mightn't like paying twice over."

"Yes—and while the preliminaries are being settled we could be learning to drive Uncle Arthur's car."

"Yes—except that it's a Daimler, and aren't they different?"

"Yes—but only about the same difference as there is between a man and a woman. A man and a woman are both human beings, you know. And Daimlers and Humbers are both cars."

"I see," said Anna-Felicitas; but she didn't.

They wrote an enthusiastic answer that very day.

The only thing they were in doubt about, they explained toward the end of the fourth sheet, when they had got to politenesses and were requesting the slightly wounded officer to allow them to express their sympathy with his wounds, was that they had not yet had an opportunity of driving a Humber car, but that this opportunity, of course, would be instantly provided by his engaging them. Also, would he kindly tell them if it was a male companion he desired to have, because if so it was very unfortunate, for neither of them were males, but quite the contrary.

They got no answer to this for three weeks, and had given up all hope and come to the depressing conclusion that they must have betrayed their want of intelligence and interestingness right away, when one day a letter came from General Headquarters in France, addressed *To Both the Miss Twinklers,* and it was a long letter, pages long, from the slightly wounded officer, telling them he had been patched up again and sent back to the front, and their answer to his advertisement had been forwarded to him there, and that he had had heaps of other answers to it, and that the one he had liked best of all was theirs; and that some day he hoped when he was back again, and able to drive himself, to show them how glorious motoring was, if their mother would bring them,—quick motoring in his racing car, sixty miles an hour motoring, flashing through the wonders of the New Forest, where he lived. And then there was a long bit about what the New Forest must be looking like just then, all quiet in the spring sunshine, with lovely dappled bits of shade underneath the big beeches, and the heather just coming alive, and all the winding solitary roads so full of peace, so empty of noise.

"Write to me, you two children," said the letter at the end. "You've no idea what it's like getting letters from home out here. Write and tell me what you do and what the garden is like these fine afternoons. The lilacs must be nearly done, but I'm sure there's the smell of them still about, and I'm sure you have a beautiful green close-cut lawn, and tea is brought out on to it, and there's no sound, no sort of sound, except birds, and you two laughing, and I daresay a jolly dog barking somewhere just for fun and not because he's angry."

The letter was signed (Captain) John Desmond, and there was a scrawl in the corner at the end: "It's for jolly little English kids like you that we're fighting, God bless you. Write to me again soon."

"English kids like us!"

They looked at each other. They had not mentioned their belligerent ancestry in their letter. They felt uncomfortable, and as if Captain Desmond were fighting for them, as it were, under false pretences. They also wondered why he should conclude they were kids.

They wrote to him again, explaining that they were not exactly what could be described as English, but on the other hand neither were they exactly what could be described as German. "We would be very glad indeed if we were really *something*," they added.

But after their letter had been gone only a few days they saw in the list of casualties in *The Times* that Captain John Desmond had been killed.

And then one day the real solution was revealed, and it was revealed to Uncle Arthur as he sat in his library on a wet Sunday morning considering his troubles in detail.

Like most great ideas it sprang full-fledged into being,—obvious, unquestionable, splendidly simple,—out of a trifle. For, chancing to raise his heavy and disgusted eyes to the bookshelves in front of him, they rested on one particular book, and on the back of this book stood out in big gilt letters the word

AMERICA

There were other words on its back, but this one alone stood out, and it had all the effect of a revelation.

There. That was it. Of course. That was the way out. Why the devil hadn't Alice thought of *that*? He knew some Americans; he didn't like them, but he knew them; and he would write to them, or Alice would write to them, and tell them the twins were coming. He would give the twins £200,—damn it, nobody could say that wasn't handsome, especially in war-time, and for a couple of girls who had no earthly sort of claim on him, whatever Alice might choose to think they had on her. Yet it was such a confounded mixed-up situation that he wasn't at all sure he wouldn't come under the Defence of the Realm Act, by giving them money, as aiding the enemy. Well, he would risk that. He would risk anything to be rid of them. Ship 'em off, that was the thing to do. They would fall on their feet right enough over there. America still swallowed Germans without making a face.

Uncle Arthur reflected for a moment with extreme disgust on the insensibility of the American palate. "Lost their chance, that's what *they've* done," he said to himself—for this was 1916, and America had not yet made her magnificent entry into the war—as he had already said to himself a hundred times. "Lost their chance of coming in on the side of civilization, and helping sweep the world up tidy of barbarism. Shoulder to shoulder with us, that's where *they* ought to have been. English-speaking races— duty to the world—" He then damned the Americans; but was suddenly interrupted by perceiving that if they had been shoulder to shoulder with him and England he wouldn't have been able to send them his wife's German nieces to take care of. There was, he conceded, that advantage resulting from their attitude. He could not, however, concede any others.

At luncheon he was very nearly gay. It was terrible to see Uncle Arthur very nearly gay, and both his wife and the twins were most uncomfortable. "I wonder what's the matter now," sighed Aunt Alice to herself, as she nervously crumbled her toast.

It could mean nothing good, Arthur in such spirits on a wet Sunday, when he hadn't been able to get his golf and the cook had overdone the joint.

CHAPTER III

And so, on a late September afternoon, the *St. Luke*, sliding away from her moorings, relieved Uncle Arthur of his burden.

It was final this time, for the two alien enemies once out of it would not be let into England again till after the war. The enemies themselves knew it was final; and the same knowledge that made Uncle Arthur feel so pleasant as he walked home across his park from golf to tea that for a moment he was actually of a mind to kiss Aunt Alice when he got in, and perhaps even address her in the language of resuscitated passion, which in Uncle Arthur's mouth was Old Girl,—an idea he abandoned, however, in case it should make her self-satisfied and tiresome—the same knowledge that produced these amiable effects in Uncle Arthur, made his alien nieces cling very close together as they leaned over the side of the *St. Luke* hungrily watching the people on the wharf.

For they loved England. They loved it with the love of youth whose enthusiasms have been led by an adored teacher always in one direction. And they were leaving that adored teacher, their mother, in England. It seemed like losing her a second time to go away, so far away, and leave her there. It was nonsense, they knew, to feel like that. She was with them just the same; wherever they went now she would be with them, and they could hear her saying at that very moment, "Little darlings, *don't* cry...." But it was a gloomy, drizzling afternoon, the sort of afternoon anybody might be expected to cry on, and not one of the people waving handkerchiefs were waving handkerchiefs to them.

"We ought to have hired somebody," thought Anna-Rose, eyeing the handkerchiefs with miserable little eyes.

"I believe I've gone and caught a cold," remarked Anna-Felicitas in her gentle, staid voice, for she was having a good deal of bother with her eyes and her nose, and could no longer conceal the fact that she was sniffing.

Anna-Rose discreetly didn't look at her. Then she suddenly whipped out her handkerchief and waved it violently.

Anna-Felicitas forgot her eyes and nose and craned her head forward. "Who are you waving to?" she asked, astonished.

"Good-bye!" cried Anna-Rose, waving, "Good-bye! Good-bye!"

"Who? Where? Who are you talking to?" asked Anna-Felicitas. "Has any one come to see us off?"

"Good-bye! Good-bye!" cried Anna-Rose.

The figures on the wharf were getting smaller, but not until they had faded into a blur did Anna-Rose leave off waving. Then she turned round and put her arm through Anna-Felicitas's and held on to her very tight for a minute.

"There wasn't anybody," she said. "Of course there wasn't. But do you suppose I was going to have us *looking* like people who aren't seen off?"

And she drew Anna-Felicitas away to the chairs, and when they were safely in them and rolled up to their chins in the rug, she added, "That man—" and then stopped. "What man?"

"Standing just behind us—"

"Was there a man?" asked Anna-Felicitas, who never saw men any more than she, in her brief career at the hospital, had seen pails.

"Yes. Looking as if in another moment he'd be sorry for us," said Anna-Rose.

"Sorry for us!" repeated Anna-Felicitas, roused to indignation.

"Yes. Did you ever?"

Anna-Felicitas said, with a great deal of energy while she put her handkerchief finally and sternly away, that she didn't ever; and after a pause Anna-Rose, remembering one of her many new responsibilities and anxieties—she had so many that sometimes for a time she didn't remember some of them—turned her head to Anna-Felicitas, and fixing a worried eye on her said, "You won't go forgetting your Bible, will you, Anna F.?"

"My Bible?" repeated Anna-Felicitas, looking blank.

"Your German Bible. The bit about *wenn die bösen Buben locken, so folge sie nicht.*"

Anna-Felicitas continued to look blank, but Anna-Rose with a troubled brow said again, "You won't go and forget that, will you, Anna F.?"

For Anna-Felicitas was very pretty. In most people's eyes she was very pretty, but in Anna-Rose's she was the most exquisite creature God had yet succeeded in turning out. Anna-Rose concealed this conviction from her. She wouldn't have told her for worlds. She considered it wouldn't have been at all good for her; and she had, up to this, and ever since they could both remember, jeered in a thoroughly sisterly fashion at her defects, concentrating particularly on her nose, on her leanness, and on the way, unless constantly reminded not to, she drooped.

But Anna-Rose secretly considered that the same nose that on her own face made no sort of a show at all, directly it got on to Anna-Felicitas's somehow was the dearest nose; and that her leanness was lovely,—the same sort of slender grace her mother had had in the days before the heart-breaking emaciation that was its last phase; and that her head was set so charmingly on her neck that when she drooped and forgot her father's constant injunction to sit up,—"For," had said her father at monotonously regular intervals, "a maiden should be as straight as a fir-tree,"—she only seemed to fall into even more attractive lines than when she didn't. And now that Anna-Rose alone had the charge of looking after this abstracted and so charming younger sister, she felt it her duty somehow to convey to her while tactfully avoiding putting ideas into the poor child's head which might make her conceited, that it behoved her to conduct herself with discretion.

But she found tact a ticklish thing, the most difficult thing of all to handle successfully; and on this occasion hers was so elaborate, and so carefully wrapped up in Scriptural language, and German Scripture at that, that Anna-Felicitas's slow mind didn't succeed in disentangling her meaning, and after a space of staring at her with a mild inquiry in her eyes, she decided that perhaps she hadn't got one. She was much too polite though, to say so, and they sat in silence under the rug till the *St. Luke* whistled and stopped, and Anna-Rose began hastily to make conversation about Christopher and Columbus.

She was ashamed of having shown so much of her woe at leaving England. She hoped Anna-Felicitas hadn't noticed. She certainly wasn't going on like that. When the *St. Luke* whistled, she was ashamed that it wasn't only Anna-Felicitas who jumped. And the amount of brightness she put into her voice when she told Anna-Felicitas it was pleasant to go and discover America was such that that young lady, who if slow was sure, said to herself, "Poor little Anna-R., she's really taking it dreadfully to heart."

The *St. Luke* was only dropping anchor for the night in the Mersey, and would go on at daybreak. They gathered this from the talk of passengers walking up and down the deck in twos and threes and passing and repassing the chairs containing the silent figures with the round heads that might be either the heads of boys or of girls, and they were greatly relieved to think they wouldn't have to begin and be sea-sick for some hours yet.

"So couldn't we walk about a little?" suggested Anna-Felicitas, who was already stiff from sitting on the hard cane chair.

But Aunt Alice had told them that the thing to do on board a ship if they wished, as she was sure they did, not only to avoid being sick but also conspicuous, was to sit down in chairs the moment the ship got under way, and not move out of them till it stopped again. "Or, at least, as rarely as possible," amended Aunt Alice, who had never herself been further on a ship than to Calais, but recognized that it might be difficult to avoid moving sooner or later if it was New York you were going to. "Two such young girls travelling alone should be seen as seldom as ever you can manage. Your Uncle is sending you second-class for that very reason, because it is so much less conspicuous."

It was also very much less expensive, and Uncle Arthur's generosities were of the kind that suddenly grow impatient and leave off. Just as in eating he was as he said, for plain roast and boiled, and messes be damned, so in benefactions he was for lump sums and done with it; and the extras, the driblets, the here a little and there a little that were necessary, or were alleged by Aunt Alice to be necessary, before he finally got rid of those blasted twins, annoyed him so profoundly that when it came to taking their passage he could hardly be got not to send them in the steerage. This was too much, however, for Aunt Alice, whose maid was going with them as far as Euston and therefore would know what sort of tickets they had, and she insisted with such quiet obstinacy that they should be sent first-class that Uncle Arthur at last split the difference and consented to make it second. To her maid Aunt Alice also explained that second-class was less conspicuous.

Anna-Rose, mindful of Aunt Alice's words, hesitated as to the wisdom of walking about and beginning to be conspicuous already, but she too was stiff, and anything the matter with one's body has a wonderful effect, as she had already in her brief career had numerous occasions to observe, in doing away with prudent determinations. So, after cautiously looking round the corners to see if the man who was on the verge of being sorry for them were nowhere in sight, they walked up and down the damp, dark deck; and the motionlessness, and silence, and mist gave them a sensation of being hung mid-air in some strange empty Hades between two worlds.

Far down below there was a faint splash every now and then against the side of the *St. Luke* when some other steamer, invisible in the mist, felt her way slowly by. Out ahead lay the sea, the immense uneasy sea that was to last ten days and nights before they got to the other side, hour after hour of it, hour after hour of tossing across it further and further away; and forlorn and ghostly as the ship felt, it yet, because on either side of it were still the shores of England, didn't seem as forlorn and ghostly as the unknown land they were bound for. For suppose, Anna-Felicitas inquired of Anna-Rose, who had been privately asking herself the same thing, America didn't like them? Suppose the same sort of difficulties were waiting for them over there that had dogged their footsteps in England?

"First of all," said Anna-Rose promptly, for she prided herself on the readiness and clearness of her explanations, "America will like us, because I don't see why it shouldn't. We're going over to it in exactly the same pleasant spirit, Anna-F.,—and don't you go forgetting it and showing your disagreeable side—that the dove was in when it flew across the waters to the ark, and with olive branches in our beaks just the same as the dove's, only they're those two letters to Uncle Arthur's friends."

"But do you think Uncle Arthur's friends—" began Anna-Felicitas, who had great doubts as to everything connected with Uncle Arthur.

"And secondly," continued Anna-Rose a little louder, for she wasn't going to be interrupted, and having been asked a question liked to give all the information in her power, "secondly, America is the greatest of the neutrals except the *liebe Gott*, and is bound particularly to prize us because we're so unusually and peculiarly neutral. What ever was more neutral than you and me? We're neither one thing nor the other, and yet at the same time we're both." Anna-Felicitas remarked that it sounded rather as if they were the Athanasian Creed.

"And thirdly," went on Anna-Rose, waving this aside, "there's £200 waiting for us over there, which is a very nice warm thing to think of. We never had £200 waiting for us anywhere in our lives before, did we,—so you remember that, and don't get grumbling."

Anna-Felicitas mildly said that she wasn't grumbling but that she couldn't help thinking what a great deal depended on the goodwill of Uncle Arthur's friends, and wished it had been Aunt Alice's friends they had letters to instead, because Aunt Alice's friends were more likely to like her.

Anna-Rose rebuked her, and said that the proper spirit in which to start on a great adventure was one of faith and enthusiasm, and that one didn't have doubts.

Anna-Felicitas said she hadn't any doubts really, but that she was very hungry, not having had anything that could be called a meal since breakfast, and that she felt like the sheep in "Lycidas," the hungry ones who looked up and were not fed, and she quoted the lines in case Anna-Rose didn't recollect them (which Anna-Rose deplored, for she knew the lines by heart, and if there was any quoting to be done liked to do it herself), and said she felt just like that,—"Empty," said Anna-Felicitas, "and yet swollen. When do you suppose people have food on board ships? I don't believe we'd mind nearly so much about—oh well, about leaving England, if it was after dinner."

"I'm not minding leaving England," said Anna-Rose quickly. "At least, not more than's just proper."

"Oh, no more am I, of course," said Anna-Felicitas airily. "Except what's proper."

"And even if we were feeling it *dreadfully*," said Anna-Rose, with a little catch in her voice, "which, of course, we're not, dinner wouldn't make any difference. Dinner doesn't alter fundamentals."

"But it helps one to bear them," said Anna-Felicitas.

"Bear!" repeated Anna-Rose, her chin in the air. "We haven't got much to bear. Don't let me hear you talk of bearing things, Anna-F."

"I won't after dinner," promised Anna-Felicitas.

They thought perhaps they had better ask somebody whether there wouldn't soon be something to eat, but the other passengers had all disappeared. They were by themselves on the gloomy deck, and there were no lights. The row of cabin windows along the wall were closely shuttered, and the door they had come through when first they came on deck was shut too, and they couldn't find it in the dark. It seemed so odd to be feeling along a wall for a door they knew was there and not be able to find it, that they began to laugh; and the undiscoverable door cheered them up more than anything that had happened since seeing the last of Uncle Arthur.

"It's like a game," said Anna-Rose, patting her hands softly and vainly along the wall beneath the shuttered windows.

"It's like something in 'Alice in Wonderland,'" said Anna-Felicitas, following in her tracks.

A figure loomed through the mist and came toward them. They left off patting, and stiffened into straight and motionless dignity against the wall till it should have passed. But it didn't pass. It was a male figure in a peaked cap, probably a steward, they thought, and it stopped in front of them and said in an American voice, "Hello."

Anna-Rose cast rapidly about in her mind for the proper form of reply to Hello.

Anna-Felicitas, instinctively responsive to example murmured "Hello" back again.

Anna-Rose, feeling sure that nobody ought to say just Hello to people they had never seen before, and that Aunt Alice would think they had brought it on themselves by being conspicuous, decided that perhaps "Good-evening" would regulate the situation, and said it.

"You ought to be at dinner," said the man, taking no notice of this.

"That's what *we* think," agreed Anna-Felicitas earnestly.

"Can you please tell us how to get there?" asked Anna-Rose, still distant, but polite, for she too very much wanted to know.

"But *don't* tell us to ask the Captain," said Anna-Felicitas, even more earnestly.

"No," said Anna-Rose, "because we won't."

The man laughed. "Come right along with me," he said, striding on; and they followed him as obediently as though such persons as possible *böse Buben* didn't exist.

"First voyage I guess," said the man over his shoulder.

"Yes," said the twins a little breathlessly, for the man's legs were long and they could hardly keep up with him.

"English?" said the man.

"Ye—es," said Anna-Rose.

"That's to say, practically," panted the conscientious Anna-Felicitas.

"What say?" said the man, still striding on. "I said," Anna-Felicitas endeavoured to explain, hurrying breathlessly after him so as to keep within reach of his ear, "practically."

"Ah," said the man; and after a silence, broken only by the pantings for breath of the twins, he added: "Mother with you?"

They didn't say anything to that, it seemed such a dreadful question to have to answer, and luckily he didn't repeat it, but, having got to the door they had been searching for, opened it and stepped into the bright light inside, and putting out his arm behind him pulled them in one after the other over the high wooden door-frame.

Inside was the same stewardess they had seen earlier in the afternoon, engaged in heatedly describing what sounded like grievances to an official in buttons, who seemed indifferent. She stopped suddenly when the man appeared, and the official took his hands out of his pockets and became alert and attentive, and the stewardess hastily picked up a tray she had set down and began to move away along a passage.

The man, however, briefly called "Hi," and she turned round and came back even more quickly than she had tried to go.

"You see," explained Anna-Rose in a pleased whisper to Anna-Felicitas, "it's Hi she answers to."

"Yes," agreed Anna-Felicitas. "It's waste of good circumlocutions to throw them away on her."

"Show these young ladies the dining-room," said the man.

"Yes, sir," said the stewardess, as polite as you please.

He nodded to them with a smile that developed for some reason into a laugh, and turned away and beckoned to the official to follow him, and went out again into the night.

"Who was that nice man?" inquired Anna-Rose, following the stewardess down a broad flight of stairs that smelt of india-rubber and machine-oil and cooking all mixed up together.

"And please," said Anna-Felicitas with mild severity, "don't tell us to ask the Captain, because we really do know better than that."

"I thought you must be relations," said the stewardess.

"We are," said Anna-Rose. "We're twins."

The stewardess stared. "Twins what of?" she asked.

"What of?" echoed Anna-Rose. "Why, of each other, of course."

"I meant relations of the Captain's," said the stewardess shortly, eyeing them with more disfavour than ever.

"You seem to have the Captain greatly on your mind," said Anna-Felicitas. "He is no relation of ours."

"You're not even friends, then?" asked the stewardess, pausing to stare round at them at a turn in the stairs as they followed her down arm-in-arm.

"Of course we're friends," said Anna-Rose with some heat. "Do you suppose we quarrel?"

"No, I didn't suppose you quarrelled with the Captain," said the stewardess tartly. "Not on board this ship anyway."

She didn't know which of the two she disliked most, the short girl or the long girl.

"You seem to be greatly obsessed by the Captain," said Anna-Felicitas gently. "Obsessed!" repeated the stewardess, tossing her head. She was unacquainted with the word, but instantly suspected it of containing a reflection on her respectability. "I've been a widow off and on for ten years now," she said angrily, "and I guess it would take more than even the Captain to obsess *me*."

They had reached the glass doors leading into the dining-room, and the stewardess, having carried out her orders, paused before indignantly leaving them and going upstairs again to say, "If you're friends, what do you want to know his name for, then?"

"Whose name?" asked Anna-Felicitas.

"The Captain's," said the stewardess.

"We don't want to know the Captain's name," said Anna-Felicitas patiently. "We don't want to know anything about the Captain."

"Then—" began the stewardess. She restrained herself, however, and merely bitterly remarking: "That gentleman *was* the Captain," went upstairs and left them.

Anna-Rose was the first to recover. "You see we took your advice," she called up after her, trying to soften her heart, for it was evident that for some reason her heart was hardened, by flattery. "You *told* us to ask the Captain."

CHAPTER IV

In their berths that night before they went to sleep, it occurred to them that perhaps what was the matter with the stewardess was that she needed a tip. At first, with their recent experiences fresh in their minds, they thought that she was probably passionately pro-Ally, and had already detected all those Junkers in their past and accordingly couldn't endure them. Then they remembered how Aunt Alice had said, "You will have to give your stewardess a little something."

This had greatly perturbed them at the time, for up to then they had been in the easy position of the tipped rather than the tippers, and anyhow they had no idea what one gave stewardesses. Neither, it appeared, had Aunt Alice; for, on being questioned, she said vaguely that as it was an American boat they were going on she supposed it would have to be American money, which was dollars, and she didn't know much about dollars except that you divided them by four and multiplied them by five, or else it was the other way about; and when, feeling still uninformed, they had begged her to tell them why one did that, she said it was the quickest way of finding out what a dollar really was, and would they mind not talking any more for a little while because her head ached.

The tips they had seen administered during their short lives had all been given at the end of things, not at the beginning; but Americans, Aunt Alice told them, were in some respects, in spite of their talking English, different, and perhaps they were different just on this point and liked to be tipped at both ends. Anna-Rose wanted to crane out her head and call up to Anna-Felicitas and ask her whether she didn't think that might be so, but was afraid of disturbing the people in the opposite berths.

Anna-Felicitas was in the top berth on their side of the cabin, and Anna-Rose as the elder and accordingly as she explained to Anna-Felicitas, needing more comfort, in the lower one. On the opposite side were two similar berths, each containing as Anna-Felicitas whispered after peeping cautiously through their closed curtains,—for at first on coming in after dinner to go to bed the cabin seemed empty, except for inanimate things, like clothes hanging up and an immense smell,—its human freight. They were awed by this discovery, for the human freight was motionless and speechless, and yet made none of the noises suggesting sleep.

They unpacked and undressed as silently and quickly as possible, but it was very difficult, for there seemed to be no room for anything, not even for themselves. Every now and then they glanced a little uneasily at the closed curtains, which bulged, and sniffed cautiously and delicately, trying to decide what the smell exactly was. It appeared to be a mixture of the sauce one had with plum pudding at Christmas, and German bedrooms in the morning. It was a smell they didn't like the idea of sleeping with, but they saw no way of getting air. They thought of ringing for the stewardess and asking her to open a window, though they could see no window, but came to the conclusion it was better not to stir her up; not yet, at least, not till they had correctly diagnosed what was the matter with her. They said nothing out loud, for fear of disturbing whatever it was behind the curtains, but they knew what each was thinking, for one isn't, as they had long ago found out, a twin for nothing.

There was a slight scuffle before Anna-Felicitas was safely hoisted up into her berth, her legs hanging helplessly down for some time after the rest of her was in it, and Anna-Rose, who had already neatly inserted herself into her own berth, after watching these legs in silence and fighting a desire to give them a tug and see what would happen, had to get out at last on hearing Anna-Felicitas begin to make sounds up there as though she were choking, and push them up in after her. Her head was then on a level with Anna-Felicitas's berth, and she could see how Anna-Felicitas, having got her legs again, didn't attempt to do anything with them in the way of orderly arrangement beneath the blankets, but lay huddled in an irregular heap, screwing her eyes up very tight and stuffing one of her pigtails into her mouth, and evidently struggling with what appeared to be an attack of immoderate and ill-timed mirth.

Anna-Rose observed her for a moment in silence, then was suddenly seized herself with a dreadful desire to laugh, and with a hasty glance round at the bulging curtains scrambled back into her own berth and pulled the sheet over her mouth.

She was sobering herself by going over her different responsibilities, checking them off on her fingers,—the two five-pound notes under her pillow for extra expenses till they were united in New York to their capital, the tickets, the passports, and Anna-Felicitas,—when two thick fair pigtails appeared dangling over the edge of her berth, followed by Anna-Felicitas's head.

"You've forgotten to turn out the light," whispered Anna-Felicitas, her eyelashes still wet from her late attack; and stretching her neck still further down till her face was scarlet with the effort and the blood rushing into it, she expressed a conviction to Anna-Rose that the human freight behind the curtains, judging from the suspicious negativeness of its behaviour, had no business in their cabin at all and was really stowaways.

"German stowaways," added Anna-Felicitas, nodding her head emphatically, which was very skilful of her, thought Anna-Rose, considering that it was upside down. "*German* stowaways," whispered Anna-Felicitas, sniffing expressively though cautiously.

Anna-Rose raised herself on her elbows and stared across at the bulging curtains. They certainly were very motionless and much curved. In spite of herself her flesh began to creep a little.

"They're men," whispered Anna-Felicitas, now dangerously congested. "Stowaways are."

There had been no one in the cabin when first they came on board and took their things down, and they hadn't been in it since till they came to bed.

"*German* men," whispered Anna-Felicitas, again with a delicate expressive sniff.

"Nonsense," whispered Anna-Rose, stoutly. "Men never come into ladies' cabins. And there's skirts on the hooks."

"Disguise," whispered Anna-Felicitas, nodding again. "Spies' disguise." She seemed quite to be enjoying her own horrible suggestions.

"Take your head back into the berth," ordered Anna-Rose quickly, for Anna-Felicitas seemed to be on the very brink of an apoplectic fit.

Anna-Felicitas, who was herself beginning to feel a little inconvenienced, obeyed, and was thrilled to see Anna-Rose presently very cautiously emerge from underneath her and on her bare feet creep across to the opposite side. She knew her to be valiant to recklessness. She sat up to watch, her eyes round with interest.

Anna-Rose didn't go straight across, but proceeded slowly, with several pauses, to direct her steps toward the pillow-end of the berths. Having got there she stood still a moment listening, and then putting a careful finger between the curtain of the lower berth and its frame, drew it the smallest crack aside and peeped in.

Instantly she started back, letting go the curtain. "I beg your pardon," she said out loud, turning very red. "I—I thought—"

Anna-Felicitas, attentive in her berth, felt a cold thrill rush down her back. No sound came from the berth on the other side any more than before the raid on it, and Anna-Rose returned quicker than she had gone. She just stopped on the way to switch off the light, and then felt along the edge of Anna-Felicitas's berth till she got to her head, and pulling it near her by its left pigtail whispered with her mouth close to its left ear, "Wide awake. Watching me all the time. Not a man. Fat."

And she crawled into her berth feeling unnerved.

CHAPTER V

The lady in the opposite berth was German, and so was the lady in the berth above her. Their husbands were American, but that didn't make them less German. Nothing ever makes a German less German, Anna-Rose explained to Anna-Felicitas.

"Except," replied Anna-Felicitas, "a judicious dilution of their blood by the right kind of mother."

"Yes," said Anna-Rose. "Only to be found in England."

This conversation didn't take place till the afternoon of the next day, by which time Anna-Felicitas already knew about the human freight being Germans, for one of their own submarines came after the *St. Luke* and no one was quite so loud in expression of terror and dislike as the two Germans.

They demanded to be saved first, on the ground that they were Germans. They repudiated their husbands, and said marriage was nothing compared to how one had been born. The curtains of their berths, till then so carefully closed, suddenly yawned open, and the berths gave up their contents just as if, Anna-Felicitas remarked afterwards to Anna-Rose, it was the resurrection and the berths were riven sepulchres chucking up their dead.

This happened at ten o'clock the next morning when the *St. Luke* was pitching about off the southwest coast of Ireland. The twins, waking about seven, found with a pained surprise that they were not where they had been dreaming they were, in the sunlit garden at home playing tennis happily if a little violently, but in a chilly yet stuffy place that kept on tilting itself upside down. They lay listening to the groans coming from the opposite berths, and uneasily wondering how long it would be before they too began to groan. Anna-Rose raised her head once with the intention of asking if she could help at all, but dropped it back again on to the pillow and shut her eyes tight and lay as quiet as the ship would let her. Anna-Felicitas didn't even raise her head, she felt so very uncomfortable.

At eight o'clock the stewardess looked in—the same stewardess, they languidly noted, with whom already they had had two encounters, for it happened that this was one of the cabins she attended to—and said that if anybody wanted breakfast they had better be quick or it would be over.

"Breakfast!" cried the top berth opposite in a heart-rending tone; and instantly was sick.

The stewardess withdrew her head and banged the door to, and the twins, in their uneasy berths, carefully keeping their eyes shut so as not to witness the behaviour of the sides and ceiling of the cabin, feebly marvelled at the stewardess for suggesting being quick to persons who were being constantly stood on their heads. And breakfast,—they shuddered and thought of other things; of fresh, sweet air, and of the scent of pinks and apricots warm with the sun.

At ten o'clock the stewardess came in again, this time right in, and with determination in every gesture.

"Come, come," she said, addressing the twins, and through them talking at the heaving and groaning occupants of the other side, "you mustn't give way like this. What you want is to be out of bed. You must get up and go on deck. And how's the cabin to get done if you stay in it all the time?"

Anna-Felicitas, the one particularly addressed, because she was more on the right level for conversation than Anna-Rose, who could only see the stewardess's apron, turned her head away and murmured that she didn't care.

"Come, come," said the stewardess. "Besides, there's life-boat drill at mid-day, and you've got to be present."

Anna-Felicitas, her eyes shut, again murmured that she didn't care.

"Come, come," said the stewardess. "Orders are orders. Every soul on the ship, sick or not, has got to be present at life-boat drill."

"Oh, I'm not a soul," murmured Anna-Felicitas, who felt at that moment how particularly she was a body, while the opposite berths redoubled their groans.

"Come, come—" said the stewardess.

Then the *St. Luke* whistled five times, and the stewardess turned pale. For a brief space, before they understood what had happened, the twins supposed she was going to be sick. But it wasn't that that was the matter with her, for after a moment's staring at nothing with horror on her face she pounced on them and pulled them bodily out of their berths, regardless by which end, and threw them on the floor anyhow. Then she plunged about and produced life-jackets; then she rushed down the passage flinging open the doors of the other cabins; then she whirled back again and tried to tie the twins into their life-jackets, but with hands that shook so that the strings immediately came undone again; and all the time she was calling out

"Quick—quick—quick—" There was a great tramping of feet on deck and cries and shouting.

The curtains of the opposite berths yawned asunder and out came the Germans, astonishingly cured of their sea-sickness, and struggled vigorously into their life-jackets and then into fur coats, and had the fur coats instantly pulled off again by a very energetic steward who ran in and said fur coats in the water were death-traps,—a steward so much bent on saving people that he began to pull off the other things the German ladies had on as well, saying while he pulled, disregarding their protests, that in the water Mother Nature was the best. "Mother Nature—Mother Nature," said the steward, pulling; and he was only stopped just in the nick of time by the stewardess rushing in again and seeing what was happening to the helpless Germans.

Anna-Rose, even at that moment explanatory, pointed out to Anna-Felicitas, who had already grasped the fact, that no doubt there was a submarine somewhere about. The German ladies, seizing their valuables from beneath their pillows, in spite of the steward assuring them they wouldn't want them in the water, demanded to be taken up and somehow signalled to the submarine, which would never dare do anything to a ship containing its own flesh and blood—and an American ship, too—there must be some awful mistake—but anyhow they must be saved—there would be terrible trouble, that they could assure the steward and the twins and the scurrying passers-by down the passage, if America allowed two Germans to be destroyed—and anyhow they would insist on having their passage money refunded....

The German ladies departed down the passage, very incoherent and very unhappy but no longer sick, and Anna-Felicitas, clinging to the edge of her berth, feeling too miserable to mind about the submarine, feebly wondered, while the steward tied her properly into her life-jacket, at the cure effected in them. Anna-Rose seemed cured too, for she was buttoning a coat round Anna-Felicitas's shoulders, and generally seemed busy and brisk, ending by not even forgetting their precious little bag of money and tickets and passports, and fastening it round her neck in spite of the steward's assuring her that it would drag her down in the water like a stone tied to a kitten.

"You're a *very* cheerful man, aren't you," Anna-Rose said, as he pushed them out of the cabin and along the corridor, holding up Anna-Felicitas on her feet, who seemed quite unable to run alone.

The steward didn't answer, but caught hold of Anna-Felicitas at the foot of the stairs and carried her up them, and then having got her on deck propped her in a corner near the life-boat allotted to the set of cabins they were in, and darted away and in a minute was back again with a big coat which he wrapped round her.

"May as well be comfortable till you do begin to drown," he said briskly, "but mind you don't forget to throw it off, Missie, the minute you feel the water."

Anna-Felicitas slid down on to the deck, her head leaning against the wall, her eyes shut, a picture of complete indifference to whatever might be going to happen next. Her face was now as white as the frill of the night-gown that straggled out from beneath her coat, for the journey from the cabin to the deck had altogether finished her. Anna-Rose was thankful that she felt too ill to be afraid. Her own heart was black with despair,—despair that Anna-Felicitas, the dear and beautiful one, should presently, at any moment, be thrown into that awful heaving water, and certainly be hurt and frightened before she was choked out of life.

She sat down beside her, getting as close as possible to keep her warm. Her own twin. Her own beloved twin. She took her cold hands and put them away beneath the coat the steward had brought. She slid an arm round her and laid her cheek against her sleeve, so that she should know somebody was there, somebody who loved her. "What's the *good* of it all—*why* were we born—" she wondered, staring at the hideous gray waves as they swept up into sight over the side of the ship and away again as the ship rose up, and at the wet deck and the torn sky, and the miserable-looking passengers in their life-jackets collected together round the life-boat.

Nobody said anything except the German ladies. They, indeed, kept up a constant wail. The others were silent, the men mostly smoking cigarettes, the women holding their fluttering wraps about them, all of them staring out to sea, watching for the track of the torpedo to appear. One shot had been fired already and had missed. The ship was zig-zagging under every ounce of steam she could lay on. An official stood by the life-boat, which was ready with water in it and provisions. That the submarine must be mad, as the official remarked, to fire on an American ship, didn't console anybody, and his further assurance that the matter would not be allowed to rest there left them cold. They felt too sure that in all probability they themselves were going to rest there, down underneath that repulsive icy water, after a struggle that was going to be unpleasant.

The man who had roused Anna-Rose's indignation as the ship left the landing-stage by looking as though he were soon going to be sorry for her, came across from the first class, where his life-boat was, to watch for the track of the expected torpedo, and caught sight of the twins huddled in their corner.

Anna-Rose didn't see him, for she was staring with wide eyes out at the desolate welter of water and cloud, and thinking of home: the home that was, that used to be till such a little while ago, the home that now seemed to have been so amazingly, so unbelievably beautiful and blest, with its daily life of love and laughter and of easy confidence that to-morrow was going to be just as good. Happiness had been the ordinary condition there, a simple matter of course. Its place was taken now by courage. Anna-Rose felt sick at all this courage there was about. There should be no occasion for it. There should be no horrors to face, no cruelties to endure. Why couldn't brotherly love continue? Why must people get killing each other? She, for her part, would be behind nobody in courage and in the defying of a Fate that could behave, as she felt, so very unlike her idea of anything even remotely decent; but it oughtn't to be necessary, this constant condition of screwed-upness; it was waste of effort, waste of time, waste of life,—oh the *stupidity* of it all, she thought, rebellious and bewildered.

"Have some brandy," said the man, pouring out a little into a small cup.

Anna-Rose turned her eyes on him without moving the rest of her. She recognized him. He was going to be sorry for them again. He had much better be sorry for himself now, she thought, because he, just as much as they were, was bound for a watery bier.

"Thank you," she said distantly, for not only did she hate the smell of brandy but Aunt Alice had enjoined her with peculiar strictness on no account to talk to strange men, "I don't drink."

"Then I'll give the other one some," said the man.

"She too," said Anna-Rose, not changing her position but keeping a drearily watchful eye on him, "is a total abstainer."

"Well, I'll go and fetch some of your warm things for you. Tell me where your cabin is. You haven't got enough on."

"Thank you," said Anna-Rose distantly, "we have quite enough on, considering the occasion. We're dressed for drowning."

The man laughed, and said there would be no drowning, and that they had a splendid captain, and were outdistancing the submarine hand over fist. Anna-Rose didn't believe him, and suspected him of supposing her to be in need of cheering, but a gleam of comfort did in spite of herself steal into her heart.

He went away, and presently came back with a blanket and some pillows.

"If you *will* sit on the floor," he said, stuffing the pillows behind their backs, during which Anna-Felicitas didn't open her eyes, and her head hung about so limply that it looked as if it might at any moment roll off, "you may at least be as comfortable as you can."

Anna-Rose pointed out, while she helped him arrange Anna-Felicitas's indifferent head on the pillow, that she saw little use in being comfortable just a minute or two before drowning. "Drowning be hanged," said the man.

"That's how Uncle Arthur used to talk," said Anna-Rose, feeling suddenly quite at home, "except that *he* would have said 'Drowning be damned.'"

The man laughed. "Is he dead?" he asked, busy with Anna-Felicitas's head, which defied their united efforts to make it hold itself up.

"Dead?" echoed Anna-Rose, to whom the idea of Uncle Arthur's ever being anything so quiet as dead and not able to say any swear words for such a long time as eternity seemed very odd.

"You said he *used* to talk like that."

"Oh, no he's not dead at all. Quite the contrary."

The man laughed again, and having got Anna-Felicitas's head arranged in a position that at least, as Anna-Rose pointed out, had some sort of self-respect in it, he asked who they were with.

Anna-Rose looked at him with as much defiant independence as she could manage to somebody who was putting a pillow behind her back. He was going to be sorry for them. She saw it coming. He was going to say "You poor things," or words to that effect. That's what the people round Uncle Arthur's had said to them. That's what everybody had said to them since the war began, and Aunt Alice's friends had said it to her too, because she had to have her nieces live with her, and no doubt Uncle Arthur's friends who played golf with him had said it to him as well, except that probably they put in a damn so as to make it clearer for him and said "You poor damned thing," or something like that, and she was sick of the very words poor things. Poor things, indeed! "We're with each other," she said briefly, lifting her chin.

"Well, I don't think that's enough," said the man. "Not half enough. You ought to have a mother or something."

"*Everybody* can't have mothers," said Anna-Rose very defiantly indeed, tears rushing into her eyes.

The man tucked the blanket round their resistless legs. "There now," he said. "That's better. What's the good of catching your deaths?"

Anna-Rose, glad that he hadn't gone on about mothers, said that with so much death imminent, catching any of it no longer seemed to her particularly to matter, and the man laughed and pulled over a chair and sat down beside her.

She didn't know what he saw anywhere in that dreadful situation to laugh at, but just the sound of a laugh was extraordinarily comforting. It made one feel quite different. Wholesome again. Like waking up to sunshine and one's morning bath and breakfast after a nightmare. He seemed altogether a very comforting man. She liked him to sit near them. She hoped he was a good man. Aunt Alice had said there were very few good men, hardly any in fact except one's husband, but this one did seem one of the few exceptions. And she thought that by now, he having brought them all those pillows, he could no longer come under the heading of strange men. When he wasn't looking she put out her hand secretly and touched his coat where he wouldn't feel it. It comforted her to touch his coat. She hoped Aunt Alice wouldn't have disapproved of seeing her sitting side by side with him and liking it.

Aunt Alice had been, as her custom was, vague, when Anna-Rose, having given her the desired promise not to talk or let Anna-Felicitas talk to strange men, and desiring to collect any available information for her guidance in her new responsible position had asked, "But when are men *not* strange?"

"When you've married them," said Aunt Alice. "After that, of course, you love them."

And she sighed heavily, for it was bed-time.

CHAPTER VI

Nothing more was seen of the submarine.

The German ladies were certain the captain had somehow let them know he had them on board, and were as full of the credit of having saved the ship as if it had been Sodom and Gomorrah instead of a ship, and they the one just man whose presence would have saved those cities if he had been in them; and the American passengers were equally sure that the submarine, on thinking it over, had decided that President Wilson was not a man to be trifled with, and had gone in search of some prey which would not have the might and majesty of America at its back.

As the day went on, and the *St. Luke* left off zig-zagging, the relief of those on board was the relief of a reprieve from death. Almost everybody was cured of sea-sickness, and quite everybody was ready to overwhelm his neighbour with cordiality and benevolence. Rich people didn't mind poor people, and came along from the first class and talked to them just as if they had been the same flesh and blood as themselves. A billionairess native to Chicago, who had crossed the Atlantic forty times without speaking to a soul, an achievement she was as justly proud of as an artist is of his best creations, actually asked somebody in a dingy mackintosh, whose little boy still looked pale, if he had been frightened; and an exclusive young man from Boston talked quite a long while to an English lady without first having made sure that she was well-connected. What could have been more like heaven? The tone on the *St. Luke* that day was very like what the tone in the kingdom of heaven must be in its simple politeness. "And so you see," said Anna-Rose, who was fond of philosophizing in season and out of season, and particularly out of season, "how good comes out of evil."

She made this observation about four o'clock in the afternoon to Anna-Felicitas in an interval of absence on the part of Mr. Twist—such, the amiable stranger had told them, was his name—who had gone to see about tea being brought up to them; and Anna-Felicitas, able by now to sit up and take notice, the hours of fresh air having done their work, smiled the ready, watery, foolishly happy smile of the convalescent. It was so nice not to feel ill; it was so nice not to have to be saved. If she had been able to talk much, she would have philosophized too, about the number and size of one's negative blessings—all the things one hasn't got, all the very horrid things; why, there's no end to them once you begin to count up, she thought, waterily happy, and yet people grumble.

Anna-Felicitas was in that cleaned-out, beatific, convalescent mood in which one is sure one will never grumble again. She smiled at anybody who happened to pass by and catch her eye. She would have smiled just like that, with just that friendly, boneless familiarity at the devil if he had appeared, or even at Uncle Arthur himself.

The twins, as a result of the submarine's activities, were having the pleasantest day they had had for months. It was the realization of this that caused Anna-Rose's remark about good coming out of evil. The background, she could not but perceive, was a very odd one for their pleasantest day for months—a rolling steamer and a cold wind flicking at them round the corner; but backgrounds, she pointed out to Anna-Felicitas, who smiled her agreement broadly and instantly, are negligible things: it is what goes on in front of them that matters. Of what earthly use, for instance, had been those splendid summer afternoons in the perfect woods and gardens that so beautifully framed in Uncle Arthur?

No use, agreed Anna-Felicitas, smiling fatuously.

In the middle of them was Uncle Arthur. You always got to him in the end.

Anna-Felicitas nodded and shook her head and was all feeble agreement.

She and Anna-Felicitas had been more hopelessly miserable, Anna-Rose remarked, wandering about the loveliness that belonged to him than they could ever have dreamed was possible. She reminded Anna-Felicitas how they used to rub their eyes to try and see more clearly, for surely these means of happiness, these elaborate arrangements for it all round them, couldn't be for nothing? There must be some of it somewhere, if only they could discover where? And there was none. Not a trace of it. Not even the faintest little swish of its skirts.

Anna-Rose left off talking, and became lost in memories. For a long time, she remembered, she had told herself it was her mother's death blotting the light out of life, but one day Anna-Felicitas said aloud that it was Uncle Arthur, and Anna-Rose knew it was true. Their mother's death was something so tender, so beautiful, that terrible as it was to them to be left without her they yet felt raised up by it somehow, raised on to a higher level than where they had been before, closer in their hearts to real things, to real values. But Uncle Arthur came into possession of their lives as a consequence of that death, and he had towered up between them and every glimpse of the sun. Suddenly there was no such thing as freedom and laughter. Suddenly everything one said and did was wrong. "And you needn't think," Anna-Felicitas had said wisely, "that he's like that because we're Germans—or *seem* to be Germans," she amended. "It's because he's Uncle Arthur. Look at Aunt Alice. *She's* not a German. And yet look at her."

And Anna-Rose had looked at Aunt Alice, though only in her mind's eye, for at that moment the twins were three miles away in a wood picnicking, and Aunt Alice was at home recovering from a *tête-à-tête* luncheon with Uncle Arthur who hadn't said a word from start to finish; and though she didn't like most of his words when he did say them, she liked them still less when he didn't say them, for then she imagined them, and what she imagined was simply awful,—Anna-Rose had, I say, looked at Aunt Alice in her mind's eye, and knew that this too was true.

Mr. Twist reappeared, followed by the brisk steward with a tray of tea and cake, and their corner became very like a cheerful picnic.

Mr. Twist was most pleasant and polite. Anna-Rose had told him quite soon after he began to talk to her, in order, as she said, to clear his mind of misconceptions, that she and Anna-Felicitas, though their clothes at that moment, and the pigtails in which their flair was done, might be misleading, were no longer children, but quite the contrary; that they were, in fact, persons who were almost ripe for going to dances, and certainly in another year would be perfectly ripe for dances supposing there were any.

Mr. Twist listened attentively, and begged her to tell him any other little thing she might think of as useful to him in his capacity of friend and attendant,—both of which, said Mr. Twist, he intended to be till he had seen them safely landed in New York.

"I hope you don't think we *need* anybody," said Anna-Rose. "We shall like being friends with you very much, but only on terms of perfect equality."

"Sure," said Mr. Twist, who was an American.

"I thought—"

She hesitated a moment.

"You thought?" encouraged Mr. Twist politely.

"I thought at Liverpool you looked as if you were being sorry for us."

"Sorry?" said Mr. Twist, in the tone of one who repudiates.

"Yes. When we were waving good-bye to—to our friends."

"Sorry?" repeated Mr. Twist.

"Which was great waste of your time."

"I should think so," said Mr. Twist with heartiness.

Anna-Rose, having cleared the ground of misunderstandings, an activity in which at all times she took pleasure, accepted Mr. Twist's attentions in the spirit in which they were offered, which was, as he said, one of mutual friendliness and esteem. As he was never sea-sick, he could move about and do things for them that might be difficult to do for themselves; as he knew a great deal about stewardesses, he could tell them what sort of tip theirs expected; as he was American, he could illuminate them about that country. He had been doing Red Cross work with an American ambulance in France for ten months, and was going home for a short visit to see how his mother, who, Anna-Rose gathered, was ancient and widowed, was getting on. His mother, he said, lived in seclusion in a New England village with his sister, who had not married.

"Then she's got it all before her," said Anna-Rose.

"Like us," said Anna-Felicitas.

"I shouldn't think she'd got as much of it before her as you," said Mr. Twist, "because she's considerably more grown up—I mean," he added hastily, as Anna-Rose's mouth opened, "she's less—well, less completely young."

"We're not completely young," said Anna-Rose with dignity. "People are completely young the day they're born, and ever after that they spend their time becoming less so."

"Exactly. And my sister has been becoming less so longer than you have. I assure you that's all I meant. She's less so even than I am."

"Then," said Anna-Rose, glancing at that part of Mr. Twist's head where it appeared to be coming through his hair, "she must have got to the stage when one is called a maiden lady."

"And if she were a German," said Anna-Felicitas suddenly, who hadn't till then said anything to Mr. Twist but only smiled widely at him whenever he happened to look her way, "she wouldn't be either a lady or a maiden, but just an It. It's very rude of Germans, I think," went on Anna-Felicitas, abstractedly smiling at the cake Mr. Twist was offering her, "never to let us be anything but Its till we've taken on some men."

Mr. Twist expressed surprise at this way of describing marriage, and inquired of Anna-Felicitas what she knew about Germans.

"The moment you leave off being sea-sick, Anna-F.," said Anna-Rose, turning to her severely, "you start being indiscreet. Well, I suppose," she added with a sigh to Mr. Twist, "you'd have had to know sooner or later. Our name is Twinkler."

She watched him to see the effect of this, and Mr. Twist, perceiving he was expected to say something, said that he didn't mind that anyhow, and that he could bear something worse in the way of revelations.

"Does it convey nothing to you?" asked Anna-Rose, astonished, for in Germany the name of Twinkler was a mighty name, and even in England it was well known.

Mr. Twist shook his head. "Only that it sounds cheerful," he said.

Anna-Rose watched his face. "It isn't only Twinkler," she said, speaking very distinctly. "It's *von* Twinkler."

"That's German," said Mr. Twist; but his face remained serene.

"Yes. And so are we. That is, we would be if it didn't happen that we weren't."

"I don't think I quite follow," said Mr. Twist.

"It *is* very difficult," agreed Anna-Rose. "You see, we used to have a German father."

"But only because our mother married him," explained Anna-Felicitas. "Else we wouldn't have."

"And though she only did it once," said Anna-Rose, "ages ago, it has dogged our footsteps ever since."

"It's very surprising," mused Anna-Felicitas, "what marrying anybody does. You go into a church, and before you know where you are, you're all tangled up with posterity."

"And much worse than that," said Anna-Rose, staring wide-eyed at her own past experiences, "posterity's all tangled up with you. It's really simply awful sometimes for posterity. Look at us."

"If there hadn't been a war we'd have been all right," said Anna-Felicitas. "But directly there's a war, whoever it is you've married, if it isn't one of your own countrymen, rises up against you, just as if he were too many meringues you'd had for dinner."

"Living or dead," said Anna-Rose, nodding, "he rises up against you."

"Till the war we never thought at all about it," said Anna-Felicitas.

"Either one way or the other," said Anna-Rose.

"We never used to bother about what we were," said Anna-Felicitas. "We were just human beings, and so was everybody else just human beings."

"We didn't mind a bit about being Germans, or about other people not being Germans."

"But you mustn't think we mind now either," said Anna-Felicitas, "because, you see, we're not."

Mr. Twist looked at them in turn. His ears were a little prominent and pointed, and they gave him rather the air, when he put his head on one side and looked at them, of an attentive fox-terrier. "I don't think I quite follow," he said again.

"It *is* very difficult," agreed Anna-Rose.

"It's because you've got into your head that we're German because of our father," said Anna-Felicitas. "But what's a father, when all's said and done?"

"Well," said Mr. Twist, "one has to have him."

"But having got him he isn't anything like as important as a mother," said Anna-Rose.

"One hardly sees one's father," said Anna-Felicitas. "He's always busy. He's always thinking of something else."

"Except when he looks at one and tells one to sit up straight," said Anna-Rose pointedly to Anna-Felicitas, whose habit of drooping still persisted in spite of her father's admonishments.

"Of course he's very kind and benevolent when he happens to remember that one is there," said Anna-Felicitas, sitting up beautifully for a moment, "but that's about everything."

"And of course," said Anna-Rose, "one's father's intentions are perfectly sound and good, but his attention seems to wander. Whereas one's mother—"

"Yes," said Anna-Felicitas, "one's mother—"

They broke off and looked straight in front of them. It didn't bear speaking of. It didn't bear thinking of.

Suddenly Anna-Felicitas, weak from excessive sea-sickness, began to cry. The tears just slopped over as though no resistance of any sort were possible.

Anna-Rose stared at her a moment horror-struck. "Look here, Anna-F.," she exclaimed, wrath in her voice, "I won't *have* you be sentimental—I won't *have* you be sentimental...."

And then she too began to cry.

Well, once having hopelessly disgraced and exposed themselves, there was nothing for it but to take Mr. Twist into their uttermost confidence. It was dreadful. It was awful. Before that strange man. A person they hardly knew. Other strangers passing. Exposing their feelings. Showing their innermost miserable places.

They writhed and struggled in their efforts to stop, to pretend they weren't crying, that it was really nothing but just tears,—odd ones left over from last time, which was years and years ago,—"But *really* years and years ago," sobbed Anna-Rose, anxiously explaining,—"the years one falls down on garden paths in, and cuts one's knees, and one's mother—one's mother—c-c-c-comforts one—"

"See here," said Mr. Twist, interrupting these incoherences, and pulling out a beautiful clean pocket-handkerchief which hadn't even been unfolded yet, "you've got to tell me all about it right away."

And he shook out the handkerchief, and with the first-aid promptness his Red Cross experience had taught him, started competently wiping up their faces.

CHAPTER VII

There was that about Mr. Twist which, once one had begun them, encouraged confidences; something kind about his eyes, something not too determined about his chin. He bore no resemblance to those pictures of efficient Americans in advertisements with which Europe is familiar,— eagle-faced gentlemen with intimidatingly firm mouths and chins, wiry creatures, physically and mentally perfect, offering in capital letters to make you Just Like Them. Mr. Twist was the reverse of eagle-faced. He was also the reverse of good-looking; that is, he would have been very handsome indeed, as Anna-Rose remarked several days later to Anna-Felicitas, when the friendship had become a settled thing,—which indeed it did as soon as Mr. Twist had finished wiping their eyes and noses that first afternoon, it being impossible, they discovered, to have one's eyes and noses wiped by somebody without being friends afterwards (for such an activity, said Anna-Felicitas, belonged to the same order of events as rescue from fire, lions, or drowning, after which in books you married him; but this having only been wiping, said Anna-Rose, the case was adequately met by friendship)—he would have been very handsome indeed if he hadn't had a face.

"But you have to *have* a face," said Anna-Felicitas, who didn't think it much mattered what sort it was so long as you could eat with it and see out of it.

"And as long as one is as kind as Mr. Twist," said Anna-Rose; but secretly she thought that having been begun so successfully at his feet, and carried upwards with such grace of long limbs and happy proportions, he might as well have gone on equally felicitously for the last little bit.

"I expect God got tired of him over that last bit," she mused, "and just put on any sort of head."

"Yes—that happened to be lying about," agreed Anna-Felicitas. "In a hurry to get done with him."

"Anyway he's very kind," said Anna-Rose, a slight touch of defiance in her voice.

"Oh, *very* kind," agreed Anna-Felicitas.

"And it doesn't matter about faces for being kind," said Anna-Rose.

"Not in the least," agreed Anna-Felicitas.

"And if it hadn't been for the submarine we shouldn't have got to know him. So you see," said Anna-Rose,—and again produced her favourite remark about good coming out of evil.

Those were the days in mid-Atlantic when England was lost in its own peculiar mists, and the sunshine of America was stretching out towards them. The sea was getting calmer and bluer every hour, and submarines more and more unlikely. If a ship could be pleasant, which Anna-Felicitas doubted, for she still found difficulty in dressing and undressing without being sea-sick and was unpopular in the cabin, this ship was pleasant. You lay in a deck-chair all day long, staring at the blue sky and blue sea that enclosed you as if you were living in the middle of a jewel, and tried not to remember—oh, there were heaps of things it was best not to remember; and when the rail of the ship moved up across the horizon too far into the sky, or moved down across it and showed too much water, you just shut your eyes and then it didn't matter; and the sun shone warm and steady on your face, and the wind tickled the tassel on the top of your German-knitted cap, and Mr. Twist came and read aloud to you, which sent you to sleep quicker than anything you had ever known.

The book he read out of and carried about with him his pocket was called "Masterpieces You Must Master," and was an American collection of English poetry, professing in its preface to be a Short Cut to Culture; and he would read with what at that time, it being new to them, seemed to the twins a strange exotic pronunciation, Wordsworth's "Ode to Dooty," and the effect was as if someone should dig a majestic Gregorian psalm in its ribs, and make it leap and giggle.

Anna-Rose, who had no reason to shut her eyes, for she didn't mind what the ship's rail did with the horizon, opened them very round when first Mr. Twist started on his Masterpieces. She was used to hearing them read by her mother in the adorable husky voice that sent such thrills through one, but she listened with the courtesy and final gratitude due to the efforts to entertain her of so amiable a friend, and only the roundness of her eyes showed her astonishment at this waltzing round, as it appeared to her, of Mr. Twist with the Stern Daughter of the Voice of God. He also read "Lycidas" to her, that same "Lycidas" Uncle Arthur took for a Derby winner, and only Anna-Rose's politeness enabled her to refrain from stopping up her ears. As it was, she fidgeted to the point of having to explain, on Mr. Twist's pausing to gaze at her questioningly through the smoke-coloured spectacles he wore on deck, which made him look so like a gigantic dragon-fly, that it was because her deck-chair was so very much harder than she was.

Anna-Felicitas, who considered that, if these things were short-cuts to anywhere, seeing she knew them all by heart she must have long ago got there, snoozed complacently. Sometimes for a few moments she would drop off really to sleep, and then her mouth would fall open, which worried Anna-Rose, who couldn't bear her to look even for a moment less beautiful than she knew she was, so that she fidgeted more than ever, unable, pinned down by politeness and the culture being administered, to make her shut her mouth and look beautiful again by taking and shaking her. Also Anna-Felicitas had a trick of waking up suddenly and forgetting to be polite, as one does when first one wakes up and hasn't had time to remember one is a lady. "To-morrow to fresh woods and pastures noo," Mr. Twist would finish, for instance, with a sort of gulp of satisfaction at having swallowed yet another solid slab of culture; and Anna-Felicitas, returning suddenly to consciousness, would murmur, with her eyes still shut and her head lolling limply, things like, "After all, it *does* rhyme with blue. I wonder why, then, one still doesn't like it."

Then Mr. Twist would turn his spectacles towards her in mild inquiry, and Anna-Rose, as always, would rush in and elaborately explain what Anna-Felicitas meant, which was so remote from anything resembling what she had said that Mr. Twist looked more mildly inquiring than ever.

Usually Anna-Felicitas didn't contradict Anna-Rose, being too sleepy or too lazy, but sometimes she did, and then Anna-Rose got angry, and would get what the Germans call a red head and look at Anna-Felicitas very severely and say things, and Mr. Twist would close his book and watch with that alert, cocked-up-ear look of a sympathetic and highly interested terrier; but sooner or later the ship would always give a roll, and Anna-Felicitas would shut her eyes and fade to paleness and become the helpless bundle of sickness that nobody could possibly go on being severe with.

The passengers in the second class were more generally friendly than those in the first class. The first class sorted itself out into little groups, and whispered about each other, as Anna-Rose observed, watching their movements across the rope that separated her from them. The second class remained to the end one big group, frayed out just a little at the edge in one or two places.

The chief fraying out was where the Twinkler kids, as the second-class young men, who knew no better, dared to call them, interrupted the circle by talking apart with Mr. Twist. Mr. Twist had no business there. He was a plutocrat of the first class; but in spite of the regulations which cut off the classes from communicating, with a view apparently to the continued sanitariness of the first class, the implication being that the second class was easily infectious and probably overrun, there he was every day and several times in every day. He must have heavily squared the officials, the second-class young men thought until the day when Mr. Twist let it somehow be understood that he had known the Twinkler young ladies for years, dandled them in their not very remote infancy on his already full-grown knee, and had been specially appointed to look after them on this journey.

Mr. Twist did not specify who had appointed him, except to the Twinkler young ladies themselves, and to them he announced that it was no less a thing, being, or creature, than Providence. The second-class young men, therefore, in spite of their rising spirits as danger lay further behind, and their increasing tendency, peculiar to those who go on ships, to become affectionate, found themselves no further on in acquaintance with the Misses Twinkler the last day of the voyage than they had been the first. Not that, under any other conditions, they would have so much as noticed the existence of the Twinkler kids. In their blue caps, pulled down tight to their eyebrows and hiding every trace of hair, they looked like bald babies. They never came to meals; their assiduous guardian, or whatever he was, feeding them on deck with the care of a mother-bird for its fledglings, so that nobody except the two German ladies in their cabin had seen them without the caps. The young men put them down as half-grown only, somewhere about fourteen they thought, and nothing but what, if they were boys instead of girls, would have been called louts.

Still, a ship is a ship, and it is wonderful what can be managed in the way of dalliance if one is shut up on one long enough; and the Misses Twinkler, in spite of their loutishness, their apparent baldness, and their constant round-eyed solemnity, would no doubt have been the objects of advances before New York was reached if it hadn't been for Mr. Twist. There wasn't a girl under forty in the second class on that voyage, the young men resentfully pointed out to each other, except these two kids who were too much under it, and a young lady of thirty who sat manicuring her nails most of the day with her back supported by a life-boat, and polishing them with red stuff till they flashed rosily in the sun. This young lady was avoided for the first two days, while the young men still remembered their mothers, because of what she looked like; but was greatly loved for the rest of the voyage precisely for that reason.

Still, every one couldn't get near her. She was only one; and there were at least a dozen active, cooped-up young men taking lithe, imprisoned exercise in long, swift steps up and down the deck, ready for any sort of enterprise, bursting with energy and sea-air and spirits. So that at last the left-overs, those of the young men the lady of the rosy nails was less kind to, actually in their despair attempted ghastly flirtations with the two German ladies. They approached them with a kind of angry amorousness. They tucked them up roughly in rugs. They brought them cushions as though they were curses. And it was through this *rapprochement*, in the icy warmth of which the German ladies expanded like bulky flowers and grew at least ten years younger, the ten years they shed being their most respectable ones, that the ship became aware of the nationality of the Misses Twinkler.

The German ladies were not really German, as they explained directly there were no more submarines about, for a good woman, they said, becomes automatically merged into her husband, and they, therefore, were merged into Americans, both of them, and as loyal as you could find, but the Twinklers were the real thing, they said,—real, unadulterated, arrogant Junkers, which is why they wouldn't talk to anybody; for no Junker, said the German ladies, thinks anybody good enough to be talked to except another Junker. The German ladies themselves had by sheer luck not been born Junkers. They had missed it very narrowly, but they had missed it, for which they were very thankful seeing what believers they were, under the affectionate manipulation of their husbands, in democracy; but they came from the part of Germany where Junkers most abound, and knew the sort of thing well.

It seemed to Mr. Twist, who caught scraps of conversation as he came and went, that in the cabin the Twinklers must have alienated sympathy. They had. They had done more; they had got themselves actively disliked.

From the first moment when Anna-Rose had dared to peep into their shrouded bunks the ladies had been prejudiced, and this prejudice had later flared up into a great and justified dislike. The ladies, to begin with, hadn't known that they were von Twinklers, but had supposed them mere Twinklers, and the von, as every German knows, makes all the difference, especially in the case of Twinklers, who, without it, were a race, the ladies knew, of small shopkeepers, laundresses and postmen in the Westphalian district, but with it were one of the oldest families in Prussia; known to all Germans; possessed of a name ensuring subservience wherever it went.

In this stage of preliminary ignorance the ladies had treated the two apparently ordinary Twinklers with the severity their conduct, age, and obvious want of means deserved; and when, goaded by their questionings, the smaller and more active Twinkler had let out her von at them much as one lets loose a dog when one is alone and weak against the attacks of an enemy, instead of falling in harmoniously with the natural change of attitude of the ladies, which became immediately perfectly polite and conciliatory, as well as motherly in its interest and curiosity, the two young Junkers went dumb. They would have nothing to do with the most motherly questioning.

And just in proportion as the German ladies found themselves full of eager milk of kindness, only asking to be permitted to nourish, so did they find themselves subsequently, after a day or two of such uncloaked repugnance to it, left with quantities of it useless on their hands and all going sour.

From first to last the Twinklers annoyed them. As plain Twinklers they had been tiresome in a hundred ways in the cabin, and as von Twinklers they were intolerable in their high-nosed indifference.

It had naturally been expected by the elder ladies at the beginning of the journey, that two obscure Twinklers of such manifest youth should rise politely and considerately each morning very early, and get themselves dressed and out of the way in at the most ten minutes, leaving the cabin clear for the slow and careful putting together bit by bit of that which ultimately emerged a perfect specimen of a lady of riper years, but the weedy Twinkler insisted on lying in her berth so late that if the ladies wished to be in time for the best parts of breakfast, which they naturally and passionately did wish, they were forced to dress in her presence, which was most annoying and awkward.

It is true she lay with closed eyes, apparently apathetic, but you never know with persons of that age. Experience teaches not to trust them. They shut their eyes, and yet seem, later on, to have seen; they apparently sleep, and afterwards are heard asking their spectacled American friend what people do on a ship, a place of so much gustiness, if their hair gets blown off into the sea. Also the weedy one had a most tiresome trick of being sick instantly every time Odol was used, or a little brandy was drunk. Odol is most refreshing; it has a lovely smell, without which no German bedroom is complete. And the brandy was not common schnaps, but an old expensive brandy that, regarded as a smell, was a credit to anybody's cabin.

The German ladies would have persisted, and indeed did persist in using Odol and drinking a little brandy, indifferent to the feeble prayer from the upper berth which floated down entreating them not to, but in their own interests they were forced to give it up. The objectionable child did not pray a second time; she passed immediately from prayer to performance. Of two disagreeables wise women choose the lesser, but they remain resentful.

The other Twinkler, the small active one, did get up early and take herself off, but she frequently mixed up her own articles of toilet with those belonging to the ladies, and would pin up her hair, preparatory to washing her face, with their hairpins.

When they discovered this they hid them, and she, not finding any, having come to the end of her own, lost no time in irresolution but picked up their nail-scissors and pinned up her pigtails with that.

It was a particularly sacred pair of nail-scissors that almost everything blunted. To use them for anything but nails was an outrage, but the grossest outrage was to touch them at all. When they told her sharply that the scissors were very delicate and she was instantly to take them out of her hair, she tugged them out in a silence that was itself impertinent, and pinned up her pigtails with their buttonhook instead.

Then they raised themselves on their elbows in their berths and asked her what sort of a bringing up she could have had, and they raised their voices as well, for though they were grateful, as they later on declared, for not having been born Junkers, they had nevertheless acquired by practice in imitation some of the more salient Junker characteristics.

"You are *salop*," said the upper berth lady,—which is untranslatable, not on grounds of propriety but of idiom. It is not, however, a term of praise.

"Yes, that is what you are—*salop*," echoed the lower berth lady. "And your sister is *salop* too—lying in bed till all hours."

"It is shameful for girls to be *salop*," said the upper berth.

"I didn't know it was your buttonhook. I thought it was ours," said Anna-Rose, pulling this out too with vehemence.

"That is because you are *salop*," said the lower berth.

"And I didn't know it wasn't our scissors either."

"*Salop, salop*," said the lower berth, beating her hand on the wooden edge of her bunk.

"And—and I'm sorry."

Anna-Rose's face was very red. She didn't look sorry, she looked angry. And so she was; but it was with herself, for having failed in discernment and grown-upness. She ought to have noticed that the scissors and buttonhook were not hers. She had pounced on them with the ill-considered haste of twelve years old. She hadn't been a lady,—she whose business it was to be an example and mainstay to Anna-Felicitas, in all things going first, showing her the way.

She picked up the sponge and plunged it into the water, and was just going to plunge her annoyed and heated face in after it when the upper berth lady said: "Your mother should be ashamed of herself to have brought you up so badly."

"And send you off like this before she has taught you even the ABC of manners," said the lower berth.

"Evidently," said the upper berth, "she can have none herself."

CHRISTOPHER AND COLUMBUS | 57

"Evidently," said the lower berth, "she is herself *salop*."

The sponge, dripping with water, came quickly out of the basin in Anna-Rose's clenched fist. For one awful instant she stood there in her nightgown, like some bird of judgment poised for dreadful flight, her eyes flaming, her knotted pigtails bristling on the top of her head.

The wet sponge twitched in her hand. The ladies did not realize the significance of that twitching, and continued to offer large angry faces as a target. One of the faces would certainly have received the sponge and Anna-Rose have been disgraced for ever, if it hadn't been for the prompt and skilful intervention of Anna-Felicitas.

For Anna-Felicitas, roused from her morning languor by the unusual loudness of the German ladies' voices, and smitten into attention and opening of her eyes, heard the awful things they were saying and saw the sponge. Instantly she knew, seeing it was Anna-Rose who held it, where it would be in another second, and hastily putting out a shaking little hand from her top berth, caught hold feebly but obstinately of the upright ends of Anna-Rose's knotted pigtails.

"I'm going to be sick," she announced with great presence of mind and entire absence of candour.

She knew, however, that she only had to sit up in order to be sick, and the excellent child—*das gute Kind*, as her father used to call her because she, so conveniently from the parental point of view, invariably never wanted to be or do anything particularly—without hesitation sacrificed herself in order to save her sister's honour, and sat up and immediately was.

By the time Anna-Rose had done attending to her, all fury had died out. She never could see Anna Felicitas lying back pale and exhausted after one of these attacks without forgiving her and everybody else everything.

She climbed up on the wooden steps to smoothe her pillow and tuck her blanket round her, and when Anna-Felicitas, her eyes shut, murmured, "Christopher—don't mind *them*—" and she suddenly realized, for they never called each other by those names except in great moments of emotion when it was necessary to cheer and encourage, what Anna-Felicitas had saved her from, and that it had been done deliberately, she could only whisper back, because she was so afraid of crying, "No, no, Columbus dear—of course—who really cares about *them*—" and came down off the steps with no fight left in her.

Also the wrath of the ladies was considerably assuaged. They had retreated behind their curtains until the so terribly unsettled Twinkler should be quiet again, and when once more they drew them a crack apart in order to keep an eye on what the other one might be going to do next and saw her doing nothing except, with meekness, getting dressed, they merely inquired what part of Westphalia she came from, and only in the tone they asked it did they convey that whatever part it was, it was anyhow a contemptible one.

"We don't come from Westphalia," said Anna-Rose, bristling a little, in spite of herself, at their persistent baiting.

Anna-Felicitas listened in cold anxiousness. She didn't want to have to be sick again. She doubted whether she could bear it.

"You must come from somewhere," said the lower berth, "and being a Twinkler it must be Westphalia."

"We don't really," said Anna-Rose, mindful of Anna-Felicitas's words and making a great effort to speak politely. "We come from England."

"England!" cried the lower berth, annoyed by this quibbling. "You were born in Westphalia. All Twinklers are born in Westphalia."

"Invariably they are," said the upper berth. "The only circumstance that stops them is if their mothers happen to be temporarily absent."

"But we weren't, really," said Anna-Rose, continuing her efforts to remain bland.

"Are you pretending—pretending to *us*," said the lower berth lady, again beating her hand on the edge of her bunk, "that you are not German?"

"Our father was German," said Anna-Rose, driven into a corner, "but I don't suppose he is now. I shouldn't think he'd want to go on being one directly he got to a really neutral place."

"Has he fled his country?" inquired the lower berth sternly, scenting what she had from the first suspected, something sinister in the Twinkler background.

"I suppose one might call it that," said Anna-Rose after a pause of consideration, tying her shoe-laces.

"Do you mean to say," said the ladies with one voice, feeling themselves now on the very edge of a scandal, "he was forced to fly from Westphalia?"

"I suppose one might put it that way," said Anna-Rose, again considering.

She took her cap off its hook and adjusted it over her hair with a deliberation intended to assure Anna-Felicitas that she was remaining calm. "Except that it wasn't from Westphalia he flew, but Prussia," she said.

"Prussia?" cried the ladies as one woman, again rising themselves on their elbows.

"That's where our father lived," said Anna-Rose, staring at them in her surprise at their surprise. "So of course, as he lived there, when he died he did that there too."

"Prussia?" cried the ladies again. "He died? You said your father fled his country."

"No. *You* said that," said Anna-Rose.

She gave her cap a final tug down over her ears and turned to the door. She felt as if she quite soon again in spite of Anna-Felicitas, might not be able to be a lady.

"After all, it *is* what you do when you go to heaven," she said as she opened the door, unable to resist, according to her custom, having the last word.

"But Prussia?" they still cried, still button-holing her, as it were, from afar. "Then—you were born in Prussia?"

"Yes, but we couldn't help it," said Anna-Rose; and shut the door quickly behind her.

CHAPTER VIII

Mr. Twist, who was never able to be anything but kind—he had the most amiable mouth and chin in the world, and his name was Edward—took a lively interest in the plans and probable future of the two Annas. He also took a lively and solicitous interest in their present, and a profoundly sympathetic one in their past. In fact, their three tenses interested him to the exclusion of almost everything else, and his chief desire was to see them safely through any shoals there might be waiting them in the shape of Uncle Arthur's friends—he distrusted Uncle Arthur, and therefore his friends—into the safe and pleasant waters of real American hospitality and kindliness.

He knew that such waters abounded for those who could find the tap. He reminded himself of that which he had been taught since childhood, of the mighty heart of America which, once touched, would take persons like the twins right in and never let them out again. But it had to be touched. It had, as it were, to be put in connection with them by means of advertisement. America, he reflected, was a little deaf. She had to be shouted to. But once she heard, once she thoroughly grasped ...

He cogitated much in his cabin—one with a private bathroom, for Mr. Twist had what Aunt Alice called ample means—on these two defenceless children. If they had been Belgians now, or Serbians, or any persons plainly in need of relief! As it was, America would be likely, he feared, to consider that either Germany or England ought to be looking after them, and might conceivably remain chilly and uninterested.

Uncle Arthur, it appeared, hadn't many friends in America, and those he had didn't like him. At least that was what Mr. Twist gathered from the conversation of Anna-Rose. She didn't positively assert but she very candidly conjectured, and Mr. Twist could quite believe that Uncle Arthur's friends wouldn't be warm ones. Their hospitality he could imagine fleeting and perfunctory. They would pass on the Twinklers as soon as possible, as indeed why should they not? And presently some dreary small job would be found for them, some job as pupil-teacher or girls' companion in the sterile atmosphere of a young ladies' school.

As much as a man of habitually generous impulses could dislike, Mr. Twist disliked Uncle Arthur. Patriotism was nothing at any time to Mr. Twist compared to humanity, and Uncle Arthur's particular kind of patriotism was very odious to him. To wreak it on these two poor aliens! Mr. Twist had no words for it. They had been cut adrift at a tender age, an age Mr. Twist, as a disciplined American son and brother, was unable to regard unmoved, and packed off over the sea indifferent to what might happen to them so long as Uncle Arthur knew nothing about it. Having flung these kittens into the water to swim or drown, so long as he didn't have to listen to their cries while they were doing it, Uncle Arthur apparently cared nothing.

All Mr. Twist's chivalry, of which there was a great deal, rose up within him at the thought of Uncle Arthur. He wanted to go and ask him what he meant by such conduct, and earnestly inquire of him whether he called himself a man; but as he knew he couldn't do this, being on a ship heading for New York, he made up for it by taking as much care of the ejected nieces as if he were an uncle himself,—but the right sort of uncle, the sort you have in America, the sort that regards you as a sacred and precious charge.

In his mind's eye Mr. Twist saw Uncle Arthur as a typical bullying, red-necked Briton, with short side-whiskers. He pictured him under-sized and heavy-footed, trudging home from golf through the soppy green fields of England to his trembling household. He was quite disconcerted one day to discover from something Anna-Rose said that he was a tall man, and not fat at all, except in one place.

"Indeed," said Mr. Twist, hastily rearranging his mind's-eye view of Uncle Arthur.

"He goes fat suddenly," said Anna-Felicitas, waking from one of her dozes. "As though he had swallowed a bomb, and it had stuck when it got to his waistcoat."

"If you can imagine it," added Anna-Rose politely, ready to explain and describe further if required.

But Mr. Twist could imagine it. He readjusted his picture of Uncle Arthur, and this time got him right,—the tall, not bad-looking man, clean-shaven and with more hair a great deal than he, Mr. Twist, had. He had thought of him as an old ruffian; he now perceived that he could be hardly more than middle-aged and that Aunt Alice, a lady for whom he felt an almost painful sympathy, had a lot more of Uncle Arthur to get through before she was done.

"Yes," said Anna-Rose, accepting the word middle-aged as correct. "Neither of his ends looks much older than yours do. He's aged in the middle. That's the only place. Where the bomb is."

"I suppose that's why it's called middle-aged," said Anna-Felicitas dreamily. "One middle-ages first, and from there it just spreads. It must be queer," she added pensively, "to watch oneself gradually rotting."

These were the sorts of observations, Mr. Twist felt, that might prejudice his mother against the twins If they could be induced not to say most of the things they did say when in her presence, he felt that his house, of all houses in America, should be offered them as a refuge whenever they were in need of one. But his mother was not, he feared, very adaptable. In her house—it was legally his, but it never felt as if it were—people adapted themselves to her. He doubted whether the twins could or would. Their leading characteristic, he had observed, was candour. They had no *savoir faire*. They seemed incapable of anything but naturalness, and their particular type of naturalness was not one, he was afraid, that his mother would understand.

She had not been out of her New England village, a place called briefly, with American economy of time, Clark, for many years, and her ideal of youthful femininity was still that which she had been herself. She had, if unconsciously, tried to mould Mr. Twist also on these lines, in spite of his being a boy, and owing to his extreme considerateness had not yet discovered her want of success. For years, indeed, she had been completely successful, and Mr. Twist arrived at and embarked on adolescence with the manners and ways of thinking of a perfect lady.

Till he was nineteen he was educated at home, as it were at his mother's knee, at any rate within reach of that sacred limb, and she had taught him to reverence women; the reason given, or rather conveyed, being that he had had and still was having a mother. Which he was never to forget. In hours of temptation. In hours of danger. Mr. Twist, with his virginal white mind, used to wonder when the hours of temptation and of danger would begin, and rather wish, in the elegant leisure of his half-holidays, that they soon would so that he might show how determined he was to avoid them.

For the ten years from his father's death till he went to Harvard, he lived with his mother and sister and was their assiduous attendant. His mother took the loss of his father badly. She didn't get over it, as widows sometimes do, and grow suddenly ten years younger. The sight of her, so black and broken, of so daily recurring a patience, of such frequent deliberate brightening for the sake of her children, kept Mr. Twist, as he grew up, from those thoughts which sometimes occur to young men and have to do with curves and dimples. He was too much absorbed by his mother to think on such lines. He was flooded with reverence and pity. Through her, all women were holy to him. They were all mothers, either actual or to be— after, of course, the proper ceremonies. They were all people for whom one leapt up and opened doors, placed chairs out of draughts, and fetched black shawls. On warm spring days, when he was about eighteen, he told himself earnestly that it would be a profanity, a terrible secret sinning, to think amorously—yes, he supposed the word was amorously—while there under his eyes, pervading his days from breakfast to bedtime, was that mourning womanhood, that lopped life, that example of brave doing without any hope or expectation except what might be expected or hoped from heaven. His mother was wonderful the way she bore things. There she was, with nothing left to look forward to in the way of pleasures except the resurrection, yet she did not complain.

But after he had been at Harvard a year a change came over Mr. Twist. Not that he did not remain dutiful and affectionate, but he perceived that it was possible to peep round the corners of his mother, the rock-like corners that had so long jutted out between him and the view, and on the other side there seemed to be quite a lot of interesting things going on. He continued, however, only to eye most of them from afar, and the nearest he got to temptation while at Harvard was to read "Madame Bovary."

After Harvard he was put into an engineering firm, for the Twists only had what would in English money be five thousand pounds a year, and belonged therefore, taking dollars as the measure of standing instead of birth, to the middle classes. Aunt Alice would have described such an income as ample means; Mrs. Twist called it straitened circumstances, and lived accordingly in a condition of perpetual self-sacrifice and doings without. She had a car, but it was only a car, not a Pierce-Arrow; and there was a bathroom to every bedroom, but there were only six bedrooms; and the house stood on a hill and looked over the most beautiful woods, but they were somebody else's woods. She felt, as she beheld the lives of those of her neighbours she let her eyes rest on, who were the millionaires dotted round about the charming environs of Clark, that she was indeed a typical widow,—remote, unfriended, melancholy, poor.

Mrs. Twist might feel poor, but she was certainly comfortable. It was her daughter Edith's aim in life to secure for her the comfort and leisure necessary for any grief that wishes to be thorough. The house was run beautifully by Edith. There were three servants, of whom Edith was one. She was the lady's maid, the head cook, and the family butler. And Mr. Twist, till he went to Harvard, might be described as the page-boy, and afterwards in his vacations as the odd man about the house. Everything centred round their mother. She made a good deal of work, because of being so anxious not to give trouble. She wouldn't get out of the way of evil, but bleakly accepted it. She wouldn't get out of a draught, but sat in it till one or other of her children remembered they hadn't shut the door. When the inevitable cold was upon her and she was lamentably coughing, she would mention the door for the first time, and quietly say she hadn't liked to trouble them to shut it, they had seemed so busy with their own affairs.

But after he had been in the engineering firm a little while, a further change came over Mr. Twist. He was there to make money, more money, for his mother. The first duty of an American male had descended on him. He wished earnestly to fulfil it creditably, in spite of his own tastes being so simple that his income of £5000—it was his, not his mother's, but it didn't feel as if it were—would have been more than sufficient for him. Out of engineering, then, was he to wrest all the things that might comfort his mother. He embarked on his career with as determined an expression on his mouth as so soft and friendly a mouth could be made to take, and he hadn't been in it long before he passed out altogether beyond the line of thinking his mother had laid down for him, and definitely grew up.

The office was in New York, far enough away from Clark for him to be at home only for the Sundays. His mother put him to board with her brother Charles, a clergyman, the rector of the Church of Angelic Refreshment at the back of Tenth Street, and the teapot out of which Uncle Charles poured his tea at his hurried and uncomfortable meals—for he practised the austerities and had no wife—dribbled at its spout. Hold it as carefully as one might it dribbled at its spout, and added to the confused appearance of the table by staining the cloth afresh every time it was used.

Mr. Twist, who below the nose was nothing but kindliness and generosity, his slightly weak chin, his lavishly-lipped mouth, being all amiability and affection, above the nose was quite different. In the middle came his nose, a nose that led him to improve himself, to read and meditate the poets, to be tenacious in following after the noble; and above were eyes in which simplicity sat side by side with appreciation; and above these was the forehead like a dome; and behind this forehead were inventions.

He had not been definitely aware that he was inventive till he came into daily contact with Uncle Charles's teapot. In his boyhood he had often fixed up little things for Edith,—she was three years older than he, and was even then canning and preserving and ironing,—little simplifications and alleviations of her labour; but they had been just toys, things that had amused him to put together and that he forgot as soon as they were done. But the teapot revealed to him clearly what his forehead was there for. He would not and could not continue, being the soul of considerateness, to spill tea on Uncle Charles's table-cloth at every meal—they had tea at breakfast, and at luncheon, and at supper—and if he were thirsty he spilled it several times at every meal. For a long time he coaxed the teapot. He was thoughtful with it. He handled it with the most delicate precision. He gave it time. He never hurried it. He never filled it more than half full. And yet at the end of every pouring, out came the same devastating dribble on to the cloth.

Then he went out and bought another teapot, one of a different pattern, with a curved spout instead of a straight one.

The same thing happened.

Then he went to Wanamaker's, and spent an hour in the teapot section trying one pattern after the other, patiently pouring water, provided by a tipped but languid and supercilious assistant, out of each different make of teapot into cups.

They all dribbled.

Then Mr. Twist went home and sat down and thought. He thought and thought, with his dome-like forehead resting on his long thin hand; and what came out of his forehead at last, sprang out of it as complete in every detail as Pallas Athene when she very similarly sprang, was that now well-known object on every breakfast table, Twist's Non-Trickler Teapot.

In five years Mr. Twist made a fortune out of the teapot. His mother passed from her straitened circumstances to what she still would only call a modest competence, but what in England would have been regarded as wallowing in money. She left off being middle-class, and was received into the lower upper-class, the upper part of this upper-class being reserved for great names like Astor, Rockefeller and Vanderbilt. With these Mrs. Twist could not compete. She would no doubt some day, for Edward was only thirty and there were still coffee-pots; but what he was able to add to the family income helped her for a time to bear the loss of the elder Twist with less of bleakness in her resignation. It was as though an east wind veered round for a brief space a little to the south.

Being naturally, however, inclined to deprecation, when every other reason for it was finally removed by her assiduous son she once more sought out and firmly laid hold of the departed Twist, and hung her cherished unhappiness up on him again as if he were a peg. When the novelty of having a great many bedrooms instead of six, and a great deal of food not to eat but to throw away, and ten times of everything else instead of only once, began to wear off, Mrs. Twist drooped again, and pulled the departed Twist out of the decent forgetfulness of the past, and he once more came to dinner in the form of his favourite dishes, and assisted in the family conversations by means of copious quotations from his alleged utterances.

Mr. Twist's income was anything between sixty and seventy thousand pounds a year by the time the war broke out. Having invented and patented the simple device that kept the table-cloths of America, and indeed of Europe, spotless, all he had to do was to receive his percentages; sit still, in fact, and grow richer. But so much had he changed since his adolescence that he preferred to stick to his engineering and his office in New York rather than go home and be happy with his mother.

She could not understand this behaviour in Edward. She understood his behaviour still less when he went off to France in 1915, himself equipping and giving the ambulance he drove.

For a year his absence, and the dangers he was running, divided Mrs. Twist's sorrows into halves. Her position as a widow with an only son in danger touched the imagination of Clark, and she was never so much called upon as during this year. Now Edward was coming home for a rest, and there was a subdued flutter about her, rather like the stirring of the funeral plumes on the heads of hearse-horses.

While he was crossing the Atlantic and Red-Crossing the Twinklers — this was one of Anna-Felicitas's epigrams and she tried Anna-Rose's patience severely by asking her not once but several times whether she didn't think it funny, whereas Anna-Rose disliked it from the first because of the suggestion it contained that Mr. Twist regarded what he did for them as works of mercy — while Mr. Twist was engaged in these activities, at his home in Clark all the things Edith could think of that he used most to like to eat were being got ready. There was an immense slaughtering of chickens, and baking and churning. Edith, who being now the head servant of many instead of three was more than double as hard-worked as she used to be, was on her feet those last few days without stopping. And she had to go and meet Edward in New York as well. Whether Mrs. Twist feared that he might not come straight home or whether it was what she said it was, that dear Edward must not be the only person on the boat who had no one to meet him, is not certain; what is certain is that when it came to the point, and Edith had to start, Mrs. Twist had difficulty in maintaining her usual brightness.

Edith would be a whole day away, and perhaps a night if the *St. Luke* got in late, for Clark is five hours' train journey from New York, and during all that time Mrs. Twist would be uncared for. She thought Edith surprisingly thoughtless to be so much pleased to go. She examined her flat and sinewy form with disapproval when she came in hatted and booted to say good-bye. No wonder nobody married Edith. And the money wouldn't help her either now—she was too old. She had missed her chances, poor thing.

Mrs. Twist forgot the young man there had been once, years before, when Edward was still in the school room, who had almost married Edith. He was a lusty and enterprising young man, who had come to Clark to stay with a neighbour, and he had had nothing to do through a long vacation, and had taken to dropping in at all hours and interrupting Edith in her housekeeping; and Edith, even then completely flat but of a healthy young uprightness and bright of eyes and hair, had gone silly and forgotten how to cook, and had given her mother, who surely had enough sorrows already, an attack of indigestion.

Mrs. Twist, however, had headed the young man off. Edith was too necessary to her at that time. She could not possibly lose Edith. And besides, the only way to avoid being a widow is not to marry. She told herself that she could not bear the thought of poor Edith's running the risk of an affliction similar to her own. If one hasn't a husband one cannot lose him, Mrs. Twist clearly saw. If Edith married she would certainly lose him unless he lost her. Marriage had only two solutions, she explained to her silent daughter,—she would not, of course, discuss with her that third one which America has so often flown to for solace and relief,—only two, said Mrs. Twist, and they were that either one died oneself, which wasn't exactly a happy thing, or the other one did. It was only a question of time before one of the married was left alone to mourn. Marriage began rosily no doubt, but it always ended black. "And think of my having to see you like *this*" she said, with a gesture indicating her sad dress.

Edith was intimidated; and the young man presently went away whistling. He was the only one. Mrs. Twist had no more trouble. He passed entirely from her mind; and as she looked at Edith dressed for going to meet Edward in the clothes she went to church in on Sundays, she unconsciously felt a faint contempt for a woman who had had so much time to get married in and yet had never achieved it. She herself had been married at twenty; and her hair even now, after all she had gone through, was hardly more gray than Edith's.

"Your hat's crooked," she said, when Edith straightened herself after bending down to kiss her good-bye; and then, after all unable to bear the idea of being left alone while Edith, with that pleased face, went off to New York to see Edward before she did, she asked her, if she still had a minute to spare, to help her to the sofa, because she felt faint.

"I expect the excitement has been too much for me," she murmured, lying down and shutting her eyes; and Edith, disciplined in affection and attentiveness, immediately took off her hat and settled down to getting her mother well again in time for Edward.

Which is why nobody met Mr. Twist on his arrival in New York, and he accordingly did things, as will be seen, which he mightn't otherwise have done.

CHAPTER IX

When the *St. Luke* was so near its journey's end that people were packing up, and the word Nantucket was frequent in the scraps of talk the twins heard, they woke up from the unworried condition of mind Mr. Twist's kindness and the dreamy monotony of the days had produced in them, and began to consider their prospects with more attention. This attention soon resulted in anxiety. Anna-Rose showed hers by being irritable. Anna-Felicitas didn't show hers at all.

It was all very well, so long as they were far away from America and never quite sure that a submarine mightn't settle their future for them once and for all, to feel big, vague, heroic things about a new life and a new world and they two Twinklers going to conquer it; but when the new world was really upon them, and the new life, with all the multitudinous details that would have to be tackled, going to begin in a few hours, their hearts became uneasy and sank within them. England hadn't liked them. Suppose America didn't like them either? Uncle Arthur hadn't liked them. Suppose Uncle Arthur's friends didn't like them either? Their hearts sank to, and remained in, their boots.

Round Anna-Rose's waist, safely concealed beneath her skirt from what Anna-Felicitas called the predatory instincts of their fellow-passengers, was a chamois-leather bag containing their passports, a letter to the bank where their £200 was, a letter to those friends of Uncle Arthur's who were to be tried first, a letter to those other friends of his who were to be the second line of defence supposing the first one failed, and ten pounds in two £5 notes.

Uncle Arthur, grievously grumbling, and having previously used in bed most of those vulgar words that made Aunt Alice so miserable, had given Anna-Rose one of the £5 notes for the extra expenses of the journey till, in New York, she should be able to draw on the £200, though what expenses there could be for a couple of girls whose passage was paid Uncle Arthur was damned, he alleged, if he knew; and Aunt Alice had secretly added the other. This was all Anna-Rose's ready money, and it would have to be changed into dollars before reaching New York so as to be ready for emergencies on arrival. She judged from the growing restlessness of the passengers that it would soon be time to go and change it. How many dollars ought she to get?

Mr. Twist was absent, packing his things. She ought to have asked him long ago, but they seemed so suddenly to have reached the end of their journey. Only yesterday there was the same old limitless sea everywhere, the same old feeling that they were never going to arrive. Now the waves had all gone, and one could actually see land. The New World. The place all their happiness or unhappiness would depend on.

She laid hold of Anna-Felicitas, who was walking about just as if she had never been prostrate on a deck-chair in her life, and was going to say something appropriate and encouraging on the Christopher and Columbus lines; but Anna-Felicitas, who had been pondering the £5 notes problem, wouldn't listen.

"A dollar," said Anna-Felicitas, worrying it out, "isn't like a shilling or a mark, but on the other hand neither is it like a pound."

"No," said Anna-Rose, brought back to her immediate business.

"It's four times more than one, and five times less than the other," said Anna-Felicitas. "That's how you've got to count. That's what Aunt Alice said."

"Yes. And then there's the exchange," said Anna-Rose, frowning. "As if it wasn't complicated enough already, there's the exchange. Uncle Arthur said we weren't to forget that."

Anna-Felicitas wanted to know what was meant by the exchange, and Anna-Rose, unwilling to admit ignorance to Anna-Felicitas, who had to be kept in her proper place, especially when one was just getting to America and she might easily become above herself, said that it was something that varied. ("The exchange, you know, varies," Uncle Arthur had said when he gave her the £5 note. "You must keep your eye on the variations." Anna-Rose was all eagerness to keep her eye on them, if only she had known what and where they were. But one never asked questions of Uncle Arthur. His answers, if one did, were confined to expressions of anger and amazement that one didn't, at one's age, already know.)

"Oh," said Anna-Felicitas, for a moment glancing at Anna-Rose out of the corner of her eye, considerately not pressing her further.

"I wish Mr. Twist would come," said Anna-Rose uneasily, looking in the direction he usually appeared from.

"We won't always have *him*" remarked Anna-Felicitas.

"I never said we would," said Anna-Rose shortly.

The young lady of the nails appeared at that moment in a hat so gorgeous that the twins stopped dead to stare. She had a veil on and white gloves, and looked as if she were going for a walk in Fifth Avenue the very next minute.

"Perhaps we ought to be getting ready too," said Anna-Felicitas.

"Yes. I wish Mr. Twist would come—"

"Perhaps we'd better begin and practise not having Mr. Twist," said Anna-Felicitas, as one who addresses nobody specially and means nothing in particular.

"If anybody's got to practise that, it'll be you," said Anna-Rose. "There'll be no one to roll you up in rugs now, remember. I won't."

"But I don't want to be rolled up in rugs," said Anna-Felicitas mildly. "I shall be walking about New York."

"Oh, *you'll* see," said Anna-Rose irritably.

She was worried about the dollars. She was worried about the tipping, and the luggage, and the arrival, and Uncle Arthur's friends, whose names were Mr. and Mrs. Clouston K. Sack; so naturally she was irritable. One is. And nobody knew and understood this better than Anna-Felicitas.

"Let's go and put on our hats and get ready," she said, after a moment's pause during which she wondered whether, in the interests of Anna-Rose's restoration to calm, she mightn't have to be sick again. She did hope she wouldn't have to. She had supposed she had done with that. It is true there were now no waves, but she knew she had only to go near the engines and smell the oil. "Let's go and put on our hats," she suggested, slipping her hand through Anna-Rose's arm.

Anna-Rose let herself be led away, and they went to their cabin; and when they came out of it half an hour later, no longer with that bald look their caps had given them, the sun catching the little rings of pale gold hair that showed for the first time, and clad, instead of in the disreputable jerseys that they loved, in neat black coats and skirts—for they still wore mourning when properly dressed—with everything exactly as Aunt Alice had directed for their arrival, the young men of the second class could hardly believe their eyes.

"You'll excuse me saying so," said one of them to Anna-Felicitas as she passed him, "but you're looking very well to-day."

"I expect that's because I *am* well," said Anna-Felicitas amiably.

Mr. Twist, when he saw them, threw up his hands and ejaculated "My!"

"Yes," said Anna-Felicitas, who was herself puzzled by the difference the clothes had made in Anna-Rose after ten solid days of cap and jersey, "I think it's our hats. They do somehow seem very splendid."

"Splendid?" echoed Mr. Twist. "Why, they'd make the very angels jealous, and get pulling off their haloes and kicking them over the edge of heaven."

"What is so wonderful is that Aunt Alice should ever have squeezed them out of Uncle Arthur," said Anna-Rose, gazing lost in admiration at Anna-Felicitas. "He didn't disgorge nice hats easily at all."

And one of the German ladies muttered to the other, as her eye fell on Anna-Felicitas, "*Ja, ja, die hat Rasse.*"

And it was only because it was the other German lady's hair that spent the night in a different part of the cabin from her head and had been seen doing it by Anna-Felicitas, that she cavilled and was grudging. "*Gewiss,*" she muttered back, "*bis auf der Nase. Die Nase aber entfremdet mich. Die ist keine echte Junkernase.*"

So that the Twinklers had quite a success, and their hearts came a little way out of their boots; only a little way, though, for there were the Clouston K. Sacks looming bigger into their lives every minute now.

Really it was a beautiful day, and, as Aunt Alice used to say, that does make such a difference. A clear pale loveliness of light lay over New York, and there was a funny sprightliness in the air, a delicate dry crispness. The trees on the shore, when they got close, were delicate too—delicate pale gold, and green, and brown, and they seemed so composed and calm, the twins thought, standing there quietly after the upheavals and fidgetiness of the Atlantic. New York was well into the Fall, the time of year when it gets nearest to beauty. The beauty was entirely in the atmosphere, and the lights and shadows it made. It was like an exquisite veil flung over an ugly woman, hiding, softening, encouraging hopes.

Everybody on the ship was crowding eagerly to the sides. Everybody was exhilarated, and excited, and ready to be friendly and talkative. They all waved whenever another boat passed. Those who knew America pointed out the landmarks to those who didn't. Mr. Twist pointed them out to the twins, and so did the young man who had remarked favourably on Anna-Felicitas's looks, and as they did it simultaneously and there was so much to look at and so many boats to wave to, it wasn't till they had actually got to the statue of Liberty that Anna-Rose remembered her £10 and the dollars.

The young man was saying how much the statue of Liberty had cost, and the word dollars made Anna-Rose turn with a jump to Mr. Twist.

"Oh," she exclaimed, clutching at her chamois leather bag where it very visibly bulged out beneath her waistband, "I forgot—I must get change.

And how much do you think we ought to tip the stewardess? I've never tipped anybody yet ever, and I wish—I wish I hadn't to."

She got quite red. It seemed to her dreadful to offer money to someone so much older than herself and who till almost that very morning had treated her and Anna-Felicitas like the naughtiest of tiresome children. Surely she would be most offended at being tipped by people such years younger than herself?

Mr. Twist thought not.

"A dollar," said the young man. "One dollar. That's the figure. Not a cent more, or you girls'll get inflating prices and Wall Street'll bust up."

Anna-Rose, not heeding him and clutching nervously the place where her bag was, told Mr. Twist that the stewardess hadn't seemed to mind them quite so much last night, and still less that morning, and perhaps some little memento—something that wasn't money—

"Give her those caps of yours," said the young man, bursting into hilarity; but indeed it wasn't his fault that he was a low young man.

Mr. Twist, shutting him out of the conversation by interposing a shoulder, told Anna-Rose he had noticed stewardesses, and also stewards, softened when journeys drew near their end, but that it didn't mean they wanted mementos. They wanted money; and he would do the tipping for her if she liked.

Anna-Rose jumped at it. This tipping of the stewardess had haunted her at intervals throughout the journey whenever she woke up at night. She felt that, not having yet in her life tipped anybody, it was very hard that she couldn't begin with somebody more her own size.

"Then if you don't mind coming behind the funnel," she said, "I can give you my £5 notes, and perhaps you would get them changed for me and deduct what you think the stewardess ought to have."

Mr. Twist, and also Anna-Felicitas, who wasn't allowed to stay behind with the exuberant young man though she was quite unconscious of his presence, went with Anna-Rose behind the funnel, where after a great deal of private fumbling, her back turned to them, she produced the two much-crumpled £5 notes.

"The steward ought to have something too," said Mr. Twist.

"Oh, I'd be glad if you'd do him as well," said Anna-Rose eagerly. "I don't think I *could* offer him a tip. He has been so fatherly to us. And imagine offering to tip one's father."

Mr. Twist laughed, and said she would get over this feeling in time. He promised to do what was right, and to make it clear that the tips he bestowed were Twinkler tips; and presently he came back with messages of thanks from the tipped—such polite ones from the stewardess that the twins were astonished—and gave Anna-Rose a packet of very dirty-looking slices of green paper, which were dollar bills, he said, besides a variety of strange coins which he spread out on a ledge and explained to her.

"The exchange was favourable to you to-day," said Mr. Twist, counting out the money.

"How nice of it," said Anna-Rose politely. "Did you keep your eye on its variations?" she added a little loudly, with a view to rousing respect in Anna-Felicitas who was lounging against a seat and showing a total absence of every kind of appropriate emotion.

"Certainly," said Mr. Twist after a slight pause. "I kept both my eyes on all of them."

Mr. Twist had, it appeared, presented the steward and stewardess each with a dollar on behalf of the Misses Twinkler, but because the exchange was so favourable this had made no difference to the £5 notes. Reducing each £5 note into German marks, which was the way the Twinklers, in spite of a year in England, still dealt in their heads with money before they could get a clear idea of it, there would have been two hundred marks; and as it took, roughly, four marks to make a dollar, the two hundred marks would have to be divided by four; which, leaving aside that extra complication of variations in the exchange, and regarding the exchange for a moment and for purposes of simplification as keeping quiet for a bit and resting, should produce, also roughly, said Anna-Rose a little out of breath as she got to the end of her calculation, fifty dollars.

"Correct," said Mr. Twist, who had listened with respectful attention. "Here they are."

"I said roughly," said Anna-Rose. "It can't be *exactly* fifty dollars. The tips anyhow would alter that."

"Yes, but you forget the exchange."

Anna-Rose was silent. She didn't want to go into that before Anna-Felicitas. Of the two, she was supposed to be the least bad at sums. Their mother had put it that way, refusing to say, as Anna-Rose industriously tried to trap her into saying, that she was the better of the two. But even so, the difference entitled her to authority on the subject with Anna-Felicitas, and by dint of doing all her calculations roughly, as she was careful to describe her method, she allowed room for withdrawal and escape where otherwise the inflexibility of figures might have caught her tight and held her down while Anna-Felicitas looked on and was unable to respect her.

Evidently the exchange was something beneficent. She decided to rejoice in it in silence, accept whatever it did, and refrain from asking questions.

"So I did. Of course. The exchange," she said, after a little.

She gathered up the dollar bills and began packing them into her bag. They wouldn't all go in, and she had to put the rest into her pocket, for which also there were too many; but she refused Anna-Felicitas's offer to put some of them in hers on the ground that sooner or later she would be sure to forget they weren't her handkerchief and would blow her nose with them.

"Thank you very much for being so kind," she said to Mr. Twist, as she stuffed her pocket full and tried by vigorous patting to get it to look inconspicuous. "We're never going to forget you, Anna-F. and me. We'll write to you often, and we'll come and see you as often as you like."

"Yes," said Anna-Felicitas dreamily, as she watched the shore of Long Island sliding past. "Of course you've got your relations, but relations soon pall, and you may be quite glad after a while of a little fresh blood."

Mr. Twist thought this very likely, and agreed with several other things Anna-Felicitas, generalizing from Uncle Arthur, said about relations, again with that air of addressing nobody specially and meaning nothing in particular, while Anna-Rose wrestled with the obesity of her pocket.

"Whether you come to see me or not," said Mr. Twist, whose misgivings as to the effect of the Twinklers on his mother grew rather than subsided, "I shall certainly come to see you."

"Perhaps Mr. Sack won't allow followers," said Anna-Felicitas, her eyes far away. "Uncle Arthur didn't. He wouldn't let the maids have any, so they had to go out and do the following themselves. We had a follower once, didn't we, Anna-R.?" she continued her voice pensive and reminiscent. "He was a friend of Uncle Arthur's. Quite old. At least thirty or forty. I shouldn't have thought he *could* follow. But he did. And he used to come home to tea with Uncle Arthur and produce boxes of chocolate for us out of his pockets when Uncle Arthur wasn't looking. We ate them and felt perfectly well disposed toward him till one day he tried to kiss one of us—I forget which. And that, combined with the chocolates, revealed him in his true colours as a follower, and we told him they weren't allowed in that house and urged him to go to some place where they were, or he would certainly be overtaken by Uncle Arthur's vengeance, and we said how surprised we were, because he was so old and we didn't know followers were as old as that ever."

"It seemed a very shady thing," said Anna-Rose, having subdued the swollenness of her pocket, "to eat his chocolates and then not want to kiss him, but we don't hold with kissing, Anna-F. and me. Still, we were full of his chocolates; there was no getting away from that. So we talked it over after he had gone, and decided that next day when he came we'd tell him he might kiss one of us if he still wanted to, and we drew lots which it was to be, and it was me, and I filled myself to the brim with chocolates so as to feel grateful enough to bear it, but he didn't come."

"No," said Anna-Felicitas. "He didn't come again for a long while, and when he did there was no follow left in him. Quite the contrary."

Mr. Twist listened with the more interest to this story because it was the first time Anna-Felicitas had talked since he knew her. He was used to the inspiriting and voluble conversation of Anna-Rose who had looked upon him as her best friend since the day he had wiped up her tears; but Anna-Felicitas had been too unwell to talk. She had uttered languid and brief observations from time to time with her eyes shut and her head lolling loosely on her neck, but this was the first time she had been, as it were, an ordinary human being, standing upright on her feet, walking about, looking intelligently if pensively at the scenery, and in a condition of affable readiness, it appeared, to converse.

Mr. Twist was a born mother. The more trouble he was given the more attached he became. He had rolled Anna-Felicitas up in rugs so often that to be not going to roll her up any more was depressing to him. He was beginning to perceive this motherliness in him himself, and he gazed through his spectacles at Anna-Felicitas while she sketched the rise and fall of the follower, and wondered with an almost painful solicitude what her fate would be in the hands of the Clouston Sacks.

Equally he wondered as to the other one's fate; for he could not think of one Twinkler without thinking of the other. They were inextricably mixed together in the impression they had produced on him, and they dwelt together in his thoughts as one person called, generally, Twinklers. He stood gazing at them, his motherly instincts uppermost, his hearty yearning over them now that the hour of parting was so near and his carefully tended chickens were going to be torn from beneath his wing. Mr. Twist was domestic. He was affectionate. He would have loved, though he had never known it, the sensation of pattering feet about his house, and small hands clinging to the apron he would never wear. And it was entirely characteristic of him that his invention, the invention that brought him his fortune, should have had to do with a teapot.

But if his heart was uneasy within him at the prospect of parting from his charges their hearts were equally uneasy, though not in the same way. The very name of Clouston K. Sack was repugnant to Anna-Rose; and Anna-Felicitas, less quick at disliking, turned it over cautiously in her mind as one who turns over an unknown and distasteful object with the nose of his umbrella. Even she couldn't quite believe that any good thing could come out of a name like that, especially when it had got into their lives through Uncle Arthur. Mr. Twist had never heard of the Clouston Sacks, which made Anna-Rose still more distrustful. She wasn't in the least encouraged when he explained the bigness of America and that nobody in it ever knew everybody—she just said that everybody had heard of Mr. Roosevelt, and her heart was too doubtful within her even to mind being told, as he did immediately tell her within ear-shot of Anna-Felicitas, that her reply was unreasonable.

Just at the end, as they were all three straining their eyes, no one with more anxiety than Mr. Twist, to try and guess which of the crowd on the landing-stage were the Clouston Sacks, they passed on their other side the *Vaterland*, the great interned German liner at its moorings, and the young man who had previously been so very familiar, as Anna-Rose said, but who was only, Mr. Twist explained, being American, came hurrying boldly up.

"You mustn't miss this," he said to Anna-Felicitas, actually seizing her by the arm. "Here's something that'll make you feel home-like right away."

And he led her off, and would have dragged her off but for Anna-Felicitas's perfect non-resistance.

"He *is* being familiar," said Anna-Rose to Mr. Twist, turning very red and following quickly after him. "That's not just being American. Everybody decent knows that if there's any laying hold of people's arms to be done one begins with the eldest sister."

"Perhaps he doesn't realize that you *are* the elder," said Mr. Twist. "Strangers judge, roughly, by size."

"I'm afraid I'm going to have trouble with her," said Anna-Rose, not heeding his consolations. "It isn't a sinecure, I assure you, being left sole guardian and protector of somebody as pretty as all that. And the worst of it is she's going on getting prettier. She hasn't nearly come to the end of what she can do in that direction. I see it growing on her. Every Sunday she's inches prettier than she was the Sunday before. And wherever I take her to live, and however out of the way it is, I'm sure the path to our front door is going to be black with suitors."

This dreadful picture so much perturbed her, and she looked up at Mr. Twist with such worried eyes, that he couldn't refrain from patting her on her shoulder.

"There, there," said Mr. Twist, and he begged her to be sure to let him know directly she was in the least difficulty, or even perplexity,—"about the suitors, for instance, or anything else. You must let me be of some use in the world, you know," he said.

"But we shouldn't like it at all if we thought you were practising being useful on us," said Anna-Rose "It's wholly foreign to our natures to enjoy being the objects of anybody's philanthropy."

"Now I just wonder where you get all your long words from," said Mr. Twist soothingly; and Anna-Rose laughed, and there was only one dimple in the Twinkler family and Anna-Rose had got it.

"What do you want to get looking at *that* for?" she asked Anna-Felicitas, when she had edged through the crowd staring at the *Vaterland,* and got to where Anna-Felicitas stood listening abstractedly to the fireworks of American slang the young man was treating her to,—that terse, surprising, swift hitting-of-the-nail-on-the-head form of speech which she was hearing in such abundance for the first time.

The American passengers appeared one and all to be rejoicing over the impotence of the great ship. Every one of them seemed to be violently pro-Ally, derisively conjecturing the feelings of the *Vaterland* as every day under her very nose British ships arrived and departed and presently arrived again,—the same ships she had seen depart coming back unharmed, unhindered by her country's submarines. Only the two German ladies, once more ignoring their American allegiance, looked angry. It was incredible to them, simply *unfassbar* as they said in their thoughts, that any nation should dare inconvenience Germans, should dare lay a finger, even the merest friendliest detaining one, on anything belonging to the mighty, the inviolable Empire. Well, these Americans, these dollar-grubbing Yankees, would soon get taught a sharp, deserved lesson—but at this point they suddenly remembered they were Americans themselves, and pulled up their thoughts violently, as it were, on their haunches.

They turned, however, bitterly to the Twinkler girl as she pushed her way through to her sister,—those renegade Junkers, those contemptible little apostates—and asked her, after hearing her question to Anna-Felicitas, with an extraordinary breaking out of pent-up emotion where she, then, supposed she would have been at that moment if it hadn't been for Germany.

"Not here I think," said Anna-Rose, instantly and fatally ready as she always was to answer back and attempt what she called reasoned conversation. "There wouldn't have been a war, so of course I wouldn't have been here."

"Why, you wouldn't so much as have been born without Germany," said the lady whose hair came off, with difficulty controlling a desire to shake this insolent and perverted Junker who could repeat the infamous English lie as to who began the war. "You owe your very existence to Germany. You should be giving thanks to her on your knees for her gift to you of life, instead of jeering at this representative—" she flung a finger out toward the *Vaterland*—"this patient and dignified-in -temporary-misfortune representative, of her power."

"I wasn't jeering," said Anna-Rose, defending herself and clutching at Anna-Felicitas's sleeve to pull her away.

"You wouldn't have had a father at all but for Germany," said the other lady, the one whose hair grew.

"And perhaps you will tell me," said the first one, "where you would have been *then*."

"I don't believe," said Anna-Rose, her nose in the air, "I don't believe I'd have ever been at a loss for a father."

The ladies, left speechless a moment by the arrogance as well as several other things about this answer gave Anna-Rose an opportunity for further reasoning with them, which she was unable to resist. "There are lots of fathers," she said, "in England, who would have I'm sure have been delighted to take me on if Germany had failed me."

"England!"

"Take you on!"

"An English father for you? For a subject of the King of Prussia?"

"I—I'm afraid I—I'm going to be sick," gasped Anna-Felicitas suddenly.

"You're never going to be sick in this bit of bathwater, Miss Twinkler?" exclaimed the young man, with the instant ungrudging admiration of one who is confronted by real talent. "My, what a gift!"

Anna-Rose darted at Anna-Felicitas's drooping head, that which she had been going to say back to the German ladies dissolving on her tongue. "Oh no—*no*—" she wailed. "Oh *no*—not in your best hat, Columbus darling—you can't—it's not done—and your hat'll shake off into the water, and then there'll only be one between us and we shall never be able to go out paying calls and things at the same time—come away and sit down—Mr. Twist—Mr. Twist—oh, please come—"

Anna-Felicitas allowed herself to be led away, just in time as she murmured, and sat down on the nearest seat and shut her eyes. She was thankful Anna-Rose's attention had been diverted to her so instantly, for it would have been very difficult to be sick with the ship as quiet as one's own bedroom. Nothing short of the engine-room could have made her sick now. She sat keeping her eyes shut and Anna-Rose's attention riveted, wondering what she would do when there was no ship and Anna-Rose was on the verge of hasty and unfortunate argument. Would she have to learn to faint? But that would terrify poor Christopher so dreadfully.

Anna-Felicitas pondered, her eyes shut, on this situation. Up to now in her life she had always found that situations solved themselves. Given time. And sometimes a little assistance. So, no doubt, would this one. Anna-Rose would ripen and mellow. The German ladies would depart hence and be no more seen; and it was unlikely she and Anna-Rose would meet at such close quarters as a ship's cabin any persons so peculiarly and unusually afflicting again. All situations solved themselves; or, if they showed signs of not going to, one adopted the gentle methods that helped them to get solved. Early in life she had discovered that objects which cannot be removed or climbed over can be walked round. A little deviousness, and the thing was done. She herself had in the most masterly manner when she was four escaped church-going for several years by a simple method, that seemed to her looking back very like an inspiration, of getting round it. She had never objected to going, had never put into words the powerful if vague dislike with which it filled her when Sunday after Sunday she had to go and dangle her legs helplessly for two hours from the chair she was put on in the enclosed pew reserved for the *hohe gräfliche Herrschaften* from the Slosh.

Her father, a strict observer of the correct and a pious believer in God for other people, attended Divine Service as regularly as he wound the clocks and paid the accounts. He *repräsentierte*, as the German phrase went; and his wife and children were expected to *repräsentieren* too. Which they did uncomplainingly; for when one has to do with determined husbands and fathers it is quickest not to complain. But the pins and needles that patient child endured, Anna-Felicitas remembered, looking back through the years at the bunched-up figure on the chair as at a stranger, were something awful. The edge of the chair just caught her legs in the pins and needles place. If she had been a little bigger or a little smaller it wouldn't have happened; as it was, St. Paul wrestling with beasts at Ephesus wasn't more heroic than Anna-Felicitas perceived that distant child to have been, silently Sunday after Sunday bearing her legs. Then one Sunday something snapped inside her, and she heard her own voice floating out into the void above the heads of the mumbling worshippers, and it said with a terrible distinctness in a sort of monotonous wail: "I only had a cold potato for breakfast,"—and a second time, in the breathless suspension of mumbling that followed upon this: "I only had a cold potato for breakfast,"—and a third time she opened her mouth to repeat the outrageous statement, regardless of her mother's startled hand laid on her arm, and of Anna-Rose's petrified stare, and of the lifted faces of the congregation, and of the bent, scandalized brows of the pastor,—impelled by something that possessed her, unable to do anything but obey it; but her father, a man of deeds, rose up in his place, took her in his arms, and carried her down the stairs and out of the church. And the minute she found herself really rescued, and out where the sun and wind, her well-known friends, were larking about among the tombstones, she laid her cheek as affectionately against her father's head as if she were a daughter to be proud of, and would have purred if she had had had a purr as loudly as the most satisfied and virtuous of cats.

"*Mein Kind*," said her father, standing her up on a convenient tomb so that her eyes were level with his, "is it then true about the cold potato?"

"No," said Anna-Felicitas patting his face, pleased at what her legs were feeling like again.

"*Mein Kind*," said her father, "do you not know it is wrong to lie?"

"No," said Anna-Felicitas placidly, the heavenly blue of her eyes, gazing straight into his, exactly like the mild sky above the trees.

"No?" echoed her father, staring at her. "But, *Kind*, you know what a lie is?"

"No," said Anna-Felicitas, gazing at him tenderly in her satisfaction at being restored to a decent pair of legs; and as he still stood staring at her she put her hands one on each of his cheeks and squeezed his face together and murmured, "Oh, I do *love* you."

CHAPTER X

Lost in the contemplation of a distant past Anna-Felicitas sat with her eyes shut long after she needn't have.

She had forgotten about the German ladies, and America, and the future so instantly pressing on her, and was away on the shores of the Baltic again, where bits of amber where washed up after a storm, and the pale rushes grew in shallow sunny water that was hardly salt, and the air seemed for ever sweet with lilac. All the cottage gardens in the little village that clustered round a clearing in the trees had lilac bushes in them, for there was something in the soil that made lilacs be more wonderful there than anywhere else in the world, and in May the whole forest as far as one could walk was soaked with the smell of it. After rain on a May evening, what a wonder it was; what a wonder, that running down the black, oozing forest paths between wet pine stems, out on to the shore to look at the sun setting below the great sullen clouds of the afternoon over on one's left where Denmark was, and that lifting of one's face to the exquisite mingling of the delicate sea smell and the lilac. And then there was home to come back to when the forest began to look too dark and its deep silence made one's flesh creep—home, and a light in the window where ones mother was. Incredible the security of those days, the safe warmth of them, the careless roominess....

"You know if you *could* manage to feel a little better, Anna-F.," said Anna-Rose's voice entreatingly in her ear, "it's time we began to get off this ship."

Anna-Felicitas opened her eyes, and got up all confused and self-reproachful. Everybody had melted away from that part of the deck except herself and Anna-Rose. The ship was lying quiet at last alongside the wharf. She had over-done being ill this time. She was ashamed of herself for having wandered off so easily and comfortably into the past, and left poor Christopher alone in the difficult present.

"I'm so sorry," she said smiling apologetically, and giving her hat a tug of determination symbolic of her being ready for anything, especially America. "I think I must have gone to sleep. Have you—" she hesitated and dropped her voice. "Are they—are the Clouston Sacks visible yet?"

"I thought I saw them," said Anna-Rose, dropping her voice too, and looking round uneasily over her shoulder. "I'd have come here sooner to see how you were getting on, but I thought I saw them, and they looked so like what I think they will look like that I went into our cabin again for a few minutes. But it wasn't them. They've found the people they were after, and have gone."

"There's a great crowd waiting," said Mr. Twist, coming up, "and I think we ought to go and look for your friends. As you don't know what they're like and they don't know what you're like it may be difficult. Heaven forbid," he continued, "that I should hurry you, but I have to catch a train if I'm to get home to-night, and I don't intend to catch it until I've handed you over safely to the Sacks."

"Those Sacks—" began Anna-Rose; and then she finished irrelevantly by remarking that it was the details of life that were discouraging,—from which Anna Felicitas knew that Christopher's heart was once more in her boots.

"Come along," said Mr. Twist, urging them to wards the gangway. "Anything you've got to say about life I shall be glad to hear, but at some time when we're more at leisure."

It had never occurred to either of the twins that the Clouston Sacks would not meet them. They had taken it for granted from the beginning that some form of Sack, either male or female, or at least their plenipotentiary, would be on the wharf to take them away to the Sack lair, as Anna-Felicitas alluded to the family mansion. It was, they knew, in Boston, but Boston conveyed nothing to them. Only Mr. Twist knew how far away it was. He had always supposed the Sacks would meet their young charges, stay that night in New York, and continue on to Boston next day. The twins were so certain they would be met that Mr. Twist was certain too. He had concluded, with a growingly empty feeling in his heart as the time of separation drew near, that all that now remained for him to do on behalf of the Twinklers was to hand them over to the Sacks. And then leave them. And then go home to that mother he loved but had for some time known he didn't like,— go home a bereft and lonely man.

But out of the crowd on the pier, any of whom might have been Sacks for all the Twinklers, eagerly scanning faces, knew, nobody in fact seemed to be Sacks. At least, nobody came forward and said, "Are you the Twinklers?" Other people fell into each other's arms; the air was full of the noise of kissing, the loud legitimate kissing of relations; but nobody took any notice of the twins. For a long while they stood waiting. Their luggage was examined, and Mr. Twist's luggage—only his was baggage—was examined, and the kissing and exclaiming crowd swayed hither and thither, and broke up into groups, and was shot through by interviewers, and got packed off into taxis, and grew thinner and thinner, and at last was so thin that the concealment of the Sacks in it was no longer possible.

There were no Sacks.

To the last few groups of people left in the great glass-roofed hall piled with bags of wool and sulphur, Mr. Twist went up boldly and asked if they were intending to meet some young ladies called Twinkler. His tone, owing to perturbation, was rather more than one of inquiry, it almost sounded menacing; and the answers he got were cold. He wandered about uncertainly from group to group, his soft felt hat on the back of his head and his brow getting more and more puckered; and Anna-Rose, anxiously looking on from afar, became impatient at last of these refusals of everybody to be Sacks, and thought that perhaps Mr. Twist wasn't making himself clear.

Impetuous by nature and little given to calm waiting, she approached a group on her own account and asked them, enunciating her words very clearly, whether they were by any chance Mr. and Mrs. Clouston Sack.

The group, which was entirely female, stared round and down at her in astonished silence, and shook its heads; and as she saw Mr. Twist being turned away for the fifth time in the distance a wave of red despair came over her, and she said, reproach in her voice and tears in her eyes, "But *somebody's* got to be the Sacks."

Upon which the group she was addressing stared at her in a more astonished silence than ever.

Mr. Twist came up mopping his brow and took he arm and led her back to Anna-Felicitas, who was taking care of the luggage and had sat down philosophically to await developments on a bag of sulphur. She didn't yet know what sulphur looked like on one's clothes after one has sat on it, and smiled cheerfully and encouragingly at Anna-Rose as she came towards her.

"There *are* no Sacks," said Anna-Rose, facing the truth.

"It's exactly like that Uncle Arthur of yours," said Mr. Twist, mopping his forehead and speaking almost vindictively. "Exactly like him. A man like that *would* have the sort of friends that don't meet one."

"Well, we must do without the Sacks," said Anna-Felicitas, rising from the sulphur bag with the look of serene courage that can only dwell on the face of one who is free from care as to what has happened to him behind. "And it isn't," she added sweetly to Mr. Twist, "as if we hadn't got *you.*"

"Yes," said Anna-Rose, suddenly seeing daylight. "Of course. What do Sacks really matter? I mean, for a day or two? You'll take us somewhere where we can wait till we've found them."

"Yes," said Anna-Felicitas. "Some nice quiet old-fashioned coffee-house sort of place, like the one the Brontes went to in St. Paul's Churchyard the first time they were launched into the world."

"Yes. Some inexpensive place."

"Suited to the frugal."

"Because although we've got £200, even that will need watching or it will go."

During this conversation Mr. Twist stood mopping his forehead. As often as he mopped it it broke out afresh and had to be mopped again. They were the only passengers left now, and had become very conspicuous. He couldn't but perceive that a group of officials with grim, locked-up-looking mouths were eyeing him and the Twinklers attentively.

Always zealous in the cause of virtue, America provided her wharves and landing-places with officials specially appointed to guard the purity of family life. Family life obviously cannot be pure without a marriage being either in it or having at some time or other passed through it. The officials engaged in eyeing Mr. Twist and the twins were all married themselves, and were well acquainted with that awful purity. But eye the Twist and Twinkler party as they might, they could see no trace of marriage anywhere about it.

On the contrary, the man of the party looked so uneasy that it amounted to conscious illegality.

"Sisters?" said the chief official, stepping forward abruptly.

"Eh?" said Mr. Twist, pausing in the wiping of his forehead.

"These here—" said the official, jerking his thumb at the twins. "They your sisters?"

"No," said Mr. Twist stiffly.

"No," said the twins, with one voice. "Do you think we look like him?"

"Daughters?"

"No," said Mr. Twist stiffly.

"No," said the twins, with an ever greater vigour of repudiation. "You can't really think we look as much like him as all that?"

"Wife and sister-in-law?"

Then the Twinklers laughed. They laughed aloud, even Anna-Rose forgetting her cares for a moment. But they were flattered, because it was at least a proof that they looked thoroughly grown-up.

"Then if they ain't your sisters, and they ain't your daughters, and they ain't your wife and sister-in-law, p'raps you'll tell me—"

"These young ladies are not anything at all of mine, sir," said Mr. Twist vehemently.

"Don't you get sir-ing me, now," said the official sticking out his jaw. "This is a free country, and I'll have no darned cheek."

"These young ladies in no way belong to me," said Mr. Twist more patiently. "They're my friends."

"Oh. Friends, are they? Then p'raps you'll tell me what you're going to do with them next."

"Do with them?" repeated Mr. Twist, as he stared with puckered brow at the twins. "That's exactly what I wish I knew."

The official scanned him from head to foot with triumphant contempt. He had got one of them, anyhow. He felt quite refreshed already. There had been a slump in sinners the past week, and he was as full of suppressed energy and as much tormented by it as an unexercised and overfed horse. "Step this way," he ordered curtly, waving Mr. Twist towards a wooden erection that was apparently an office. "Oh, don't you worry about the girls," he added, as his prey seemed disinclined to leave them.

But Mr. Twist did worry. He saw Ellis Island looming up behind the two figures that were looking on in an astonishment that had not yet had time to turn into dismay as he was marched off out of sight. "I'll be back in a minute," he called over his shoulder.

"That's as may be," remarked the official grimly.

But he was back; if not in a minute in a little more than five minutes, still accompanied by the official, but an official magically changed into tameness and amiability, desirous to help, instructing his inferiors to carry Mr. Twist's and the young ladies' baggage to a taxi.

It was the teapot that had saved him,—that blessed teapot that was always protruding itself benevolently into his life. Mr. Twist had identified himself with it, and it had instantly saved him. In the shelter of his teapot Mr. Twist could go anywhere and do anything in America. Everybody had it. Everybody knew it. It was as pervasive of America as Ford's cars, but cosily, quietly pervasive. It was only less visible because it stayed at home. It was more like a wife than Ford's cars were. From a sinner caught red-handed,

Mr. Twist, its amiable creator, leapt to the position of one who can do no wrong, for he had not only placed his teapot between himself and judgment but had accompanied his proofs of identity by a suitable number of dollar bills, pressed inconspicuously into the official's conveniently placed hand.

The twins found themselves being treated with distinction. They were helped into the taxi by the official himself, and what was to happen to them next was left entirely to the decision and discretion of Mr. Twist—a man so much worried that at that moment he hadn't any of either. He couldn't even answer when asked where the taxi was to go to. He had missed his train, and he tried not to think of his mother's disappointment, the thought was so upsetting. But he wouldn't have caught it if he could, for how could he leave these two poor children?

"I'm more than ever convinced," he said, pushing his hat still further off his forehead, and staring at the back of the Twinkler trunks piled up in front of him next to the driver, while the disregarded official at the door still went on asking him where he wished the cab to go to, "that children should all have parents."

CHAPTER XI

The hotel they were finally sent to by the official, goaded at last by Mr. Twist's want of a made-up mind into independent instructions to the cabman, was the Ritz. He thought this very suitable for the evolver of Twist's Non-Trickler, and it was only when they were being rushed along at what the twins, used to the behaviour of London taxis and not altogether unacquainted with the prudent and police-supervised deliberation of the taxis of Berlin, regarded as a skid-collision-and-mutilation-provoking speed, that a protest from Anna-Rose conveyed to Mr. Twist where they were heading for.

"An hotel called Ritz sounds very expensive," she said. "I've heard Uncle Arthur talk of one there is in London and one there is in Paris, and he said that only damned American millionaires could afford to stay in them. Anna-Felicitas and me aren't American millionaires—"

"Or damned," put in Anna-Felicitas.

"—but quite the contrary," said Anna-Rose, "hadn't you better take us somewhere else?"

"Somewhere like where the Brontes stayed in London," said Anna-Felicitas harping on this idea. "Where cheapness is combined with historical associations."

"Oh Lord, it don't matter," said Mr. Twist, who for the first time in their friendship seemed ruffled.

"Indeed it does," said Anna-Rose anxiously.

"You forget we've got to husband our resources," said Anna-Felicitas.

"You mustn't run away with the idea that because we've got £200 we're the same as millionaires," said Anna-Rose.

"Uncle Arthur," said Anna-Felicitas, "frequently told us that £200 is a very vast sum; but he equally frequently told us that it isn't."

"It was when he was talking about having given to us that he said it was such a lot," said Anna-Rose.

"He said that as long as we had it we would be rich," said Anna-Felicitas, "but directly we hadn't it we would be poor."

"So we'd rather not go to the Ritz, please," said Anna-Rose, "if you don't mind."

The taxi was stopped, and Mr. Twist got out and consulted the driver. The thought of his Uncle Charles as a temporary refuge for the twins floated across his brain, but was rejected because Uncle Charles would speak to no woman under fifty except from his pulpit, and approached those he did speak to with caution till they were sixty. He regarded them as one of the chief causes of modern unrest. He liked them so much that he hated them. He could practise abstinence, but not temperance. Uncle Charles was no good as a refuge.

"Well now, see here," said the driver at last, after Mr. Twist had rejected such varied suggestions of something small and quiet as the Waldorf-Astoria, the Plaza and the Biltmore, "you tell me where you want to go to and I'll take you there."

"I want to go to the place your mother would stay in if she came up for a day or two from the country," said Mr. Twist helplessly.

"Get right in then, and I'll take you back to the Ritz," said the driver.

But finally, when his contempt for Mr. Twist, of whose identity he was unaware, had grown too great even for him to bandy pleasantries with him, he did land his party at an obscure hotel in a street off the less desirable end of Fifth Avenue, and got rid of him.

It was one of those quiet and cheap New York hotels that yet are both noisy and expensive. It was full of foreigners,—real foreigners, the twins perceived, not the merely technical sort like themselves, but people with yellow faces and black eyes. They looked very seedy and shabby, and smoked very much, and talked volubly in unknown tongues. The entrance hall, a place of mottled marble, with clerks behind a counter all of whose faces looked as if they were masks, was thick with them; and it was when they turned to stare and whisper as Anna-Felicitas passed and Anna-Rose was thinking proudly, "Yes, you don't see anything like that every day, do you," and herself looked fondly at her Columbus, that she saw that it wasn't Columbus's beauty at all but the sulphur on the back of her skirt.

This spoilt Anna-Rose's arrival in New York. All the way up in the lift to the remote floor on which their bedroom was she was trying to brush it off, for the dress was Anna-F.'s very best one.

"That's all your grips, ain't it?" said the youth in buttons who had come up with them, dumping their bags down on the bedroom floor.

"Our what?" said Anna-Rose, to whom the expression was new. "Do you mean our bags?"

"No. Grips. These here," said the youth.

"Is that what they're called in America?" asked Anna-Felicitas, with the intelligent interest of a traveller determined to understand and appreciate everything, while Anna-Rose, still greatly upset by the condition of the best skirt but unwilling to expatiate upon it before the youth, continued to brush her down as best she could with her handkerchief.

"I don't call them. It's what they are," said the youth. "What I want to know is, are they all here?"

"How interesting that you don't drop your h's," said Anna-Felicitas, gazing at him. "The rest of you is so *like* no h's."

The youth said nothing to that, the line of thought being one he didn't follow.

"Those *are* all our—grips, I think," said Anna-Rose counting them round the corner of Anna-Felicitas's skirt. "Thank you very much," she added after a pause, as he still lingered.

But this didn't cause him to disappear as it would have in England. Instead, he picked up a metal bottle with a stopper off the table, and shook it and announced that their ice-water bottle was empty. "Want some ice water?" he inquired.

"What for?" asked Anna-Felicitas.

"What for?" echoed the youth.

"Thank you," said Anna-Rose, who didn't care about the youth's manner which seemed to her familiar, "we don't want ice water, but we should be glad of a little hot water."

"You'll get all you want of that in there," said the youth, jerking his head towards a door that led into a bathroom. "It's ice water and ink that you get out of me."

"Really?" said Anna-Felicitas, gazing at him with even more intelligent interest, almost as if she were prepared, it being America, a country, she had heard, of considerable mechanical ingenuity, to find his person bristling with taps which only needed turning.

"We don't want either, thank you," said Anna-Rose.

The youth lingered. Anna-Rose's brushing began to grow vehement. Why didn't he go? She didn't want to have to be rude to him and hurt his feelings by asking him to go, but why didn't he? Anna-Felicitas, who was much too pleasantly detached, thought Anna-Rose, for such a situation, the door being wide open to the passage and the ungetridable youth standing there staring, was leisurely taking off her hat and smoothing her hair.

"Suppose you're new to this country," said the youth after a pause.

"Brand," said Anna-Felicitas pleasantly.

"Then p'raps," said the youth, "you don't know that the feller who brings up your grips gets a tip."

"Of course we know that," said Anna-Rose, standing up straight and trying to look stately.

"Then if you know why don't you do it?"

"Do it?" she repeated, endeavouring to chill him into respectfulness by haughtily throwing back her head. "Of course we shall do it. At the proper time and place."

"Which is, as you must have noticed," added Anna-Felicitas gently, "departure and the front door."

"That's all right," said the youth, "but that's only one of the times and places. That's the last one. Where we've got to now is the first one."

"Do I understand," said Anna-Rose, trying to be very dignified, while her heart shrank within her, for what sort of sum did one offer people like this?—"that to America one tips at the beginning as well?"

"Yep," said the youth. "And in the middle too. Right along through. Never miss an opportunity, is as good a slogan as you'll get when it comes to tipping."

"I believe you'd have liked Kipps," said Anna-Felicitas meditatively, shaking some dust off her hat and remembering the orgy of tipping that immortal young man went in for at the seaside hotel.

"What I like now," said the youth, growing more easy before their manifest youth and ignorance, "is tips. Guess you can call it Kipps if it pleases you."

Anna-Rose began to fumble nervously in her purse "It's horrid, I think, to ask for presents," she said to the youth in deep humiliation, more on his account than hers.

"Presents? I'm not asking for presents. I'm telling you what's done," said the youth. And he had spots on his face. And he was repugnant to her.

Anna-Rose gave him what looked like a shilling. He took it, and remarking that he had had a lot of trouble over it went away; and Anna-Rose was still flushed by this encounter when Mr. Twist knocked and asked if they were ready to be taken down to tea.

"He might have said thank you," she said indignantly to Anna-Felicitas, giving a final desperate brushing to the sulphur.

"I expect he'll come to a bad end," said Anna-Felicitas soothingly.

They had tea in the restaurant and were the only people doing such a thing, a solitary cluster in a wilderness of empty tables laid for dinner. It wasn't the custom much in America, explained Mr. Twist, to have tea, and no preparations were made for it in hotels of that sort. The very waiters, feeling it was a meal to be discouraged, were showing their detachment from it by sitting in a corner of the room playing dominoes. It was a big room, all looking-glasses and windows, and the street outside was badly paved and a great noise of passing motor-vans came in and drowned most of what Mr. Twist was saying. It was an unlovely place, a place in which one might easily feel homesick and that the world was empty of affection, if one let oneself go that way. The twins wouldn't. They stoutly refused, in their inward recesses, to be daunted by these externals. For there was Mr. Twist, their friend and stand-by, still with them, and hadn't they got each other? But they felt uneasy all the same; for Mr. Twist, though he plied them with buttered toast and macaroons and was as attentive as usual, had a somnambulatory quality in his attention. He looked like a man who is doing things in a dream. He looked like one who is absorbed in something else. His forehead still was puckered, and what could it be puckered about, seeing that he had got home, and was going back to his mother, and had a clear and uncomplicated future ahead of him, and anyhow was a man?

"Have you got something on your mind?" asked Anna-Rose at last, when he hadn't even heard a question she asked,—he, the polite, the interested, the sympathetic friend of the journey across.

Mr. Twist, sitting tilted back in his chair, his hands deep in his pockets, looked up from the macaroons he had been staring at and said, "Yes."

"Tell us what it is," suggested Anna-Felicitas.

"You," said Mr. Twist.

"Me?"

"Both of you. You both of you go together. You're in one lump in my mind. And on it too," finished Mr. Twist ruefully.

"That's only because," explained Anna-Felicitas, "you've got the idea we want such a lot of taking care of. Get rid of that, and you'll feel quite comfortable again. Why not regard us merely as pleasant friends?"

Mr. Twist looked at her in silence.

"Not as objects to be protected," continued Anna Felicitas, "but as co-equals. Of a reasonable soul and human flesh subsisting."

Mr. Twist continued to look at her in silence.

CHRISTOPHER AND COLUMBUS | 93

"We didn't come to America to be on anybody's mind," said Anna-Rose, supporting Anna-Felicitas.

"We had a good deal of that in England," said Anna-Felicitas. "For instance, we're quite familiar with Uncle Arthur's mind, we were on it so heavily and so long."

"It's our fixed determination," said Anna-Rose, "now that we're starting a new life, to get off any mind we find ourselves on *instantly*."

"We wish to carve out our own destinies," said Anna-Felicitas.

"We more than wish to," corrected Anna-Rose, "we intend to. What were we made in God's image for if it wasn't to stand upright on our own feet?"

"Anna-Rose and I had given this a good deal of thought," said Anna-Felicitas, "first and last, and we're prepared to be friends with everybody, but only as co-equals and of a reasonable soul and human flesh subsisting."

"I don't know exactly," said Mr. Twist, "what that means, but it seems to give you a lot of satisfaction."

"It does. It's out of the Athanasian Creed, and suggests such perfect equality. If you'll regard us as co-equals instead of as objects to be looked after, you'll see how happy we shall all be."

"Not," said Anna-Rose, growing tender, for indeed in her heart she loved and clung to Mr. Twist, "that we haven't very much liked all you've done for us and the way you were so kind to us on the boat,—we've been *most* obliged to you, and we shall miss you very much indeed, I know."

"But we'll get over that of course in time," put in Anna-Felicitas, "and we've got to start life now in earnest."

"Well then," said Mr. Twist, "will you two Annas kindly tell me what it is you propose to do next?"

"Next? After tea? Go and look at the sights."

"I mean to-morrow," said Mr. Twist.

"To-morrow," said Anna-Rose, "we proceed to Boston."

"To track the Clouston Sacks to their lair," said Anna-Felicitas.

"Ah. You've made up your minds to do that. They've behaved abominably," said Mr. Twist.

"Perhaps they missed the train," said Anna-Felicitas mildly.

"It's the proper course to pursue," said Anna-Rose. "To proceed to Boston."

"I suppose it is," said Mr. Twist, again thinking that the really proper and natural course was for him to have been able to take them to his mother. Pity one's mother wasn't—

He pulled himself up on the brink of an unfiliality. He was on the verge of thinking it a pity one's mother wasn't a different one.

CHAPTER XII

"Then," said Mr. Twist, "if this is all you're going to see of New York, this one evening, let us go and look at it."

He beckoned to the waiter who came up with the bill. Anna-Rose pulled out her purse. Mr. Twist put up his hand with severe determination.

"You're my guest," he said, "as long as I am with you. Useless to protest, young lady. You'll not get me to belie my American manhood. I only listened with half an ear to all the things you both said in the taxi, because I hadn't recovered from the surprise of finding myself still with you instead of on the train for Clark, and because you both of you do say so very many things. But understand once and for all that in this country everything female has to be paid for by some man. I'm that man till I've left you on the Sack doorstep, and then it'll be Sack—confound him," finished Mr. Twist suddenly.

And he silenced Anna-Rose's protests, which persisted and were indignant, by turning on her with, an irascibility she hadn't yet seen in him, and inquiring of her whether then she really wished to put him to public shame? "You wouldn't wish to go against an established custom, surely," he said more gently.

So the twins gave themselves up for that one evening to what Anna-Felicitas called government by wealth, otherwise plutocracy, while reserving complete freedom of action in regard to Mr. Sack, who was, in their ignorance of his circumstances, an unknown quantity. They might be going to be mothers' helps in the Sack *ménage* for all they knew,—they might, they said, be going to be anything, from honoured guests to typists.

"Can you type?" asked Mr. Twist.

"No," said the twins.

He took them in a taxi to Riverside Drive, and then they walked down to the charming footpath that runs along by the Hudson for three enchanting miles. The sun had set some time before they got there, and had left a clear pale yellow sky, and a wonderful light on the river. Lamps were being lit, and hung like silver globes in the thin air. Steep grass slopes, and groups of big trees a little deeper yellow than the sky, hid that there were houses and a street above them on their right. Up and down the river steamers passed, pierced with light, their delicate smoke hanging in the air long after they had gone their way. It was so great a joy to walk in all this after ten days shut up on the *St. Luke* and to see such blessed things as grass and leaves again, that the twins felt suddenly extraordinarily brisked up and cheerful. It was impossible not to be cheerful, translated from the *St. Luke* into such a place, trotting along in the peculiar dry air that made one all tingly.

The world seemed suddenly quite good,—the simplest, easiest of objects to tackle. All one had to do was not to let it weigh on one, to laugh rather than cry. They trotted along humming bits of their infancy's songs, feeling very warm and happy inside, felicitously full of tea and macaroons and with their feet comfortably on something that kept still and didn't heave or lurch beneath them. Mr. Twist, too, was gayer than he had been for some hours. He seemed relieved; and he was. He had sent a telegram to his mother, expressing proper sorrow at being detained in New York, but giving no reason for it, and promising he would be with her rather late the next evening; and he had sent a telegram to the Clouston Sacks saying the Twinklers, who had so unfortunately missed them in New York, would arrive in Boston early next afternoon. His mind was clear again owing to the determination of the twins to go to the Sacks. He was going to take them there, hand them over, and then go back to Clark, which fortunately was only three hours' journey from Boston.

If the twins had shown a disinclination to go after the Sacks who, in Mr. Twist's opinion, had behaved shamefully already, he wouldn't have had the heart to press them to go; and then what would he have done with them? Their second and last line of defence, supposing they had considered the Sacks had failed and were to be ruled out, was in California, a place they spoke of as if it were next door to Boston and New York. How could he have let them set out alone on that four days' journey, with the possibility of once more at its end not being met? No wonder he had been abstracted at tea. He was relieved to the extent of his forehead going quite smooth again at their decision to proceed to the Sacks. For he couldn't have taken them to his mother without preparation and explanation, and he couldn't have left them in New York while he went and prepared and explained. Great, reflected Mr. Twist, the verb dropping into his mind with the *aplomb* of an inspiration, are the difficulties that beset a man directly he begins to twinkle. Already he had earnestly wished to knock the reception clerk in the hotel office down because of, first, his obvious suspicion of the party before he had heard Mr. Twist's name, and because of, second, his politeness, his confidential manner as of an understanding sympathizer with a rich man's recreations, when he had. The tea, which he, had poured out of one of his own teapots, had been completely spoilt by the knowledge that it was only this teapot that had saved him from being treated as a White Slave Trafficker. He wouldn't have got into that hotel at all with the Twinklers, or into any other decent one, except for his teapot. What a country, Mr. Twist had thought, fresh from his work in France, fresh from where people were profoundly occupied with the great business of surviving at all. Here he came back from a place where civilization toppled, where deadly misery, deadly bravery, heroism that couldn't be uttered, staggered month after month among ruins, and found America untouched, comfortable, fat, still with time to worry over the suspected amorousness of the rich, still putting people into uniforms in order to buttonhole a man on landing and cross-question him as to his private purities.

He had been much annoyed, but he too couldn't resist the extreme pleasure of real exercise on such a lovely evening, nor could he resist the infection of the cheerfulness of the Twinklers. They walked along, talking and laughing, and seeming to walk much faster than he did, especially Anna-Rose who had to break into a run every few steps because of his so much longer legs, his face restored to all its usual kindliness as he listened benevolently to their remarks, and just when they were beginning to feel as if they soon might be tired and hungry a restaurant with lamp-hung gardens appeared as punctually as if they had been in Germany, that land of nicely arranged distances between meals. They had an extremely cheerful little supper out of doors, with things to eat that thrilled the Twinklers in their delicious strangeness; heavenly food, they thought it after the rigours of the second-class cooking on the *St. Luke*, and the biggest ices they had seen in their lives,—great dollops of pink and yellow divineness.

Then Mr. Twist took them in a taxi to look at the illuminated advertisements in Broadway, and they forgot everything but the joy of the moment. Whatever the next day held, this evening was sheer happiness. Their eyes shone and their cheeks flushed, and Mr. Twist was quite worried that they were so pretty. People at the other tables at the restaurant had stared at them with frank admiration, and so did the people in the streets whenever the taxi was blocked. On the ship he had only sometimes been aware of it,—there would come a glint of sunshine and settle on Anna-Rose's little cheek where the dimple was, or he would lift his eyes from the Culture book and suddenly see the dark softness of Anna-Felicitas's eyelashes as she slept in her chair. But now, dressed properly, and in their dryland condition of cheerful animation, he perceived that they were very pretty indeed, and that Anna-Felicitas was more than very pretty. He couldn't help thinking they were a most unsuitable couple to be let loose in America with only two hundred pounds to support them. Two hundred pounds was just enough to let them slip about if it should enter their heads to slip about,—go off without explanation, for instance, if they wanted to leave the Clouston Sacks,—but of course ridiculous as a serious background to life. A girl should either have enough money or be completely dependent on her male relations. As a girl was usually young reflected Mr. Twist, his spectacles with the Broadway lights in them blazing on the two specimens opposite him, it was safest for her to be dependent. So were her actions controlled, and kept within the bounds of wisdom.

And next morning, as he sat waiting for the twins for breakfast at ten o'clock according to arrangement the night before, their grape-fruit in little beds of ice on their plates and every sort of American dish ordered, from griddle cakes and molasses to chicken pie, a page came in with loud cries for Mr. Twist, which made him instantly conspicuous—a thing he particularly disliked—and handed him a letter.

The twins had gone.

CHAPTER XIII

They had left early that morning for Boston, determined, as they wrote, no longer to trespass on his kindness. There had been a discussion in their bedroom the night before when they got back in which Anna-Rose supplied the heat and Anna-Felicitas the arguments, and it ended in Anna-Felicitas succeeding in restoring Anna-Rose to her original standpoint of proud independence, from which, lured by the comfort and security of Mr. Twist's companionship, she had been inclined to slip.

It took some time, because of Anna-Rose being the eldest. Anna-Felicitas had had to be as wary, and gentle, and persistently affectionate as a wife whom necessity compels to try and get reason into her husband. Anna-Rose's feathers, even as the feathers of a husband, bristled at the mere breath of criticism of her superior intelligence and wisdom. She was the leader of the party, the head and guide, the one who had the dollars in her pocket, and being the eldest naturally must know best. Besides, she was secretly nervous about taking Anna-Felicitas about alone. She too had observed the stares of the public, and had never supposed that any of them might be for her. How was she to get to Boston successfully with so enchanting a creature, through all the complications of travel in an unknown country, without the support and counsel of Mr. Twist? Just the dollars and quarters and dimes and cents cowed her. The strangeness of everything, while it delighted her so long as she could peep at it from behind Mr. Twist, appalled her the minute she was left alone with it. America seemed altogether a foreign country, a strange place whose inhabitants by accident didn't talk in a strange language. They talked English; or rather what sounded like English till you found that it wasn't really.

But Anna-Felicitas prevailed. She had all Anna-Rose's inborn horror of accepting money or other benefits from people who had no natural right to exercise their benevolences upon her, to appeal to. Christopher, after long wrestling restored at last to pride, did sit down and write the letter that so much spoilt Mr. Twist's breakfast next morning, while Columbus slouched about the room suggesting sentences.

It was a letter profuse in thanks for all Mr. Twist had done for them, and couched in language that betrayed the particular share Anna-Felicitas had taken in the plan; for though they both loved long words Anna-Felicitas's were always a little the longer. In rolling sentences that made Mr. Twist laugh in spite of his concern, they pointed out that his first duty was to his mother, and his second was not to squander his possessions in paying the hotel and railway bills of persons who had no sort of claim on him, except those general claims of humanity which he had already on the *St. Luke* so amply discharged. They would refrain from paying their hotel bill, remembering his words as to the custom of the country, though their instincts were altogether against this course, but they could and would avoid causing him the further expense and trouble and waste of his no doubt valuable time of taking them to Boston, by the simple process of going there without him. They promised to write from the Sacks and let him know of their arrival to the address at Clark he had given them, and they would never forget him as long as they lived and remained his very sincerely, A.-R., and A.-F. Twinkler.

Mr. Twist hurried out to the office.

The clerk who had been so confidential in his manner the evening before looked at him curiously. Yes, the young ladies had left on the 8.15 for Boston. They had come downstairs, baggage and all, at seven o'clock, had asked for a taxi, had said they wished to go to Boston, inquired about the station, etc., and had specially requested that Mr. Twist should not be disturbed.

"They seemed in a slight hurry to be off," said the clerk, "and didn't like there being no train before the 8.15. I thought you knew all about it, Mr. Twist," he added inquisitively.

"So I did—so I did," said Mr. Twist, turning away to go back to his breakfast for three.

"So he did—so he did," muttered the clerk with a wink to the other clerk; and for a few minutes they whispered, judging from the expressions on their faces, what appeared to be very exciting things to each other.

Meanwhile the twins, after a brief struggle of extraordinary intensity at the station in getting their tickets, trying to understand the black man who seized and dealt with their luggage, and closely following him wherever he went in case he should disappear, were sitting in a state of relaxation and relief in the Boston express, their troubles over for at least several hours.

The black porter, whose heart happened not to be black and who had children of his own, perceived the helpless ignorance that lay behind the twins' assumption a of severe dignity, and took them in hand and got seats for them in the parlour car. As they knew nothing about cars, parlour or otherwise, but had merely and quite uselessly reiterated to the booking-clerk, till their porter intervened, that they wanted third-class tickets, they accepted these seats, thankful in the press and noise round them to get anything so roomy and calm as these dignified arm-chairs; and it wasn't till they had been in them some time, their feet on green footstools, with attendants offering them fruit and chocolates and magazines at intervals just as if they had been in heaven, as Anna-Felicitas remarked admiringly, that counting their money they discovered what a hole the journey had made in it. But they were too much relieved at having accomplished so much on their own, quite uphelped for the first time since leaving Aunt Alice, to take it particularly to heart; and, as Anna-Felicitas said, there was still the £200, and, as Anna-Rose said, it wasn't likely they'd go in a train again for ages; and anyhow, as Anna-Felicitas said, whatever it had cost they were bound to get away from being constant drains on Mr. Twist's purse.

The train journey delighted them. To sit so comfortably and privately in chairs that twisted round, so that if a passenger should start staring at Anna-Felicitas one could make her turn her back altogether on him; to have one's feet on footstools when they were the sort of feet that don't reach the ground; to see the lovely autumn country flying past, hills and woods and fields and gardens golden in the October sun, while the horrible Atlantic was nowhere in sight; to pass through towns so queerly reminiscent of English and German towns shaken up together and yet not a bit like either; to be able to have the window wide open without getting soot in one's eyes because one of the ministering angels—clad, this one, appropriately to heaven, in white, though otherwise black—pulled up the same sort of wire screen they used to have in the windows at home to keep out the mosquitoes; to imitate about twelve, when they grew bold because they were so hungry, the other passengers and cause the black angel to spread a little table between them and bring clam broth, which they ordered in a spirit of adventure and curiosity and concealed from each other that they didn't like; to have the young man who passed up and down with the candy, and whose mouth was full of it, grow so friendly that he offered them toffee from his own private supply at last when they had refused regretfully a dozen suggestions to buy—"Have a bit," he said, thrusting it under their noses. "As a gentleman to ladies—no pecuniary obligations—come on, now;" all this was to the twins too interesting and delightful for words.

They accepted the toffee in the spirit in which it was offered, and since nobody can eat somebody's toffee without being pleasant in return, intermittent amenities passed between them and the young man as he journeyed up and down through the cars.

"First visit to the States?" he inquired, when with some reluctance, for presently it appeared to the twins that the clam broth and the toffee didn't seem to be liking each other now they had got together inside them, and also for fear of hurting his feelings if they refused, they took some more.

They nodded and smiled stickily.

"English, I guess."

They hesitated, covering their hesitation with the earnest working of their toffee-filled jaws.

Then Anna-Felicitas, her cheek distorted, gave him the answer she had given the captain of the *St. Luke,* and said, "Practically."

"Ah," said the young man, turning this over in his mind, the r in "practically" having rolled as no English or American r ever did; but the conductor appearing in the doorway he continued on his way.

"It's evident," said Anna-Rose, speaking with difficulty, for her jaws clave together because of the toffee, "that we're going to be asked that the first thing every time a fresh person speaks to us. We'd better decide what we're going to say, and practise saying it without hesitation."

Anna-Felicitas made a sound of assent.

"That answer of yours about practically," continued Anna-Rose, swallowing her bit of toffee by accident and for one moment afraid it would stick somewhere and make her die, "causes first surprise, then reflection, and then suspicion."

"But," said Anna-Felicitas after a pause during which she had disentangled her jaws, "it's going to be difficult to say one is German when America seems to be so very neutral and doesn't like Germans. Besides, it's only in the eye of the law that we are. In God's eye we're not, and that's the principal eye after all."

Her own eyes grew thoughtful. "I don't believe," she said, "that parents when they marry have any idea of all the difficulties they're going to place their children in."

"I don't believe they think about it at all," said Anna-Rose. "I mean," she added quickly, lest she should be supposed to be questioning the perfect love and forethought of their mother, "fathers don't."

They were silent a little after this, each thinking things tinged to sobriety by the effect of the inner conflict going on between the clam broth and the toffee. Also Boston was rushing towards them, and the Clouston Sacks. Quite soon they would have to leave the peaceful security of the train and begin to be active again, and quick and clever. Anna-Felicitas, who was slow, found it difficult ever to be clever till about the week after, and Anna-Rose, who was impetuous, was so impetuous that she entirely outstripped her scanty store of cleverness and landed panting and surprised in situations she hadn't an idea what to do with. The Clouston Sacks, now—Aunt Alice had said, "You must take care to be very tactful with Mr. and Mrs. Clouston Sack;" and when Anna-Rose, her forehead as much puckered as Mr. Twist's in her desire to get exactly at what tactful was in order to be able diligently to be it, asked for definitions, Aunt Alice only said it was what gentlewomen were instinctively.

"Then," observed Anna-Felicitas, when on nearing Boston Anna-Rose repeated Aunt Alice's admonishment and at the same time provided Anna-Felicitas for her guidance with the definition, "seeing that we're supposed to be gentlewomen, all we've got to do is to behave according to our instincts."

But Anna-Rose wasn't sure. She doubted their instincts, especially Anna-Felicitas's. She thought her own were better, being older, but even hers were extraordinarily apt to develop in unexpected directions according to the other person's behaviour. Her instinct, for instance, when engaged by Uncle Arthur in conversation had usually been to hit him. Was that tact? Yet she knew she was a gentlewoman. She had heard that, since first she had heard words at all, from every servant, teacher, visitor and relation—except her mother—in her Prussian home. Indeed, over there she had been told she was more than a gentlewoman, for she was a noblewoman and therefore her instincts ought positively to drip tact.

"Mr. Dodson," Aunt Alice had said one afternoon towards the end, when the twins came in from a walk and found the rector having tea, "says that you can't be too tactful in America. He's been there."

"Sensitive—sensitive," said Mr. Dodson, shaking his head at his cup. "Splendidly sensitive, just as they are splendidly whatever else they are. A great country. Everything on a vast scale, including sensitiveness. It has to be met vastly. But quite easy really—-" He raised a pedagogic finger at the twins. "You merely add half as much again to the quantity of your tact as the quantity you encounter of their sensitiveness, and it's all right."

"Be sure you remember that now," said Aunt Alice, pleased.

As Boston got nearer, Anna-Rose, trying to learn Mr. Dodson's recipe for social success by heart, became more silent. On the ship, when the meeting with the Sacks was imminent, she had fled in sudden panic to her cabin to hide from them. That couldn't have been tact. But it was instinct. And she was a gentlewoman. Now once again dread took possession of her and she wanted to hide, not to get there, to stay in the train and go on and on. She said nothing, of course, of her dread to Anna-Felicitas in order not to undermine that young person's *morale*, but she did very much wish that principles weren't such important things and one needn't have cut oneself off from the protecting figure of Mr. Twist.

"Now remember what Aunt Alice said," she whispered severely to Anna-Felicitas, gripping her arm as they stood jammed in the narrow passage to the door waiting to be let out at Boston.

On the platform, they both thought, would be the Sacks,—certainly one Sack, and they had feverishly made themselves tidy and composed their faces into pleasant smiles preparatory to the meeting. But once again no Sacks were there. The platform emptied itself just as the great hall of the landing-stage had emptied itself, and nobody came to claim the Twinklers.

"These Sacks," remarked Anna-Felicitas patiently at last, when it was finally plain that there weren't any, "don't seem to have acquired the meeting habit."

"No," said Anna-Rose, vexed but relieved. "They're like what Aunt Alice used to complain about the housemaids,—neither punctual nor methodical."

"But it doesn't matter," said Anna-Felicitas. "They shall not escape us. I'm getting quite hungry for the Sacks as a result of not having them. We will now proceed to track them to their lair."

For one instant Anna-Rose looked longingly at the train. It was still there. It was going on further and further away from the Sacks. Happy train. One little jump, and they'd be in it again. But she resisted, and engaged a porter.

Even as soon as this the twins were far less helpless than they had been the day before. The Sack address was in Anna-Rose's hand, and they knew what an American porter looked like. The porter and a taxi were engaged with comparative ease and assurance, and on giving the porter, who had staggered beneath the number of their grips, a dime, and seeing a cloud on his face, they doubled it instantly sooner than have trouble, and trebled it equally quickly on his displaying yet further dissatisfaction, and they departed for the Sacks, their grips piled up round them in the taxi as far as their chins, congratulating themselves on how much easier it was to get away from a train than to get into one.

But the minute their activities were over and they had time to think, silence fell upon them again. They were both nervous. They both composed their faces to indifference to hide that they were nervous, examining the streets they passed through with a calm and *blasé* stare worthy of a lorgnette. It was the tact part of the coming encounter that was chiefly unnerving Anna-

Rose, and Anna-Felicitas was dejected by her conviction that nobody who was a friend of Uncle Arthur's could possibly be agreeable. "By their friends ye shall know them," thought Anna-Felicitas, staring out of the window at the Boston buildings. Also the persistence of the Sacks in not being on piers and railway stations was discouraging. There was no eagerness about this persistence; there wasn't even friendliness. Perhaps they didn't like her and Anna-Rose being German.

This was always the twins' first thought when anybody wasn't particularly cordial. Their experiences in England had made them a little jumpy. They were conscious of this weak spot, and like a hurt finger it seemed always to be getting in the way and being knocked. Anna-Felicitas once more pondered on the inscrutable behaviour of Providence which had led their mother, so safely and admirably English, to leave that blessed shelter and go and marry somebody who wasn't. Of course there was this to be said for it, that she wasn't their mother then. If she had been, Anna-Felicitas felt sure she wouldn't have. Then, perceiving that her thoughts were getting difficult to follow she gave them up, and slid her hand through Anna-Rose's arm and gave it a squeeze.

"Now for the New World, Christopher," she said, pretending to be very eager and brave and like the real Columbus, as the taxi stopped.

CHAPTER XIV

The taxi had stopped in front of a handsome apartment house, and almost before it was quiet a boy in buttons darted out across the intervening wide pavement and thrust his face through the window.

"Who do you want?" he said, or rather jerked out.

He then saw the contents of the taxi, and his mouth fell open; for it seemed to him that grips and passengers were piled up inside it in a seething mass.

"We want Mr. and Mrs. Clouston Sack," said Anna-Rose in her most grown-up voice. "They're expecting us."

"They ain't," said the boy promptly.

"They ain't?" repeated Anna-Rose, echoing his language in her surprise.

"How do you know?" asked Anna-Felicitas.

"That they ain't? Because they ain't," said the boy. "I bet you my Sunday shirt they ain't."

The twins stared at him. They were not accustomed in their conversations with the lower classes to be talked to about shirts.

The boy seemed extraordinarily vital. His speech was so quick that it flew out with the urgency and haste of squibs going off.

"Please open the door," said Anna-Rose recovering herself. "We'll go up and see for ourselves."

"You won't see," said the boy.

"Kindly open the door," repeated Anna-Rose.

"You won't see," he said, pulling it open, "but you can look. If you do see Sacks up there I'm a Hun."

The minute the door opened, grips fell out. There were two umbrellas, two coats, a knapsack of a disreputable bulged appearance repugnant to American ideas of baggage which run on big simple lines of huge trunks, an *attaché* case, a suit case, a hold-all, a basket and a hat-box. Outside beside the driver were two such small and modest trunks that they might almost as well have been grips themselves.

"Do you mind taking those in?" asked Anna-Rose, getting out with difficulty over the umbrella that had fallen across the doorway, and pointing to the gutter in which the other umbrella and the knapsack lay and into which the basket, now that her body no longer kept it in, was rolling.

"In where?" crackled the boy.

"In," said Anna-Rose severely. "In to wherever Mr. and Mrs. Clouston Sack are."

"It's no good your saying they are when they ain't," said the boy, increasing the loudness of his crackling.

"Do you mean they don't live here?" asked Anna-Felicitas, in her turn disentangling herself from that which was still inside the taxi, and immediately followed on to the pavement by the hold-all and the *attaché* case.

"They did live here till yesterday," said the boy, "but now they don't. One does. But that's not the same as two. Which is what I meant when you said they're expecting you and I said they ain't."

"Do you mean to say—" Anna-Rose stopped with a catch of her breath. "Do you mean," she went on in an awe-struck voice, "that one of them—one of them is dead?"

"Dead? Bless you, no. Anything but dead. The exact opposite. Gone. Left. Got," said the boy.

"Oh," said Anna-Rose greatly relieved, passing over his last word, whose meaning escaped her, "oh—you mean just gone to meet us. And missed us. You see," she said, turning to Anna-Felicitas, "they did try to after all."

Anna-Felicitas said nothing, but reflected that whichever Sack had tried to must have a quite unusual gift for missing people.

"Gone to meet you?" repeated the boy, as one surprised by a new point of view. "Well, I don't know about that—"

"We'll go up and explain," said Anna-Rose. "Is it Mr. or Mrs. Clouston Sack who is here?"

"Mr.," said the boy.

"Very well then. Please bring in our things." And Anna-Rose proceeded, followed by Anna-Felicitas, to walk into the house.

The boy, instead of bringing them in, picked up the articles lying on the pavement and put them back again into the taxi. "No hurry about them,

I guess," he said to the driver. "Time enough to take them up when the gurls ask again—" and he darted after the gurls to hand them over to his colleague who worked what he called the elevator.

"Why do you call it the elevator," inquired Anna-Felicitas, mildly inquisitive, of this boy, who on hearing that they wished to see Mr. Sack stared at them with profound and unblinking interest all the way up, "when it is really a lift?"

"Because it is an elevator," said the boy briefly.

"But we, you see," said Anna-Felicitas, "are equally convinced that it's a lift."

The boy didn't answer this. He was as silent as the other one wasn't; but there was a thrill about him too, something electric and tense. He stared at Anna-Felicitas, then turned quickly and stared at Anna-Rose, then quickly back to Anna-Felicitas, and so on all the way up. He was obviously extraordinarily interested. He seemed to have got hold of an idea that had not struck the squib-like boy downstairs, who was entertaining the taxi-driver with descriptions of the domestic life of the Sacks.

The lift stopped at what the twins supposed was going to be the door of a landing or public corridor, but it was, they discovered, the actual door of the Sack flat. At any moment the Sacks, if they wished to commit suicide, could do so simply by stepping out of their own front door. They would then fall, infinitely far, on to the roof of the lift lurking at the bottom.

The lift-boy pressed a bell, the door opened, and there, at once exposed to the twins, was the square hall of the Sack flat with a manservant standing in it staring at them.

Obsessed by his idea, the lift-boy immediately stepped out of his lift, approached the servant, introduced his passengers to him by saying, "Young ladies to see Mr. Sack," took a step closer, and whispered in his ear, but perfectly audibly to the twins who, however, regarded it as some expression peculiarly American and were left unmoved by it, "The co-respondents."

The servant stared uncertainly at them. His mistress had only been gone a few hours, and the flat was still warm with her presence and authority. She wouldn't, he well knew, have permitted co-respondents to be about the place if she had been there, but on the other hand she wasn't there. Mr. Sack was in sole possession now. Nobody knew where Mrs. Sack was. Letters and telegrams lay on the table for her unopened, among them Mr. Twist's announcing the arrival of the Twinklers. In his heart the servant sided with Mr. Sack, but only in his heart, for the servant's wife was the cook, and she, as she frequently explained, was all for strict monogamy. He stared therefore uncertainly at the twins, his brain revolving round their colossal impudence in coming there before Mrs. Sack's rooms had so much as had time to get, as it were, cold.

"We want to see Mr. Clouston Sack," began Anna-Rose in her clear little voice; and no sooner did she begin to speak than a door was pulled open and the gentleman himself appeared.

"I heard a noise of arrival—" he said, stopping suddenly when he saw them. "I heard a noise of arrival, and a woman's voice—"

"It's us," said Anna-Rose, her face covering itself with the bright conciliatory smiles of the arriving guest. "Are you Mr. Clouston Sack?"

She went up to him and held out her hand. They both went up to him and held out their hands.

"We're the Twinklers," said Anna-Rose.

"We've come," said Anna-Felicitas, in case he shouldn't have noticed it.

Mr. Sack let his hand be shaken, and it was a moist hand. He looked like a Gibson young man who has grown elderly. He had the manly profile and shoulders, but they sagged and stooped. There was a dilapidation about him, a look of blurred edges. His hair lay on his forehead in disorder, and his tie had been put on carelessly and had wriggled up to the rim of his collar.

"The Twinklers," he repeated. "The Twinklers. Do I remember, I wonder?"

"There hasn't been much time to forget," said Anna-Felicitas. "It's less than two months since there were all those letters."

"Letters?" echoed Mr. Sack. "Letters?"

"So now we've got here," said Anna-Rose, the more brightly that she was unnerved.

"Yes. We've come," said Anna-Felicitas, also with feverish brightness.

Bewildered, Mr. Sack, who felt that he had had enough to bear the last few hours, stood staring at them. Then he caught sight of the lift-boy, lingering and he further saw the expression on his servant's face Even to his bewilderment it was clear what he was thinking.

Mr. Sack turned round quickly and led the way into the dining-room. "Come in, come in," he said distractedly.

They went in. He shut the door. The lift-boy and the servant lingered a moment making faces at each other; then the lift-boy dropped away in his lift, and the servant retired to the kitchen. "I'm darned," was all he could articulate. "I'm darned."

"There's our luggage," said Anna-Rose, turning to Mr. Sack on getting inside the room, her voice gone a little shrill in her determined cheerfulness. "Can it be brought up?"

"Luggage?" repeated Mr. Sack, putting his hand to his forehead. "Excuse me, but I've got such a racking headache to-day—it makes me stupid—"

"Oh, I'm *very* sorry," said Anna-Rose solicitously.

"And so am I—*very*," said Anna-Felicitas, equally solicitous. "Have you tried aspirin? Sometimes some simple remedy like that—"

"Oh thank you—it's good of you, it's good of you. The effect, you see, is that I can't think very clearly. But do tell me—why luggage? Luggage—luggage. You mean, I suppose, baggage."

"Why luggage?" asked Anna-Rose nervously. "Isn't there—isn't there always luggage in America too when people come to stay with one?"

"You've come to stay with me," said Mr. Sack, putting his hand to his forehead again.

"You see," said Anna-Felicitas, "we're the Twinklers."

"Yes, yes—I know. You've told me that."

"So naturally we've come."

"But *is* it natural?" asked Mr. Sack, looking at them distractedly.

"We sent you a telegram," said Anna-Rose, "or rather one to Mrs. Sack, which is the same thing—"

"It isn't, it isn't," said the distressed Mr. Sack. "I wish it were. It ought to be. Mrs. Sack isn't here—"

"Yes—we're very sorry to have missed her. Did she go to meet us in New York, or where?"

"Mrs. Sack didn't go to meet you. She's—gone."

"Gone where?"

"Oh," cried Mr. Sack, "somewhere else, but not to meet you. Oh," he went on after a moment in which, while the twins gazed at him, he fought with and overcame emotion, "when I heard you speaking in the hall I thought—I had a moment's hope—for a minute I believed—she had come back. So I went out. Else I couldn't have seen you. I'm not fit to see strangers—"

The things Mr. Sack said, and his fluttering, unhappy voice, were so much at variance with the stern lines of his Gibson profile that the twins viewed him with the utmost surprise. They came to no conclusion and passed no judgment because they didn't know but what if one was an American one naturally behaved like that.

"I don't think," said Anna-Felicitas gently, "that you can call us strangers. We're the Twinklers."

"Yes, yes—I know—you keep on telling me that," said Mr. Sack. "But I can't call to mind—"

"Don't you remember all Uncle Arthur's letters about us? We're the nieces he asked you to be kind to for a bit—as I'm sure," Anna-Felicitas added politely, "you're admirably adapted for being."

Mr. Sack turned his bewildered eyes on to her. "Oh, aren't you a pretty girl," he said, in the same distressed voice.

"You mustn't make her vain," said Anna-Rose, trying not to smile all over her face, while Anna-Felicitas remained as manifestly unvain as a person intent on something else would be.

"We know you got Uncle Arthur's letters about us," she continued, "because he showed us your answers back. You invited us to come and stay with you. And, as you perceive, we've done it."

"Then it must have been months ago—months ago," said Mr. Sack, "before all this—do I remember something about it? I've had such trouble since—I've been so distracted one way and another—it may have slipped away out of my memory under the stress—Mrs. Sack—" He paused and looked round the room helplessly. "Mrs. Sack—well, Mrs. Sack isn't here now."

"We're *very* sorry you've had trouble," said Anna-Felicitas sympathetically. "It's what everybody has, though. Man that is born of woman is full of misery. That's what the Burial Service says, and it ought to know."

Mr. Sack again turned bewildered eyes on to her. "Oh, aren't you a pretty—" he again began.

"When do you think Mrs. Sack will be back?" interrupted Anna-Rose.

"I wish I knew—I wish I could hope—but she's gone for a long while, I'm afraid—"

"Gone not to come back at all, do you mean?" asked Anna-Felicitas.

Mr. Sack gulped. "I'm afraid that is her intention," he said miserably.

There was a silence, in which they all stood looking at each other.

"Didn't she like you?" then inquired Anna-Felicitas.

Anna-Rose, sure that this wasn't tactful, gave her sleeve a little pull.

"Were you unkind to her?" asked Anna-Felicitas, disregarding the warning.

Mr. Sack, his fingers clasping and unclasping themselves behind his back, started walking up and down the room. Anna-Felicitas, forgetful of what Aunt Alice would have said, sat down on the edge of the table and began to be interested in Mrs. Sack.

"The wives I've seen," she remarked, watching Mr. Sack with friendly and interested eyes, "who were chiefly Aunt Alice—that's Uncle Arthur's wife, the one we're the nieces of—seemed to put up with the utmost contumely from their husbands and yet didn't budge. You must have been something awful to yours."

"I worshipped Mrs. Sack," burst out Mr. Sack. "I worshipped her. I do worship her. She was the handsomest, brightest woman in Boston. I was as proud of her as any man has ever been of his wife."

"Then why did she go?" asked Anna-Felicitas.

"I don't think that's the sort of thing you should ask," rebuked Anna-Rose.

"But if I don't ask I won't be told," said Ann Felicitas, "and I'm interested."

"Mrs. Sack went because I was able—I was so constructed—that I could be fond of other people as well as of her," said Mr. Sack.

"Well, *that's* nothing unusual," said Anna-Felicitas.

"No," said Anna-Rose, "I don't see anything in that."

"I think it shows a humane and friendly spirit," said Anna-Felicitas.

"Besides, it's enjoined in the Bible," said Anna-Rose.

"I'm sure when we meet Mrs. Sack," said Anna-Felicitas very politely indeed, "much as we expect to like her we shall nevertheless continue to like other people as well. You, for instance. Will she mind that?"

"It wasn't so much that I liked other people," said Mr. Sack, walking about and thinking tumultuously aloud rather than addressing anybody, "but that I liked other people so *much*."

"I see," said Anna-Felicitas, nodding. "You overdid it. Like over-eating whipped cream. Only it wasn't you but Mrs. Sack who got the resulting ache."

"And aren't I aching? Aren't I suffering?"

"Yes, but you did the over-eating," said Anna-Felicitas.

"The world," said the unhappy Mr. Sack, quickening his pace, "is so full of charming and delightful people. Is one to shut one's eyes to them?"

"Of course not," said Anna-Felicitas. "One must love them."

"Yes, yes," said Mr. Sack. "Exactly. That's what I did."

"And though I wouldn't wish," said Anna-Felicitas, "to say anything against somebody who so very nearly was my hostess, yet really, you know, wasn't Mrs. Sack's attitude rather churlish?"

Mr. Sack gazed at her. "Oh, aren't you a pretty—" he began again, with a kind of agonized enthusiasm; but he was again cut short by Anna-Rose, on whom facts of a disturbing nature were beginning to press.

"Aunt Alice," she said, looking and feeling extremely perturbed as the situation slowly grew clear to her, "told us we were never to stay with people whose wives are somewhere else. Unless they have a mother or other female relative living with them. She was most particular about it, and said whatever else we did we weren't ever to do this. So I'm afraid," she continued in her politest voice, determined to behave beautifully under circumstances that were trying, "much as we should have enjoyed staying with you and Mrs. Sack if she had been here to stay with, seeing that she isn't we manifestly can't."

"You can't stay with me," murmured Mr. Sack, turning his bewildered eyes to her. "Were you going to?"

"Of course we were going to. It's what we've come for," said Anna-Felicitas.

"And I'm afraid," said-Anna-Rose, "disappointed as we are, unless you can produce a mother—"

"But where on earth are we to go to, Anna-R.?" inquired Anna-Felicitas, who, being lazy, having got to a place preferred if possible to stay in it, and who besides was sure that in their forlorn situation a Sack in the hand was worth two Sacks not in it, any day. Also she liked the look of Mr. Sack, in spite of his being so obviously out of repair. He badly wanted doing up she said to herself, but on the other hand he seemed to her lovable in his distress, with much of the pathetic helplessness her own dear Irish terrier, left behind in Germany, had had the day he caught his foot in a rabbit trap.

He had looked at Anna-Felicitas, while she was trying to get him out of it, with just the same expression on his face that Mr. Sack had on his as he walked about the room twisting and untwisting his fingers behind his back. Only, her Irish terrier hadn't had a Gibson profile. Also, he had looked much more efficient.

"Can't you by any chance produce a mother?" she asked.

Mr. Sack stared at her.

"Of course we're very sorry," said Anna-Rose.

Mr. Sack stared at her.

"But you understand, I'm sure, that under the circumstances—"

"Do you say," said Mr. Sack, stopping still after a few more turns in front of Anna-Rose, and making a great effort to collect his thoughts, "that I—that we—had arranged to look after you?"

"Arranged with Uncle Arthur," said Anna-Rose. "Uncle Arthur Abinger. Of course you had. That's why we're here. Why, you wrote bidding us welcome. He showed us the letter."

"Abinger. Abinger. Oh—*that* man," said Mr. Sack, his mind clearing.

"We thought you'd probably feel like that about him," said Anna-Felicitas sympathetically.

"Why, then," said Mr. Sack, his mind getting suddenly quite clear, "you must be—why, you *are* the Twinklers."

"We've been drawing your attention to that at frequent intervals since we got here," said Anna-Felicitas.

"But whether you now remember or still don't realize," said Anna-Rose with great firmness, "I'm afraid we've got to say good-bye."

"That's all very well, Anna-R.," again protested Anna-Felicitas, "but where are we to go to?"

"Go?" said Anna-Rose with a dignity very creditable in one of her size, "Ultimately to California, of course, to Uncle Arthur's other friends. But now, this afternoon, we get back into a train and go to Clark, to Mr. Twist. He at least has a mother."

CHAPTER XV

And so it came about that just as the reunited Twists, mother, son and daughter, were sitting in the drawing-room, a little tired after a long afternoon of affection, waiting for seven o'clock to strike and, with the striking, Amanda the head maid to appear and announce supper, but waiting with lassitude, for they had not yet recovered from an elaborate welcoming dinner, the Twinklers, in the lovely twilight of a golden day, were hastening up the winding road from the station towards them. Silent, and a little exhausted, the unconscious Twists sat in their drawing-room, a place of marble and antimacassars, while these light figures, their shoes white with the dust of a country-side that had had no rain for weeks, sped every moment nearer.

The road wound gently upwards through fields and woods, through quiet, delicious evening country, and there was one little star twinkling encouragingly at the twins from over where they supposed Clark would be. At the station there had been neither porter nor conveyance, nor indeed anybody or anything at all except themselves, their luggage, and a thin, kind man who represented authority. Clark is two miles away from its station, and all the way to it is uninhabited. Just at the station are a cluster of those hasty buildings America flings down in out-of-the-way places till she shall have leisure to make a splendid city; but the road immediately curved away from these up into solitude and the evening sky.

"You can't miss it," encouraged the station-master. "Keep right along after your noses till they knock up against Mrs. Twist's front gate. I'll look after the menagerie—" thus did he describe the Twinkler luggage. "Guess Mrs. Twist'll be sending for it as soon as you get there. Guess she forgot you. Guess she's shaken up by young Mr. Twist's arriving this very day. *I* wouldn't have forgotten you. No, not for a dozen young Mr. Twists," he added gallantly.

"Why do you call him young Mr. Twist," inquired Anna-Felicitas, "when he isn't? He must be at least thirty or forty or fifty."

"You see, we know him quite well," said Anna-Rose proudly, as they walked off. "He's a *great* friend of ours."

"You don't say," said the station-master, who was chewing gum; and as the twins had not yet seen this being done they concluded he had been interrupted in the middle of a meal by the arrival of the train.

"Now mind," he called after them, "you do whatever the road does. Give yourselves up to it, and however much it winds about stick to it. You'll meet other roads, but don't you take any notice of them."

Freed from their luggage, and for a moment from all care, the twins went up the hill. It was the nicest thing in the world to be going to see their friend again in quite a few minutes. They had, ever since the collapse of the Sack arrangements, been missing him very much. As they hurried on through the scented woods, past quiet fields, between yellow-leaved hedges, the evening sky growing duskier and the beckoning star lighter, they remembered Mr. Twist's extraordinary kindness, his devoted and unfailing care, with the warmest feelings of gratitude and affection. Even Anna-Felicitas felt warm. How often had he rearranged her head when it was hopelessly rolling about; how often had he fed her when she felt better enough to be hungry. Anna-Felicitas was very hungry. She still thought highly of pride and independence, but now considered their proper place was after a good meal. And Anna-Rose, with all the shameless cheerfulness of one who for a little has got rid of her pride and is feeling very much more comfortable in consequence remarked that one mustn't overdo independence.

"Let's hurry," said Anna-Felicitas. "I'm so dreadfully hungry. I do so terribly want supper. And I'm sure it's supper-time, and the Twists will have finished and we mightn't get any."

"As though Mr. Twist wouldn't see to that!" exclaimed Anna-Rose, proud and confident.

But she did begin to run, for she too was very hungry, and they raced the rest of the way; which is why they arrived on the Twist doorstep panting, and couldn't at first answer Amanda the head maid's surprised and ungarnished inquiry as to what they wanted, when she opened the door and found them there.

"We want Mr. Twist," said Anna-Rose, as soon as she could speak.

Amanda eyed them. "You from the village?" she asked, thinking perhaps they might be a deputation of elder school children sent to recite welcoming poems to Mr. Twist on his safe return from the seat of war. Yet she knew all the school children and everybody else in Clark, and none of them were these.

"No—from the station," panted Anna-Rose.

"We didn't see any village," panted Anna-Felicitas.

"We want Mr. Twist please," said Anna-Rose struggling with her breath.

Amanda eyed them. "Having supper," she said curtly.

"Fortunate creature," gasped Anna-Felicitas, "I hope he isn't eating it all."

"Will you announce us please?" said Anna-Rose putting on her dignity. "The Miss Twinklers."

"The who?" said Amanda.

"The Miss Twinklers," said Anna-Rose, putting on still more dignity, for there was that in Amanda's manner which roused the Junker in her.

"Can't disturb him at supper," said Amanda briefly.

"I assure you," said Anna-Felicitas, with the earnestness of conviction, "that he'll like it. I think I can undertake to promise he'll show no resentment whatever."

Amanda half shut the door.

"We'll come in please," said Anna-Rose, inserting herself into what was left of the opening. "Will you kindly bear in mind that we're totally unaccustomed to the doorstep?"

Amanda, doubtful, but unpractised in such a situation, permitted herself, in spite of having as she well knew the whole of free and equal America behind her, to be cowed. Well, perhaps not cowed, but taken aback. It was the long words and the awful politeness that did it. She wasn't used to beautiful long words like that, except on Sundays when the clergyman read the prayers in church, and she wasn't used to politeness. That so much of it should come out of objects so young rendered Amanda temporarily dumb.

She wavered with the door. Instantly Anna-Rose slipped through it; instantly Anna-Felicitas followed her.

"Kindly tell your master the Miss Twinklers have arrived," said Anna-Rose, looking every inch a Junker. There weren't many inches of Anna-Rose, but every one of them at that moment, faced by Amanda's want of discipline, was sheer Junker.

Amanda, who had never met a Junker in her happy democratic life, was stirred into bristling emotion by the word master. She was about to fling the insult of it from her by an impetuous and ill-considered assertion that if he was her master she was his mistress and so there now, when the bell which had rung once already since they had been standing parleying rang again and more impatiently, and the dining-room door opened and a head appeared. The twins didn't know that it was Edith's head, but it was.

"Amanda—" began Edith, in the appealing voice that was the nearest she ever dared get to rebuke without Amanda giving notice; but she stopped on seeing what, in the dusk of the hall, looked like a crowd. "Oh—" said Edith, taken aback. "Oh—" And was for withdrawing her head and shutting the door.

But the twins advanced towards her and the stream of light shining behind her and the agreeable smell streaming past her, with outstretched hands.

"How do you do," they both said cordially. "*Don't* go away again."

Edith, feeling that here was something to protect her quietly feeding mother from, came rather hastily through the door and held it to behind her, while her unresponsive and surprised hand was taken and shaken even as Mr. Sack's had been.

"We've come to see Mr. Twist," said Anna-Rose.

"He's our friend," said Anna-Felicitas.

"He's our best friend," said Anna-Rose.

"Is he in there?" asked Anna-Felicitas, appreciatively moving her nose, a particularly delicate instrument, round among the various really heavenly smells that were issuing from the dining-room and sorting them out and guessing what they probably represented, the while water rushed into her mouth.

The sound of a chair being hastily pushed back was heard and Mr. Twist suddenly appeared in the doorway.

"What is it, Edward?" a voice inside said.

Mr. Twist was a pale man, whose skin under no circumstances changed colour except in his ears. These turned red when he was stirred, and they were red now, and seemed translucent with the bright light behind him shining through them.

The twins flew to him. It was wonderful how much pleased they were to see him again. It was as if for years they had been separated from their dearest friend. The few hours since the night before had been enough to turn their friendship and esteem for him into a warm proprietary affection.

They felt that Mr. Twist belonged to them. Even Anna-Felicitas felt it, and her eyes as she beheld him were bright with pleasure.

"Oh there you are," cried Anna-Rose darting forward, gladness in her voice, and catching hold of his arm.

"We've come," said Anna-Felicitas, beaming and catching hold of his other arm.

"We got into difficulties," said Anna-Rose.

"We got into them at once," said Anna-Felicitas.

"They weren't our difficulties—"

"They were the Sacks'—"

"But they reacted on us—"

"And so here we are."

"Who is it, Edward?" asked the voice inside.

"Mrs. Sack ran away yesterday from Mr. Sack," went on Anna-Rose eagerly.

"Mr. Sack was still quite warm and moist from it when we got there," said Anna-Felicitas.

"Aunt Alice said we weren't ever to stay in a house where they did that," said Anna-Rose.

"Where there wasn't a lady," said Anna-Felicitas

"So when we saw that she wasn't there because she'd gone, we turned straight round to you," said Anna. Rose.

"Like flowers turning to the sun," said Anna-Felicitas, even in that moment of excitement not without complacency at her own aptness.

"And left our things at the station," Anna-Rose rushed on.

"And ran practically the whole way," said Anna-Felicitas, "because of perhaps being late for supper and you're having eaten it all, and we so dreadfully hungry—"

"Who is it, Edward?" again called the voice inside, louder and more insistently.

Mr. Twist didn't answer. He was quickly turning over the situation in his mind.

He had not mentioned the twins to his mother, which would have been natural, seeing how very few hours he had of reunion with her, if she hadn't happened to have questioned him particularly as to his fellow-passengers on the boat. Her questions had been confined to the first-class passengers, and he had said, truthfully, that he had hardly spoken to one of them, and not at all to any of the women.

Mrs. Twist had been relieved, for she lived in dread of Edward's becoming, as she put it to herself, entangled with ladies. Sin would be bad enough—for Mrs. Twist was obliged reluctantly to know that even with ladies it is possible to sin—but marriage for Edward would be even worse, because it lasted longer. Sin, terrible though it was, had at least this to be said for it, that it could be repented of and done with, and repentance after all was a creditable activity; but there was no repenting of marriage with any credit. It was a holy thing, and you don't repent of holy things,—at least, you oughtn't to. If, as ill-advised young men so often would, Edward wanted as years went on to marry in spite of his already having an affectionate and sympathetic home with feminine society in it, then it seemed to Mrs. Twist most important, most vital to the future comfort of the family, that it should be someone she had chosen herself. She had observed him from infancy, and knew much better than he what was needed for his happiness; and she also knew, if there must be a wife, what was needed for the happiness of his mother and sister. She had not thought to inquire about the second-class passengers, for it never occurred to her that a son of hers could drift out of his natural first-class sphere into the slums of a ship, and Mr. Twist had seen no reason for hurrying the Twinklers into her mental range. Not during those first hours, anyhow. There would be plenty of hours, and he felt that sufficient unto the day would be the Twinklers thereof.

But the part that was really making his ears red was that he had said nothing about the evening with the twins in New York. When his mother asked with the fondness of the occasion what had detained him, he said as many another honest man, pressed by the searching affection of relations, has said before him, that it was business. Now it appeared that he would have to go into the dining-room and say, "No. It wasn't business. It was these."

His ears glowed just to think of it. He hated to lie. Specially he hated to have lied,—at the moment, one plunged in spurred by sudden necessity, and then was left sorrowfully contemplating one's degradation. His own desire was always to be candid; but his mother, he well knew, could not bear the pains candour gave her. She had been so terribly hurt, so grievously wounded when, fresh from praying,—for before he went to Harvard he used to pray—he had on one or two occasions for a few minutes endeavoured not to lie to her that sheer fright at the effect of his unfiliality made him apologize and beg her to forget it and forgive him. Now she was going to be still more wounded by his having lied.

The meticulous tortuousness of family life struck Mr. Twist with a sudden great impatience. After that large life over there in France, to come back to this dreary petticoat lying, this feeling one's way about among tender places ...

"Who is it, Edward?" called the voice inside for the third time.

"There's someone in there seems quite particularly to want to know who we are," said Anna-Felicitas. "Why not tell her?"

"I expect it's your mother," said Anna-Rose, feeling the full satisfaction of having got to a house from which the lady hadn't run anywhere.

"It is," said Mr. Twist briefly.

"Edith!" called the voice, much more peremptorily.

Edith started and half went in, but hesitated and quite stayed out. She was gazing at the Twinklers with the same kind eyes her brother had, but without the disfiguring spectacles. Astonishment and perplexity and anxiety were mixed with the kindness. Amanda also gazed; and if the twins hadn't been so sure of their welcome, even they might gradually have begun to perceive that it wasn't exactly open-armed.

"Edith—Edward—Amanda," called the voice, this time with unmistakable anger.

For one more moment Mr. Twist stood uncertain, looking down at the happy confident faces turned up to him exactly, as Anna-Felicitas had just said, like flowers turning to the sun. Visions of France flashed before him, visions of what he had known, what he had just come back from. His friends over there, the gay courage, the helpfulness, the ready, uninquiring affection, the breadth of outlook, the quick friendliness, the careless assumption that one was decent, that one's intentions were good,—why shouldn't he pull some of the splendid stuff into his poor, lame little home? Why should he let himself drop back from heights like those to the old ridiculous timidities, the miserable habit of avoiding the truth? Rebellion, hope, determination, seized Mr. Twist. His eyes shone behind his spectacles. His ears were two red flags of revolution. He gripped hold of the twins, one under each arm.

"You come right in," he said, louder than he had ever spoken in his life. "Edith, see these girls? They're the two Annas. Their other name is Twinkler, but Anna'll see you through. They want supper, and they want beds, and they want affection, and they're going to get it all. So hustle with the food, and send the Cadillac for their baggage, and fix up things for them as comfortably as you know how. And as for Mrs. Sack," he said, looking first at one twin and then at the other, "if it hadn't been for her running away from her worthless husband—I'm convinced that fellow Sack is worthless— you might never have come here at all. So you see," he finished, laughing at Anna-Rose, "how good comes out of evil."

And with the sound of these words preceding him he pushed open the dining-room door and marched them in.

CHAPTER XVI

At the head of the table sat his mother; long, straight, and grave. She was in the seat of authority, the one with its back to the windows and its face to the door, from whence she could see what everybody did, especially Amanda. Having seen what Amanda did, she then complained to Edith. She didn't complain direct to Amanda, because Amanda could and did give notice.

Her eyes were fixed on the door. Between it and her was the table, covered with admirable things to eat, it being supper and therefore, according to a Twist tradition surviving from penurious days, all the food, hot and cold, sweet and salt, being brought in together, and Amanda only attending when rung for. Half-eaten oyster patties lay on Mrs. Twist's plate. In her glass neglected champagne had bubbled itself flat. Her hand still held her fork, but loosely, as an object that had lost its interest, and her eyes and ears for the last five minutes had not departed from the door.

At first she had felt mere resigned annoyance that Amanda shouldn't have answered the bell, but she didn't wish to cast a shadow over Edward's homecoming by drawing poor Edith's attention before him to how very badly she trained the helps, and therefore she said nothing at the moment; then, when Edith, going in search of Amanda, had opened the door and let in sounds of argument, she was surprised, for she knew no one so intimately that they would be likely to call at such an hour; but when Edward too leapt up, and went out and stayed out and failed to answer her repeated calls, she was first astonished, then indignant, and then suddenly was overcome by a cold foreboding.

Mrs. Twist often had forebodings, and they were always cold. They seized her with bleak fingers; and one of Edith's chief functions was to comfort and reassure her for as long a while each time as was required to reach the stage of being able to shake them off. Here was one, however, too icily convincing to be shaken off. It fell upon her with the swiftness of a revelation. Something unpleasant was going to happen to her; something perhaps worse than unpleasant,—disastrous. And something immediate.

Those excited voices out in the hall,—they were young, surely, and they were feminine. Also they sounded most intimate with Edward. What had he been concealing from her? What disgracefulness had penetrated through him, through the son the neighbourhood thought so much of, into her very home? She was a widow. He was her only son. Impossible to believe he would betray so sacred a position, that he whom she had so lovingly and proudly welcomed a few hours before would allow his—well, she really didn't know what to call them, but anyhow female friends of whom she had been told nothing, to enter that place which to every decent human being is inviolable, his mother's home. Yet Mrs. Twist did instantly believe it.

Then Edward's voice, raised and defiant—surely defiant?—came through the crack in the door, and every word he said was quite distinct. Anna; supper; affection ... Mrs. Twist sat frozen. And then the door was flung open and Edward tumultuously entered, his ears crimson, his face as she had never seen it and in each hand, held tightly by the arm, a girl.

Edward had been deceiving her.

"Mother—" he began.

"How do you do," said the girls together, and actually with smiles.

Edward had been deceiving her. That whole afternoon how quiet he had been, how listless. Quite gentle, quite affectionate, but listless and untalkative. She had thought he must be tired; worn out with his long journey across from Europe. She had made allowances for him; been sympathetic, been considerate. And look at him now. Never had she seen him with a face like that. He was—Mrs. Twist groped for the word and reluctantly found it—rollicking. Yes; that was the word that exactly described him— rollicking. If she hadn't observed his languor up to a few minutes ago at supper, and seen him with her own eyes refuse champagne and turn his back on cocktails, she would have been forced to the conclusion, dreadful though it was to a mother, that he had been drinking. And the girls! Two of them. And so young.

Mrs. Twist had known Edward, as she sometimes informed Edith, all his life, and had not yet found anything in his morals which was not blameless. Watch him with what loving care she might she had found nothing; and she was sure her mother's instinct would not have failed her. Nevertheless, even with that white past before her—he hadn't told her about "Madame Bovary"—she now instantly believed the worst.

It was the habit of Clark to believe the worst. Clark was very small, and therefore also very virtuous. Each inhabitant was the careful guardian of his neighbour's conduct. Nobody there ever did anything that was wrong; there wasn't a chance. But as Nature insists on a balance, the minds of Clark dwelt curiously on evil. They were minds active in suspicion. They leapt with an instantaneous agility at the worst conclusions. Nothing was ever said in Clark, but everything was thought. The older inhabitants, made fast prisoners in their mould of virtue by age, watched with jealous care the behaviour of those still young enough to attract temptation. The younger ones, brought up in inhibitions, settled down to wakefulness in regard to each other. Everything was provided and encouraged in Clark, a place of pleasant orchards and gentle fields, except the things that had to do with love. Husbands were there; and there was a public library, and social afternoons, and an Emerson society. The husbands died before the wives, being less able to cope with virtue; and a street in Clark of smaller houses into which their widows gravitated had been christened by the stationmaster—a more worldly man because of his three miles off and all the trains—Lamentation Lane.

In this village Mrs. Twist had lived since her marriage, full of dignity and honour. As a wife she had been full of it, for the elder Mr. Twist had been good even when alive, and as a widow she had been still fuller, for the elder Mr. Twist positively improved by being dead. Not a breath had ever touched her and her children. Not the most daring and distrustful Clark mind had ever thought of her except respectfully. And now here was this happening to her; at her age; when she was least able to bear it.

She sat in silence, staring with sombre eyes at the three figures.

"Mother—" began Edward again; but was again interrupted by the twins, who said together, as they had now got into the habit of saying when confronted by silent and surprised Americans, "We've come."

It wasn't that they thought it a particularly good conversational opening, it was because silence and surprise on the part of the other person seemed to call for explanation on theirs, and they were constitutionally desirous of giving all the information in their power.

"How do you do," they then repeated, loosening themselves from Mr. Twist and advancing down the room with outstretched hands.

Mr. Twist came with them. "Mother," he said, "these are the Twinkler girls. Their name's Twinkler. They—-"

Freed as he felt he was from his old bonds, determined as he felt he was on emulating the perfect candour and simplicity of the twins and the perfect candour and simplicity of his comrades in France, his mother's dead want of the smallest reaction to this announcement tripped him up for a moment and prevented his going on.

But nothing ever prevented the twins going on. If they were pleased and excited they went on with cheerful gusto, and if they were unnerved and frightened they still went on,—perhaps even more volubly, anxiously seeking cover behind a multitude of words.

Mrs. Twist had not yet unnerved and frightened them, because they were too much delighted that they had got to her at all. The relief Anna-Rose experienced at having safely piloted that difficult craft, the clumsy if adorable Columbus, into a respectable Port was so immense that it immediately vented itself in words of warmest welcome to the lady in the chair to her own home.

"We're *so* glad to see you here," she said, smiling till her dimple seemed to be everywhere at once hardly able to refrain from giving the lady a welcome hug instead of just inhospitably shaking her hand. She couldn't even shake her hand, however, because it still held, immovably, the fork. "It would have been too awful," Anna-Rose therefore finished, putting the heartiness of the handshake she wanted to give into her voice instead, "if *you* had happened to have run away too."

"As Mrs. Sack has done from her husband," Anna-Felicitas explained, smiling too, benevolently, at the black lady who actually having got oyster patties on her plate hadn't bothered to eat them. "But of course you couldn't," she went on, remembering in time to be tactful and make a Sympathetic reference to the lady's weeds; which, indeed, considering Mr. Twist had told her and Anna-Rose that his father had died when he was ten, nearly a quarter of a century ago, seemed to have kept their heads up astonishingly and stayed very fresh. And true to her German training, and undaunted by the fork, she did that which Anna-Rose in her contentment had forgotten, and catching up Mrs. Twist's right hand, fork and all, to her lips gave it the brief ceremonious kiss of a well brought up Junker.

Like Amanda's, Mrs. Twist's life had been up to this empty of Junkers. She had never even heard of them till the war, and pronounced their name, and so did the rest of Clark following her lead, as if it had been junket, only with an r instead of a t at the end. She didn't therefore recognize the action; but even she, outraged as she was, could not but see its grace. And looking up in sombre hostility at the little head bent over her hand and at the dark line of eyelashes on the the flushed face, she thought swiftly, "*She's* the one."

"You see, mother," said Mr. Twist, pulling a chair vigorously and sitting on it with determination, "it's like this. (Sit down, you two, and get eating. Start on anything you see in this show that hits your fancy. Edith'll be fetching you something hot, I expect—soup, or something—but meanwhile here's enough stuff to go on with.) You see, mother—" he resumed, turning squarely to her, while the twins obeyed him with immense alacrity and sat down and began to eat whatever happened to be nearest them, "these two girls—well, to start with they're twins—-"

Mr. Twist was stopped again by his mother's face. She couldn't conceive why he should lie. Twins the world over matched in size and features; it was notorious that they did. Also, it was the custom for them to match in age, and the tall one of these was at least a year older than the other one. But still, thought Mrs. Twist, let that pass. She would suffer whatever it was she had to suffer in silence.

The twins too were silent, because they were so busy eating. Perfectly at home under the wing they knew so well, they behaved with an easy naturalness that appeared to Mrs. Twist outrageous. But still—let that too pass. These strangers helped themselves and helped each other, as if everything belonged to them; and the tall one actually asked her—her, the mistress of the house—if she could get *her* anything. Well, let that pass too.

"You see, mother—" began Mr. Twist again.

He was finding it extraordinarily difficult. What a tremendous hold one's early training had on one, he reflected, casting about for words; what a deeply rooted fear there was in one, subconscious, lurking in one's foundations, of one's mother, of her authority, of her quickly wounded affection. Those Jesuits, with their conviction that they could do what they liked with a man if they had had the bringing up of him till he was seven, were pretty near the truth. It took a lot of shaking off, the unquestioning awe, the habit of obedience of one's childhood.

Mr. Twist sat endeavouring to shake it off. He also tried to bolster himself up by thinking he might perhaps be able to assist his mother to come out from her narrowness, and discover too how warm and glorious the sun shone outside, where people loved and helped each other. Then he rejected that as priggish.

"You see, mother," he started again, "I came across them—across these two girls—they're both called Anna, by the way, which seems confusing but isn't really—I came across them on the boat——"

He again stopped dead.

Mrs. Twist had turned her dark eyes to him. They had been fixed on Anna-Felicitas, and on what she was doing with the dish of oyster patties in front of her. What she was doing was not what Mrs. Twist was accustomed to see done at her table. Anna-Felicitas was behaving badly with the patties, and not even attempting to conceal, as the decent do, how terribly they interested her.

"You came across them on the boat," repeated Mrs. Twist, her eyes on her son, moved in spite of her resolution to speech. And he had told her that very afternoon that he had spoken to nobody except men. Another lie. Well, let that pass too ...

Mr. Twist sat staring back at her through his big gleaming spectacles. He well knew the weakness of his position from his mother's point of view; but why should she have such a point of view, such a niggling, narrow one, determined to stay angry and offended because he had been stupid enough to continue, under the influence of her presence, the old system of not being candid with her, of being slavishly anxious to avoid offending? Let her try for once to understand and forgive. Let her for once take the chance offered her of doing a big, kind thing. But as he stared at her it entered his mind that he couldn't very well start moving her heart on behalf of the twins in their presence. He couldn't tell her they were orphans, alone in the world, helpless, poor, and so unfortunately German, with them sitting there. If he did, there would be trouble. The twins seemed absorbed for the moment in getting fed, but he had no doubt their ears were attentive, and at the first suggestion of sympathy being invoked for them they would begin to say a few of those things he was so much afraid his mother mightn't be able to understand. Or, if she understood, appreciate.

He decided that he would be quiet until Edith came back, and then ask his mother to go to the drawing-room with him, and while Edith was looking after the Annas he would, well out of earshot, explain them to his mother, describe their situation, commend them to her patience and her love. He sat silent therefore, wishing extraordinarily hard that Edith would be quick.

But Anna-Felicitas's eyes were upon him now, as well as his mother's. "Is it possible," she asked with her own peculiar gentleness, balancing a piece of patty on her fork, "that you haven't yet mentioned us to your mother?"

And Anna-Rose, struck in her turn at such an omission, paused too with food on the way to her mouth, and said, "And we such friends?"

"Almost, as it were, still red-hot from being with you?" said Anna-Felicitas.

Both the twins looked at Mrs. Twist in their surprise.

"I thought the first thing everybody did when they got back to their mother," said Anna-Rose, addressing her, "was to tell her everything from the beginning."

Mrs. Twist, after an instant's astonishment at this unexpected support, bowed her head—it could hardly be called a nod—in her son's direction. "You see—" the movement seemed to say, "even these ..."

"And ever since the first day at sea," said Anna-Felicitas, also addressing Mrs. Twist, "up to as recently as eleven o'clock last night, he has been what I think can be quite accurately described as our faithful two-footed companion."

"Yes," said Anna-Rose. "As much as that we've been friends. Practically inseparable."

"So that it really is *very* surprising," said Anna-Felicitas to Mr. Twist, "that you didn't tell your mother about us."

Mr. Twist got up. He wouldn't wait for Edith. It was unhealthy in that room.

He took his mother's arm and helped her to get up. "You're very wise, you two," he flung at the twins in the voice of the goaded, "but you may take it from me you don't know everything yet. Mother, come into the drawing-room, and we'll talk. Edith'll see to these girls. I expect I ought to have talked sooner," he went on, as he led her to the door, "but confound it all, I've only been home about a couple of hours."

"Five," said Mrs. Twist.

"Five then. What's five? No time at all."

"Ample," said Mrs Twist; adding icily, "and did I you say confound, Edward?"

"Well, damn then," said Edward very loud, in a rush of rank rebellion.

CHAPTER XVII

This night was the turning-point in Mr. Twist's life. In it he broke loose from his mother. He spent a terrible three hours with her in the drawing-room, and the rest of the night he strode up and down his bedroom. The autumn morning, creeping round the house in long white wisps, found him staring out of his window very pale, his mouth pulled together as tight as it would go.

His mother had failed him. She had not understood. And not only simply not understood, but she had said things when at last she did speak, after he had explained and pleaded for at least an hour, of an incredible bitterness and injustice. She had seemed to hate him. If she hadn't been his mother Mr. Twist would have been certain she hated him, but he still believed that mothers couldn't hate their children. It was stark against nature; and Mr. Twist still believed in the fundamental rightness of that which is called nature. She had accused him of gross things—she, his mother, who from her conversation since he could remember was unaware, he had judged, of the very existence of such things. Those helpless children ... Mr. Twist stamped as he strode. Well, he had made her take that back; and indeed she had afterwards admitted that she said it in her passion of grief and disappointment, and that it was evident these girls were not like that.

But before they reached that stage, for the first time in his life he had been saying straight out what he wanted to say to his mother just as if she had been an ordinary human being. He told her all he knew of the twins, asked her to take them in for the present and be good to them, and explained the awkwardness of their position, apart from its tragedy, as Germans by birth stranded in New England, where opinion at that moment was so hostile to Germans. Then, continuing in candour, he had told his mother that here was her chance of doing a fine and beautiful thing, and it was at this point that Mrs. Twist suddenly began, on her side, to talk.

She had listened practically in silence to the rest; had only started when he explained the girls' nationality; but when he came to offering her these girls as the great opportunity of her life to do something really good at last, she, who felt she had been doing nothing else but noble and beautiful things, and doing them with the most single-minded devotion to duty and the most consistent disregard of inclination, could keep silence no longer. Had she not borne her great loss without a murmur? Had she not devoted all her years to bringing up her son to be a good man? Had she ever considered herself? Had she ever flagged in her efforts to set an example of patience in grief, of dignity in misfortune? She began to speak. And just as amazed as she had been at the things this strange, unknown son had been saying to her and at the manner of their delivery, so was he amazed at the things this strange, unknown mother was saying to him, and at the manner of their delivery.

Yet his amazement was not so great after all as hers. Because for years, away down hidden somewhere inside him, he had doubted his mother; for years he had, shocked at himself, covered up and trampled on these unworthy doubts indignantly. He had doubted her unselfishness; he had doubted her sympathy and kindliness; he had even doubted her honesty, her ordinary honesty with money and accounts; and lately, before he went to Europe, he had caught himself thinking she was cruel. Nevertheless this unexpected naked justification of his doubts was shattering to him.

But Mrs. Twist had never doubted Edward. She thought she knew him inside out. She had watched him develop. Watched him during the long years of his unconsciousness. She had been quite secure; and rather disposed, also somewhere down inside her, to a contempt for him, so easy had he been to manage, so ready to do everything she wished. Now it appeared that she no more knew Edward than if he had been a stranger in the street.

The bursting of the dykes of convention between them was a horrible thing to them both. Mr. Twist had none of the cruelty of the younger generation to support him: he couldn't shrug his shoulder and take comfort in the thought that this break between them was entirely his mother's fault, for however much he believed it to be her fault the belief merely made him wretched; he had none of the pitiless black pleasure to be got from telling himself it served her right. So naturally kind was he—weak, soft, stupid, his mother shook out at him—that through all his own shame at this naked vision of what had been carefully dressed up for years in dignified clothes of wisdom and affection, he was actually glad, when he had time in his room to think it over, glad she should be so passionately positive that he, and only he, was in the wrong. It would save her from humiliation; and of the painful things of late Mr. Twist could least bear to see a human being humiliated.

That was, however, towards morning. For hours raged, striding about his room, sorting out the fragments into which his life as a son had fallen, trying to fit them into some sort of a pattern, to see clear about the future.

Clearer. Not clear. He couldn't hope for that yet. The future seemed one confused lump. All he could see really clear of it was that he was going, next day, and taking the twins. He would take them to the other people they had a letter to, the people in California, and then turn his face back to Europe, to the real thing, to the greatness of life where death is. Not an hour longer than he could help would he or they stay in that house. He had told his mother he would go away, and she had said, "I hope never to see you again." Who would have thought she had so much of passion in her? Who would have thought he had so much of it in him?

Fury against her injustice shook and shattered Mr. Twist. Not so could fair and affectionate living together be conducted, on that basis of suspicion, distrust, jealousy. Through his instinct, though not through his brain, shot the conviction that his mother was jealous of the twins,—jealous of the youth of the twins, and of their prettiness, and goodness, and of the power, unknown to them, that these things gave them. His brain was impervious to such a conviction, because it was an innocent brain, and the idea would never have entered it that a woman of his mother's age, well over sixty, could be jealous in that way; but his instinct knew it.

The last thing his mother said as he left the drawing-room was, "You have killed me. You have killed your own mother. And just because of those girls."

And Mr. Twist, shocked at this parting shot of unfairness, could find, search as he might, nothing to be said for his mother's point of view. It simply wasn't true. It simply was delusion.

Nor could she find anything to be said for his, but then she didn't try to, it was so manifestly unforgivable. All she could do, faced by this bitter sorrow, was to leave Edward to God. Sternly, as he flung out of the room at last, unsoftened, untouchable, deaf to her even when she used the tone he had always obeyed the tone of authority, she said to herself she must leave her son to God. God knew. God would judge. And Clark too would know; and Clark too would judge.

Left alone in the drawing-room on this terrible night of her second great bereavement, Mrs. Twist was yet able, she was thankful to feel, to resolve she would try to protect her son as long as she could from Clark. From God she could not, if she would, protect him; but she would try to protect him even now, as she had always protected him, from earthly harm and hurt. Clark would, however, surely know in time, protect as she might, and judge between her and Edward. God knew already, and was already judging. God and Clark.... Poor Edward.

CHAPTER XVIII

The twins, who had gone to bed at half-past nine, shepherded by Edith, in the happy conviction that they had settled down comfortably for some time, were surprised to find at breakfast that they hadn't.

They had taken a great fancy to Edith, in spite of a want of restfulness on her part that struck them while they were finishing their supper, and to which at last they drew her attention. She was so kind, and so like Mr. Twist; but though she looked at them with hospitable eyes and wore an expression of real benevolence, it didn't escape their notice that she seemed to be listening to something that wasn't, anyhow, them, and to be expecting something that didn't, anyhow, happen. She went several times to the door through which her brother and mother had disappeared, and out into whatever part of the house lay beyond it, and when she came back after a minute or two was as wanting in composure as ever.

At last, finding these abrupt and repeated interruptions hindered any real talk, they pointed out to her that reasoned conversation was impossible if one of the parties persisted in not being in the room, and inquired of her whether it were peculiar to her, or typical of the inhabitants of America, to keep on being somewhere else. Edith smiled abstractedly at them, said nothing, and went out again.

She was longer away this time, and the twins having eaten, among other things, a great many meringues, grew weary of sitting with those they hadn't eaten lying on the dish in front of them reminding them of those they had. They wanted, having done with meringues, to get away from them and forget them. They wanted to go into another room now, where there weren't any. Anna-Felicitas felt, and told Anna-Rose who was staring listlessly at the left-over meringues, that it was like having committed murder, and being obliged to go on looking at the body long after you were thoroughly tired of it. Anna-Rose agreed, and said that she wished now she hadn't committed meringues,—anyhow so many of them.

Then at last Edith came back, and told them she was sure they were very tired after their long day, and suggested their going upstairs to their rooms. The rooms were ready, said Edith, the baggage had come, and she was sure they would like to have nice hot baths and go to bed.

The twins obeyed her readily, and she checked a desire on their part to seek out her mother and brother first and bid them good-night, on the ground that her mother and brother were busy; and while the twins were expressing polite regret, and requesting her to convey their regret for them to the proper quarter in a flow of well-chosen words that astonished Edith, who didn't know how naturally Junkers make speeches, she hurried them by the drawing-room door through which, shut though it was, came sounds of people being, as Anna-Felicitas remarked, very busy indeed; and Anna-Rose, impressed by the quality and volume of Mr. Twist's voice as it reached her passing ears, told Edith that intimately as she knew her brother she had never known him as busy as that before.

Edith said nothing, but continued quickly up the stairs.

They found they each had a bedroom, with a door between, and that each bedroom had a bathroom of its own, which filled them with admiration and pleasure. There had only been one bathroom at Uncle Arthur's, and at home in Pomerania there hadn't been any at all. The baths there had been vessels brought into one's bedroom every night, into which servants next morning poured water out of buckets, having previously pumped the water into the bucket from the pump in the backyard. They put Edith in possession of these facts while she helped them unpack and brushed and plaited their hair for them, and she was much astonished,—both at the conditions of discomfort and slavery they revealed as prevalent in other countries, and at the fact that they, the Twinklers, should hail from Pomerania.

Pomerania, reflected Edith as she tied up their pigtails with the ribbons handed to her for that purpose, used to be in Germany when she went to school, and no doubt still was. She became more thoughtful than ever, though she still smiled at them, for how could she help it? Everyone, Edith was certain, must needs smile at the Twinklers even if they didn't happen to be one's own dear brother's *protegees*. And when they came out, very clean and with scrubbed pink ears, from their bath, she not only smiled at them as she tucked them up in bed, but she kissed them good-night.

Edith, like her brother, was born to be a mother,—one of the satisfactory sort that keeps you warm and doesn't argue with you. Germans or no Germans the Twinklers were the cutest little things, thought Edith; and she kissed them, with the same hunger with which, being now thirty-eight, she was beginning to kiss puppies.

"You remind me so of Mr. Twist," murmured Anna-Felicitas sleepily, as Edith tucked her up and kissed her.

"You do all the sorts of things he does," murmured Anna-Rose, also sleepily, when it was her turn to be tucked up and kissed; and in spite of a habit now fixed in her of unquestioning acceptance and uncritical faith. Edith went downstairs to her restless vigil outside the drawing-room door a little surprised.

At breakfast the twins learnt to their astonishment that, though appearances all pointed the other way what they were really doing was not being stationary at all, but merely having a night's lodging and breakfast between, as it were, two trains.

Mr. Twist, who looked pale and said shortly when the twins remarked solicitously on it that he felt pale, briefly announced the fact.

"What?" exclaimed Anna-Rose, staring at Mr. Twist and then at Edith—Mrs. Twist, they were told, was breakfasting in bed—"Why, we've unpacked."

"You will re-pack," said Mr. Twist.

They found difficulty in believing their ears.

"But we've settled in," remonstrated Anna-Felicitas, after an astonished pause.

"You will settle out," said Mr. Twist.

He frowned. He didn't look at them, he frowned at his own teapot. He had made up his mind to be very short with the Annas until they were safely out of the house, and not permit himself to be entangled by them in controversy. Also, he didn't want to look at them if he could help it. He was afraid that if he did he might be unable not to take them both in his arms and beg their pardon for the whole horridness of the world.

But if he didn't look at them, they looked at him. Four round, blankly surprised eyes were fixed, he knew, unblinkingly on him.

"We're seeing you in quite a new light," said Anna-Rose at last, troubled and upset.

"Maybe," said Mr. Twist, frowning at his teapot.

"Perhaps you will be so good," said Anna-Felicitas stiffly, for at all times she hated being stirred up and uprooted, "as to tell us where you think we're going to."

"Because," said Anna-Rose, her voice trembling a little, not only at the thought of fresh responsibilities, but also with a sense of outraged faith, "our choice of residence, as you may have observed, is strictly limited."

Mr. Twist, who had spent an hour before breakfast with Edith, whose eyes were red, informed them that they were *en route* for California.

"To those other people," said Anna-Rose. "I see."

She held her head up straight.

"Well, I expect they'll be very glad to see us," she said after a silence; and proceeded, her chin in the air, to look down her nose, because she didn't want Mr. Twist, or Edith or Anna-Felicitas, to notice that her eyes had gone and got tears in them. She angrily wished she hadn't got such damp eyes. They were no better than swamps, she thought—undrained swamps; and directly fate's foot came down a little harder than usual, up oozed the lamentable liquid. Not thus should the leader of an expedition behave. Not thus, she was sure, did the original Christopher. She pulled herself together; and after a minute's struggle was able to leave off looking down her nose.

But meanwhile Anna-Felicitas had informed Mr. Twist with gentle dignity that he was obviously tired of them.

"Not at all," said Mr. Twist.

Anna-Felicitas persisted. "In view of the facts," she said gently, "I'm afraid your denial carries no weight."

"The facts," said Mr. Twist, taking up his teapot and examining it with care, "are that I'm coming with you."

"Oh are you," said Anna-Felicitas much more briskly; and it was here that Anna-Rose's eyes dried up.

"That rather dishes your theory," said Mr. Twist, still turning his teapot about in his hands. "Or would if it didn't happen that I—well, I happen to have some business to do in California, and I may as well do it now as later. Still, I could have gone by a different route or train, so you see your theory *is* rather dished, isn't it?"

"A little," admitted Anna-Felicitas. "Not altogether. Because if you really like our being here, here we are. So why hurry us off somewhere else so soon?"

Mr. Twist perceived that he was being led into controversy in spite of his determination not to be. "You're very wise," he said shortly, "but you don't know everything. Let us avoid conjecture and stick to facts. I'm going to take you to California, and hand you over to your friends. That's all you know, and all you need to know."

"As Keats very nearly said," said Anna-Rose

"And if our friends have run away?" suggested Anna-Felicitas.

"Oh Lord," exclaimed Mr. Twist impatiently, putting the teapot down with a bang, "do you think we're running away all the time in America?"

"Well, I think you seem a little restless," said Anna-Felicitas.

Thus it was that two hours later the twins found themselves at the Clark station once more, once more starting into the unknown, just as if they had never done it before, and gradually, as they adapted themselves to the sudden change, such is the india-rubber-like quality of youth, almost with the same hopefulness. Yet they couldn't but meditate, left alone on the platform while Mr. Twist checked the baggage, on the mutability of life. They seemed to live in a kaleidoscope since the war began what a series of upheavals and readjustments had been theirs! Silent, and a little apart on the Clark platform, they reflected retrospectively; and as they counted up their various starts since the days, only fourteen months ago, when they were still in their home in Germany, apparently as safely rooted, as unshakably settled as the pine trees in their own forests, they couldn't but wonder at the elusiveness of the unknown, how it wouldn't let itself be caught up with and at the trouble it was giving them.

They had had so many changes in the last year that they did want now to have time to become familiar with some one place and people. Already however, being seventeen, they were telling themselves, and each other that after all, since the Sacks had failed them, California was their real objective. Not Clark at all. Clark had never been part of their plans. Uncle Arthur and Aunt Alice didn't even know it existed. It was a side-show; just a little thing of their own, an extra excursion slipped in between the Sacks and the Delloggs. True they had hoped to stay there some time, perhaps even for months,—anyhow, time to mend their stockings in, which were giving way at the toes unexpectedly, seeing how new they were; but ultimately California was the place they had to go to. It was only that it was a little upsetting to be whisked out of Clark at a moment's notice.

"I expect you'll explain everything to us when we're in the train and have lots of time," Anna-Rose had said to Mr. Twist as the car moved away from the house and Edith, red-eyed, waved her handkerchief from the doorstep.

Mrs. Twist had not come down to say good-bye, and they had sent her many messages.

"I expect I will," Mr. Twist had answered.

But it was not till they were the other side of Chicago that he really began to be himself again. Up to then—all that first day, and the next morning in New York where he took them to the bank their £200 was in and saw that they got a cheque-book, and all the day after that waiting in the Chicago hotel for the train they were to go on in to California—Mr. Twist was taciturn.

They left Chicago in the evening; a raw, wintery October evening with cold rain in the air, and the twins, going early to bed in their compartment, a place that seemed to them so enchanting that their spirits couldn't fail to rise, saw no more of him till breakfast next morning. They then noticed that the cloud had lifted a little; and as the day went on it lifted still more. They were going to be three days together in that train, and it would be impossible for Mr. Twist, they were sure, to go on being taciturn as long as that. It wasn't his nature. His nature was conversational. And besides, shut up like that in a train, the sheer getting tired of reading all day would make him want to talk.

So after lunch, when they were all three on the platform of the observation car, though there was nothing to observe except limitless flat stretches of bleak and empty country, the twins suggested that he should now begin to talk again. They pointed out that his body was bound to get stiff on that long journey from want of exercise, but that his mind needn't, and he had better stretch it by conversing agreeably with them as he used to before the day, which seemed so curiously long ago, when they landed in America.

"It does indeed seem long ago," agreed Mr. Twist, lighting another cigarette. "I have difficulty in realizing it isn't a week yet."

And he reflected that the Annas had managed to produce pretty serious havoc in America considering they had only been in it five days. He and his mother permanently estranged; Edith left alone at Clark sitting there in the ruins of her loving preparations for his return, with nothing at all that he could see to look forward to and live for except the hourly fulfilment of what she regarded as duty; every plan upset; the lives, indeed, of his mother and of his sister and of himself completely altered,—it was a pretty big bag in the time, he thought, flinging the match back towards Chicago.

Mr. Twist felt sore. He felt like somebody who had had a bad tumble, and is sore and a little dizzy; but he recognized that these great ruptures cannot take place without aches and doubts. He ached, and he doubted and he also knew through his aches and doubts that he was free at last from what of late years he had so grievously writhed under—the shame of pretence. And the immediate cause of his being set free was, precisely, the Annas.

It had been a violent, a painful setting free, but it had happened; and who knew if, without their sudden appearance at Clark and the immediate effect they produced on his mother, he wouldn't have lapsed after all, in spite of the feelings and determinations he had brought back with him from Europe, into the old ways again under the old influence, and gone on ignobly pretending to agree, to approve, to enjoy, to love, when he was never for an instant doing anything of the sort? He might have trailed on like that for years—Mr. Twist didn't like the picture of his own weakness, but he was determined to look at himself as he was—trailed along languidly when he was at home, living another life when he was away, getting what he absolutely must have, the irreducible minimum of personal freedom necessary to sanity, by means of small and shabby deceits. My goodness, how he hated deceits, how tired he was of the littleness of them!

He turned his head and looked at the profiles of the Annas sitting alongside him. His heart suddenly grew warm within him. They had on the blue caps again which made them look so bald and cherubic, and their eyes were fixed on the straight narrowing lines of rails that went back and back to a point in the distance. The dear little things; the dear, dear little things,—so straightforward, so blessedly straight and simple, thought Mr. Twist. Fancy his mother losing a chance like this. Fancy *anybody*, thought the affectionate and kind man, missing an opportunity of helping such unfortunately placed children.

The twins felt he was looking at them, and together they turned and looked at him. When they saw his expression they knew the cloud had lifted still more, and their faces broke into broad smiles of welcome.

"It's pleasant to see you back again," said Anna-Felicitas heartily, who was next to him.

"We've missed you very much," said Anna-Rose.

"It hasn't been like the same place, the world hasn't," said Anna-Felicitas, "since you've been away."

"Since you walked out of the dining-room that night at Clark," said Anna-Rose.

"Of course we know you can't always be with us," said Anna-Felicitas.

"Which we deeply regret," interjected Anna-Rose.

"But while you are with us," said Anna-Felicitas, "for these last few days, I would suggest that we should be happy. As happy as we used to be on the *St. Luke* when we weren't being sea-sick." And she thought she might even go so far as to enjoy hearing the "Ode to Dooty," now.

"Yes," said Anna-Rose, leaning forward. "In three days we shall have disappeared into the maw of the Delloggs. Do let us be happy while we can. Who knows what their maw will be like? But whatever it's like," she added firmly, "we're going to stick in it."

"And perhaps," said Anna-Felicitas, "now that you're a little restored to your normal condition, you'll tell us what has been the matter."

"For it's quite clear," said Anna-Rose, "that something *has* been the matter."

"We've been talking it over," said Anna-Felicitas, "and putting two and two together, and perhaps you'll tell us what it was, and then we shall know if we're right."

"Perhaps I will," said Mr. Twist, cogitating, as he continued benevolently to gaze at them. "Let's see—" He hesitated, and pushed his hat off his forehead. "I wonder if you'd understand—"

"We'll give our minds to it," Anna-Felicitas assured him.

"These caps make us look more stupid than we are," Anna-Rose assured him, deducing her own appearance from that of Anna-Felicitas.

Encouraged, but doubtful of their capabilities of comprehension on this particular point, Mr. Twist embarked rather gingerly on his explanations. He was going to be candid from now on for the rest of his days, but the preliminary plunges were, he found, after all a little difficult. Even with the pellucidly candid Annas, all ready with ears pricked up attentively and benevolently and minds impartial, he found it difficult. It was because, on the subject of mothers, he feared he was up against their one prejudice. He felt rather than knew that their attitude on this one point might be uncompromising,—mothers were mothers, and there was an end of it; that sort of attitude, coupled with extreme reprobation of himself for supposing anything else.

He was surprised and relieved to find he was wrong. Directly they got wind of the line his explanations were taking, which was very soon for they were giving their minds to it as they promised and Mr. Twist's hesitations were illuminating, they interrupted.

"So we were right," they said to each other.

"But you don't know yet what I'm going to say," said Mr. Twist. "I've only started on the preliminaries."

"Yes we do. You fell out with your mother," said Anna-Rose.

"Quarrelled," said Anna-Felicitas, nodding

"We didn't think so at the time," said Anna-Rose.

"We just felt there was an atmosphere of strain about Clark," said Anna-Felicitas.

"But talking it over privately, we concluded that was what had happened."

Mr. Twist was so much surprised that for a moment he could only say "Oh." Then he said, "And you're terribly shocked, I suppose."

"Oh no," they said airily and together.

"No?"

"You see—" began Anna-Felicitas.

"You see—" began Anna-Rose.

"You see, as a general principle," said Anna-Felicitas, "it's reprehensible to quarrel with one's mother."

"But we've not been able to escape observing—" said Anna-Rose.

"In the course of our brief and inglorious career," put in Anna-Felicitas.

"—that there are mothers and mothers," said Anna-Rose.

"Yes," said Mr. Twist; and as they didn't go on he presently added, "Yes?"

"Oh, that's all," said the twins, once more airily and together.

CHAPTER XIX

After this brief *éclaircissement* the rest of the journey was happy. Indeed, it is doubtful if any one can journey to California and not be happy.

Mr. Twist had never been further west than Chicago and break up or no break up of his home he couldn't but have a pleasant feeling of adventure. Every now and then the realization of this feeling gave his conscience a twinge, and wrung out of it a rebuke. He was having the best of it in this business; he was the party in the quarrel who went away, who left the dreariness of the scene of battle with all its corpses of dead illusions, and got off to fresh places and people who had never heard of him. Just being in a train, he found, and rushing on to somewhere else was extraordinarily nerve-soothing. At Clark there would be gloom and stagnation, the heavy brooding of a storm that has burst but not moved on, a continued anger on his mother's side, naturally increasing with her inactivity, with her impotence. He was gone, and she could say and do nothing more to him. In a quarrel, thought Mr. Twist, the morning he pushed up his blinds and saw the desert at sunrise, an exquisite soft thing just being touched into faint colours,—in a quarrel the one who goes has quite unfairly the best of it. Beautiful new places come and laugh at him, people who don't know him and haven't yet judged and condemned him are ready to be friendly. He must, of course, go far enough; not stay near at hand in some familiar place and be so lonely that he ends by being remorseful. Well, he was going far enough. Thanks to the Annas he was going about as far as he could go. Certainly he was having the best of it in being the one in the quarrel who went; and he was shocked to find himself cynically thinking, on top of that, that one should always, then, take care to be the one who did go.

But the desert has a peculiarly exhilarating air. It came in everywhere, and seemed to tickle him out of the uneasy mood proper to one who has been cutting himself off for good and all from his early home. For the life of him he couldn't help feeling extraordinarily light and free. Edith—yes, there was Edith, but some day he would make up to Edith for everything. There was no helping her now: she was fast bound in misery and iron, and didn't even seem to know it. So would he have been, he supposed, if he had never left home at all. As it was, it was bound to come, this upheaval. Just the mere fact of inevitable growth would have burst the bands sooner or later. There oughtn't, of course, to have been any bands; or, there being bands, he ought long ago to have burst them.

He pulled his kind slack mouth firmly together and looked determined. Long ago, repeated Mr. Twist, shaking his head at his own weak past. Well, it was done at last, and never again—never, never again, he said to himself, sniffing in through his open window the cold air of the desert at sunrise.

By that route, the Santa Fé, it is not till two or three hours before you get to the end of the journey that summer meets you. It is waiting for you at a place called San Bernardino. There is no trace of it before. Up to then you are still in October; and then you get to the top of the pass, and with a burst it is June,—brilliant, windless, orange-scented.

The twins and Mr. Twist were in the restaurant-car lunching when the miracle happened. Suddenly the door opened and in came summer, with a great warm breath of roses. In a moment the car was invaded by the scent of flowers and fruit and of something else strange and new and very aromatic. The electric fans were set twirling, the black waiters began to perspire, the passengers called for cold things to eat, and the twins pulled off their knitted caps and jerseys.

From that point on to the end of the line in Los Angeles the twins could only conclude they were in heaven. It was the light that did it, the extraordinary glow of radiance. Of course there were orchards after orchards of orange trees covered with fruit, white houses smothered in flowers, gardens overrun with roses, tall groups of eucalyptus trees giving an impression of elegant nakedness, long lines of pepper trees with frail fern-like branches, and these things continued for the rest of the way; but they would have been as nothing without that beautiful, great bland light. The twins had had their hot summers in Pomerania, and their July days in England, but had not yet seen anything like this. Here was summer without sultriness, without gnats, mosquitoes, threatening thunderstorms, or anything to spoil it; it was summer as it might be in the Elysian fields, perfectly clear, and calm, and radiant. When the train stopped they could see how not a breath of wind stirred the dust on the quiet white roads, and the leaves of the magnolia trees glistened motionless in the sun. The train went slowly and stopped often, for there seemed to be one long succession of gardens and villages. After the empty, wind-driven plains they had come through, those vast cold expanses without a house or living creature in sight, what a laughing plenty, what a gracious fruitfulness, was here. And when they went back to their compartment it too was full of summer smells,—the smell of fruit, and roses, and honey.

For the first time since the war began and with it their wanderings, the twins felt completely happy. It was as though the loveliness wrapped them round and they stretched themselves in it and forgot. No fear of the future, no doubt of it at all, they thought, gazing out of the window, the soft air patting their faces, could possibly bother them here. They never, for instance, could be cold here, or go hungry. A great confidence in life invaded them. The Delloggs, sun-soaked and orange-fed for years in this place, couldn't but be gentle too, and kind and calm. Impossible not to get a sort of refulgence oneself, they thought, living here, and absorb it and give it out again. They pictured the Delloggs as bland pillars of light coming forward effulgently to greet them, and bathing them in the beams of their hospitality. And the feeling of responsibility and anxiety that had never left Anna-Rose since she last saw Aunt Alice dropped off her in this place, and she felt that sun and oranges, backed by £200 in the bank, would be difficult things for misfortune to get at.

As for Mr. Twist, he was even more entranced than the twins as he gazed out of the window, for being older he had had time to see more ugly things, had got more used to them and to taking them as principally making up life. He stared at what he saw, and thought with wonder of his mother's drawing-room at Clark, of its gloomy, velvet-upholstered discomforts, of the cold mist creeping round the house, and of that last scene in it, with her black figure in the middle of it, tall and thin and shaking with bitterness. He had certainly been in that drawing-room and heard her so terribly denouncing him, but it was very difficult to believe; it seemed so exactly like a nightmare, and this the happy normal waking up in the morning.

They all three were in the highest spirits when they got out at Los Angeles and drove across to the Southern Pacific station—the name alone made their hearts leap—to catch the afternoon train on to where the Delloggs lived, and their spirits were the kind one can imagine in released souls on their first arriving in paradise,—high, yet subdued; happy, but reverential; a sort of rollicking awe. They were subdued, in fact, by beauty. And the journey along the edge of the Pacific to Acapulco, where the Delloggs lived, encouraged and developed this kind of spirits, for the sun began to set, and, as the train ran for miles close to the water with nothing but a strip of sand between it and the surf, they saw their first Pacific sunset. It happened to be even in that land of wonderful sunsets an unusually wonderful one, and none of the three had ever seen anything in the least like it. They could but sit silent and stare. The great sea, that little line of lovely islands flung down on it like a chain of amethysts, that vast flame of sky, that heaving water passionately reflecting it, and on the other side, through the other windows, a sharp wall of black mountains,—it was fantastically beautiful, like something in a poem or a dream.

By the time they got to Acapulco it was dark. Night followed upon the sunset with a suddenness that astonished the twins, used to the leisurely methods of twilight on the Baltic; and the only light in the country outside the town as they got near it was the light from myriads of great stars.

No Delloggs were at the station, but the twins were used now to not being met and had not particularly expected them; besides, Mr. Twist was with them this time, and he would see that if the Delloggs didn't come to them they would get safely to the Delloggs.

The usual telegram had been sent announcing their arrival, and the taxi-driver, who seemed to know the Dellogg house well when Mr. Twist told him where they wanted to go, apparently also thought it natural they should want to go exactly there. In him, indeed, there did seem to be a trace of expecting them,—almost as if he had been told to look out for them; for hardly had Mr. Twist begun to give him the address than glancing at the twins he said, "I guess you're wanting Mrs. Dellogg"; and got down and actually opened the door for them, an attention so unusual in the taxi-drivers the twins had up to then met in America that they were more than ever convinced that nothing in the way of unfriendliness or unkindness could stand up against sun and oranges.

"Relations?" he asked them through the window as he shut the door gently and carefully, while Mr. Twist went with a porter to see about the luggage.

"I beg your pardon?" said Anna-Rose.

"Relations of Delloggses?"

"No," said Anna-Rose. "Friends."

"At least," amended Anna-Felicitas, "practically."

"Ah," said the driver, leaning with both his arms on the window-sill in the friendliest possible manner, and chewing gum and eyeing them with thoughtful interest.

Then he said, after a pause during which his jaw rolled regularly from side to side and the twins watched the rolling with an interest equal to his interest in them, "From Los Angeles?"

"No," said Anna-Rose. "From New York."

"At least," amended Anna-Felicitas, "practically."

"Well I call that a real compliment," said the driver slowly and deliberately because of his jaw going on rolling. "To come all that way, and without being relations—I call that a real compliment, and a friendship that's worth something. Anybody can come along from Los Angeles, but it takes a real friend to come from New York," and he eyed them now with admiration.

The twins for their part eyed him. Not only did his rolling jaws fascinate them, but the things he was saying seemed to them quaint.

"But we wanted to come," said Anna-Rose, after a pause.

"Of course. Does you credit," said the driver.

The twins thought this over.

The bright station lights shone on their faces, which stood out very white in the black setting of their best mourning. Before getting to Los Angeles they had dressed themselves carefully in what Anna-Felicitas called their favourable-impression-on-arrival garments,—those garments Aunt Alice had bought for them on their mother's death, expressing the wave of sympathy in which she found herself momentarily engulfed by going to a very good and expensive dressmaker; and in the black perfection of these clothes the twins looked like two well-got-up and very attractive young crows. These were the clothes they had put on on leaving the ship, and had been so obviously admired in, to the uneasiness of Mr. Twist, by the public; it was in these clothes that they had arrived within range of Mr. Sack's distracted but still appreciative vision, and in them that they later roused the suspicions and dislike of Mrs. Twist. It was in these clothes that they were now about to start what they hoped would be a lasting friendship with the Delloggs, and remembering they had them on they decided that perhaps it wasn't only sun and oranges making the taxi-driver so attentive, but also the effect on him of their grown-up and awe-inspiring hats.

This was confirmed by what he said next. "I guess you're old friends, then," he remarked, after a period of reflective jaw-rolling. "Must be, to come all that way."

"Well—not exactly," said Anna-Rose, divided between her respect for truth and her gratification at being thought old enough to be somebody's old friend.

"You see," explained Anna-Felicitas, who was never divided in her respect for truth, "we're not particularly old anything."

The driver in his turn thought this over, and finding he had no observations he wished to make on it he let it pass, and said, "You'll miss Mr. Dellogg."

"Oh?" said Anna-Rose, pricking up her ears, "Shall we?"

"We don't mind missing Mr. Dellogg," said Anna-Felicitas. "It's Mrs. Dellogg we wouldn't like to miss."

The driver looked puzzled.

"Yes—that would be too awful," said Anna-Rose, who didn't want a repetition of the Sack dilemma. "You did say," she asked anxiously, "didn't you, that we were going to miss Mr. Dellogg?"

The driver, looking first at one of them and then at the other, said, "Well, and who wouldn't?"

And this answer seemed so odd to the twins that they could only as they stared at him suppose it was some recondite form of American slang, provided with its own particular repartee which, being unacquainted with the language, they were not in a position to supply. Perhaps, they thought, it was of the same order of mysterious idioms as in England such sentences as I don't think, and Not half,—forms of speech whose exact meaning and proper use had never been mastered by them.

"There won't be another like Mr. Dellogg in these parts for many a year," said the driver, shaking his head. "Ah no. And that's so."

"Isn't he coming back?" asked Anna-Rose.

The driver's jaws ceased for a moment to roll. He stared at Anna-Rose with unblinking eyes. Then he turned his head away and spat along the station, and then, again fixing his eyes on Anna-Rose, he said, "Young gurl, you may be a spiritualist, and a table-turner, and a psychic-rummager, and a ghost-fancier, and anything else you please, and get what comfort you can out of your coming backs and the rest of the blessed truck, but I know better. And what I know, being a Christian, is that once a man's dead he's either in heaven or he's in hell, and whichever it is he's in, in it he stops."

Anna-Felicitas was the first to speak. "Are we to understand," she inquired, "that Mr. Dellogg—" She broke off.

"That Mr. Dellogg is—" Anna-Rose continued for her, but broke off too.

"That Mr. Dellogg isn't—" resumed Anna-Felicitas with determination, "well, that he isn't alive?"

"Alive?" repeated the driver. He let his hand drop heavily on the window-sill. "If that don't beat all," he said, staring at her. "What do you come his funeral for, then?"

"His funeral?"

"Yes, if you don't know that he ain't?"

"Ain't—isn't what?"

"Alive, of course. No, I mean dead. You're getting me all tangled up."

"But we haven't."

"But we didn't."

"We had a letter from him only last month."

"At least, an uncle we've got had."

"And he didn't say a word in it about being dead—I mean, there was no sign of his being going to be—I mean, he wasn't a bit ill or anything in his letter—"

"Now see here," interrupted the driver, sarcasm in his voice, "it ain't exactly usual is it—I put it to you squarely, and say it ain't *exactly* usual (there may be exceptions, but it ain't exactly *usual*) to come to a gentleman's funeral, and especially not all the way from New York, without some sort of an idea that he's dead. Some sort of a *general* idea, anyhow," he added still more sarcastically; for his admiration for the twins had given way to doubt and discomfort, and a suspicion was growing on him that with incredible and horrible levity, seeing what the moment was and what the occasion, they were filling up the time waiting for their baggage, among which were no doubt funeral wreaths, by making game of him.

"Gurls like you shouldn't behave that way," he went on, his voice aggrieved as he remembered how sympathetically he had got down from his seat when he saw their mourning clothes and tired white faces and helped them into his taxi,—only for genuine mourners, real sorry ones, going to pay their last respects to a gentleman like Mr. Dellogg, would he, a free American have done that. "Nicely dressed gurls, well-cared for gurls. Daughters of decent people. Here you come all this way, I guess sent by your parents to represent them properly, and properly fitted out in nice black clothes and all, and you start making fun. Pretending. Playing kind of hide-and-seek with me about the funeral. Messing me up in a lot of words. I don't like it. I'm a father myself, and I don't like it. I don't like to see daughters going on like this when their father ain't looking. It don't seem decent to me. But I suppose you Easterners—"

The twins, however, were not listening. They were looking at each other in dismay. How extraordinary, how terrible, the way Uncle Arthur's friends gave out. They seemed to melt away at one's mere approach. People who had been living with their husbands all their lives ran away just as the twins came on the scene; people who had been alive all their lives went and died, also at that very moment. It almost seemed as if directly anybody knew that they, the Twinklers, were coming to stay with them they became bent on escape. They could only look at each other in stricken astonishment at this latest blow of Fate. They heard no more of what the driver said. They could only sit and look at each other.

And then Mr. Twist came hurrying across from the baggage office, wiping his forehead, for the night was hot. Behind him came the porter, ruefully balancing the piled-up grips on his truck.

"I'm sorry to have been so—" began Mr. Twist, smiling cheerfully: but he stopped short in his sentence and left off smiling when he saw the expression in the four eyes fixed on him. "What has happened?" he asked quickly.

"Only what we might have expected," said Anna-Rose.

"Mr. Dellogg's dead," said Anna-Felicitas.

"You don't say," said Mr. Twist; and after a pause he said again, "You don't say."

Then he recovered himself. "I'm very sorry to hear it, of course," he said briskly, picking himself up, as it were, from this sudden and unexpected tumble, "but I don't see that it matters to you so long as Mrs. Dellogg isn't dead too."

"Yes, but—" began Anna-Rose.

"Mr. Dellogg isn't *very* dead, you see," said Anna-Felicitas.

Mr. Twist looked from them to the driver, but finding no elucidation there and only disapproval, looked back again.

"He isn't dead and settled *down*," said Anna-Rose.

"Not *that* sort of being dead," said Anna-Felicitas. "He's *just* dead."

"Just got to the stage when he has a funeral," said Anna-Rose.

"His funeral, it seems, is imminent," said Anna-Felicitas. "Did you not give us to understand," she asked, turning to the driver, "that it was imminent?"

"I don't know about imminent," said the driver, who wasn't going to waste valuable time with words like that, "but it's to-morrow."

"And you see what that means for us," said Anna-Felicitas, turning to Mr. Twist.

Mr. Twist did.

He again wiped his forehead, but not this time because the night was hot.

CHAPTER XX

Manifestly it is impossible to thrust oneself into a house where there is going to be a funeral next day, even if one has come all the way from New York and has nowhere else to go. Equally manifestly it is impossible to thrust oneself into it after the funeral till a decent interval has elapsed. But what the devil, Mr. Twist asked himself in language become regrettably natural to him since his sojourn at the front, is a decent interval?

This Mr. Twist asked himself late that night, pacing up and down the sea-shore in the warm and tranquil darkness in front of the Cosmopolitan Hotel, while the twins, utterly tired out by their journey and the emotions at the end of it, crept silently into bed.

How long does it take a widow to recover her composure? Recover, that is, the first beginnings of it? At what stage in her mourning is it legitimate to intrude on her with reminders of obligations incurred before she was a widow,—with, in fact, the Twinklers? Delicacy itself would shrink from doing it under a week thought Mr. Twist, or even under a fortnight, or even if you came to that, under a month; and meanwhile what was he to do with the Twinklers?

Mr. Twist, being of the artistic temperament for otherwise he wouldn't have been so sympathetic nor would he have minded, as he so passionately did mind, his Uncle Charles's teapot dribbling on to the tablecloth—was sometimes swept by brief but tempestuous revulsions of feeling, and though he loved the Twinklers he did at this moment describe them mentally and without knowing it in the very words of Uncle Arthur, as those accursed twins. It was quite unjust, he knew. They couldn't help the death of the man Dellogg. They were the victims, from first to last, of a cruel and pursuing fate; but it is natural to turn on victims, and Mr. Twist was for an instant, out of the very depth of his helpless sympathy, impatient with the Twinklers.

He walked up and down the sands frowning and pulling his mouth together, while the Pacific sighed sympathetically at his feet. Across the road the huge hotel standing in its gardens was pierced by a thousand lights. Very few people were about and no one at all was on the sands. There was an immense noise of what sounded like grasshoppers or crickets, and also at intervals distant choruses of frogs, but these sounds seemed altogether beneficent,—so warm, and southern, and far away from less happy places where in October cold winds perpetually torment the world. Even in the dark Mr. Twist knew he had got to somewhere that was beautiful. He could imagine nothing more agreeable than, having handed over the twins safely to the Delloggs, staying on a week or two in this place and seeing them every day,—perhaps even, as he had pictured to himself on the journey, being invited to stay with the Delloggs. Now all that was knocked on the head. He supposed the man Dellogg couldn't help being dead but he, Mr. Twist, equally couldn't help resenting it. It was so awkward; so exceedingly awkward. And it was so like what one of that creature Uncle Arthur's friends would do.

Mr. Twist, it will be seen, was frankly unreasonable, but then he was very much taken aback and annoyed. What was he to do with the Annas? He was obviously not a relation of theirs—and indeed no profiles could have been less alike—and he didn't suppose Acapulco was behind other parts of America in curiosity and gossip. If he stayed on at the Cosmopolitan with the twins till Mrs. Dellogg was approachable again, whenever that might be, every sort of question would be being asked in whispers about who they were and what was their relationship, and presently whenever they sat down anywhere the chairs all round them would empty. Mr. Twist had seen the kind of thing happening in hotels before to other people,—never to himself; never had he been in any situation till now that was not luminously regular. And quite soon after this with the chairs had begun to happen, the people who created these vacancies were told by the manager—firmly in America, politely in England, and sympathetically in France—that their rooms had been engaged a long time ago for the very next day, and no others were available.

The Cosmopolitan was clearly an hotel frequented by the virtuous rich. Mr. Twist felt that he and the Annas wouldn't, in their eyes, come under this heading, not, that is, when the other guests became aware of the entire absence of any relationship between him and the twins. Well, for a day or two nothing could happen; for a day or two, before his party had had time to sink into the hotel consciousness and the manager appeared to tell him the rooms were engaged, he could think things out and talk them over with his companions. Perhaps he might even see Mrs. Dellogg. The funeral, he had heard on inquiring of the hall porter was next day. It was to be a brilliant affair, said the porter. Mr. Dellogg had been a prominent inhabitant, free with his money, a supporter of anything there was to support. The porter talked of him as the taxi-driver had done, regretfully and respectfully; and Mr. Twist went to bed angrier than ever with a man who, being so valuable and so necessary, should have neglected at such a moment to go on living.

Mr. Twist didn't sleep very well that night. He lay in his rosy room, under a pink silk quilt, and most of the time stared out through the open French windows with their pink brocade curtains at the great starry night, thinking.

In that soft bed, so rosy and so silken as to have been worthy of the relaxations of, at least, a prima donna, he looked like some lean and alien bird nesting temporarily where he had no business to. He hadn't thought of buying silk pyjamas when the success of his teapot put him in the right position for doing so, because his soul was too simple for him to desire or think of anything less candid to wear in bed than flannel, and he still wore the blue flannel pyjamas of a careful bringing up. In that beautiful bed his pyjamas didn't seem appropriate. Also his head, so frugal of hair, didn't do justice to the lace and linen of a pillow prepared for the hairier head of, again at least, a prima donna. And finding he couldn't sleep, and wishing to see the stars he put on his spectacles, and then looked more out of place than ever. But as nobody was there to see him,—which, Mr. Twist sometimes thought when he caught sight of himself in his pyjamas at bed-time, is one of the comforts of being virtuously unmarried,—nobody minded.

His reflections were many and various, and they conflicted with and contradicted each other as the reflections of persons in a difficult position who have Mr. Twist's sort of temperament often do. Faced by a dribbling teapot, an object which touched none of the softer emotions, Mr. Twist soared undisturbed in the calm heights of a detached and concentrated intelligence, and quickly knew what to do with it; faced by the derelict Annas his heart and his tenderness got in the ways of any clear vision.

About three o'clock in the morning, when his mind was choked and strewn with much pulled-about and finally discarded plans, he suddenly had an idea. A real one. As far as he could see, a real good one. He would place the Annas in a school.

Why shouldn't they go to school? he asked himself, starting off answering any possible objections. A year at a first-rate school would give them and everybody else time to consider. They ought never to have left school. It was the very place for luxuriant and overflowing natures like theirs. No doubt Acapulco had such a thing as a finishing school for young ladies in it, and into it the Annas should go, and once in it there they should stay put, thought Mr. Twist in vigorous American, gathering up his mouth defiantly.

Down these lines of thought his relieved mind cantered easily. He would seek out a lawyer the next morning, regularize his position to the twins by turning himself into their guardian, and then get them at once into the best school there was. As their guardian he could then pay all their expenses, and faced by this legal fact they would, he hoped, be soon persuaded of the propriety of his paying whatever there was to pay.

Mr. Twist was so much pleased by his idea that he was able to go to sleep after that. Even three months' school—the period he gave Mrs. Dellogg for her acutest grief—would do. Tide them over. Give them room to turn round in. It was a great solution. He took off his spectacles, snuggled down into his rosy nest, and fell asleep with the instantaneousness of one whose mind is suddenly relieved.

But when he went down to breakfast he didn't feel quite so sure. The twins didn't look, somehow, as though they would want to go to school. They had been busy with their luggage, and had unpacked one of the trunks for the first time since leaving Aunt Alice, and in honour of the heat and sunshine and the heavenly smell of heliotrope that was in the warm air, had put on white summer frocks.

Impossible to imagine anything cooler, sweeter, prettier and more angelically good than those two Annas looked as they came out on to the great verandah of the hotel to join Mr. Twist at breakfast. They instantly sank into the hotel consciousness. Mr. Twist had thought this wouldn't happen for a day or two, but he now perceived his mistake. Not a head that wasn't turned to look at them, not a newspaper that wasn't lowered. They were immediate objects of interest and curiosity, entirely benevolent interest and curiosity because nobody yet knew anything about them, and the wives of the rich husbands—those halves of the virtuous-rich unions which provided the virtuousness—smiled as they passed, and murmured nice words to each other like cute and cunning.

Mr. Twist, being a good American, stood up and held the twins' chairs for them when they appeared. They loved this; it seemed so respectful, and made them feel so old and looked-up to. He had done it that night in New York at supper, and at all the meals in the train in spite of the train being so wobbly and each time they had loved it. "It makes one have such self-respect," they agreed, commenting on this agreeable practice in private.

They sat down in the chairs with the gracious face of the properly treated, and inquired, with an amiability and a solicitous politeness on a par with their treatment how Mr. Twist had slept. They themselves had obviously slept well, for their faces were cherubic in their bland placidity, and already after one night wore what Mr. Twist later came to recognize as the Californian look, a look of complete unworriedness.

Yet they ought to have been worried. Mr. Twist had been terribly worried up to the moment in the night when he got his great idea, and he was worried again, now that he saw the twins, by doubts. They didn't look as though they would easily be put to school. His idea still seemed to him magnificent, a great solution, but would the Annas be able to see it? They might turn out impervious to it; not rejecting it, but simply non-absorbent. As they slowly and contentedly ate their grape-fruit, gazing out between the spoonfuls at the sea shining across the road through palm trees, and looking unruffled itself, he felt it was going to be rather like suggesting to two cherubs to leave their serene occupation of adoring eternal beauty and learn lessons instead. Still, it was the one way out, as far as Mr. Twist could see, of the situation produced by the death of the man Dellogg. "When you've done breakfast," he said, pulling himself together on their reaching the waffle stage, "we must have a talk."

"When we've done breakfast," said Anna-Rose, "we must have a walk."

"Down there," said Anna-Felicitas, pointing with her spoon. "On the sands. Round the curve to where the pink hills begin."

"Mr. Dellogg's death," said Mr. Twist, deciding it was necessary at once to wake them up out of the kind of happy somnolence they seemed to be falling into, "has of course completely changed—"

"How unfortunate," interrupted Anna-Rose, her eyes on the palms and the sea and the exquisite distant mountains along the back of the bay, "to have to be dead on a day like this."

"It's not only his missing the fine weather that makes it unfortunate," said Mr. Twist.

"You mean," said Anna-Rose, "it's our missing him."

"Precisely," said Mr. Twist.

"Well, we know that," said Anna-Felicitas placidly.

"We knew it last night, and it worried us," said Anna-Rose. "Then we went to sleep and it didn't worry us. And this morning it still doesn't."

"No," said Mr. Twist dryly. "You don't look particularly worried, I must say."

"No," said Anna-Felicitas, "we're not. People who find they've got to heaven aren't usually worried, are they."

"And having got to heaven," said Anna-Rose, "we've thought of a plan to enable us to stay in it."

"Oh have you," said Mr. Twist, pricking up his ears.

"The plan seemed to think of us rather than we of it," explained Anna-Felicitas. "It came and inserted itself, as it were, into our minds while we were dressing."

"Well, I've thought of a plan too," said Mr. Twist firmly, feeling sure that the twins' plan would be the sort that ought to be instantly nipped in the bud.

He was therefore greatly astonished when Anna-Rose said, "Have you? Is it about schools?"

He stared at her in silence. "Yes," he then said slowly, for he was very much surprised. "It is."

"So is ours," said Anna-Rose.

"Indeed," said Mr. Twist.

"Yes," said Anna-Felicitas. "We don't think much of it, but it will tide us over."

"Exactly," said Mr. Twist, still more astonished at this perfect harmony of ideas.

"Tide us over till Mrs. Dellogg is—-" began Anna-Rose in her clear little voice that carried like a flute to all the tables round them.

Mr. Twist got up quickly. "If you've finished let us go out of doors," he said; for he perceived that silence had fallen on the other tables, and attentiveness to what Anna-Rose was going to say next.

"Yes. On the sands," said the twins, getting up too.

On the sands, however, Mr. Twist soon discovered that the harmony of ideas was not as complete as he had supposed; indeed, something very like heated argument began almost as soon as they were seated on some rocks round the corner of the shore to the west of the hotel and they became aware, through conversation, of the vital difference in the two plans.

The Twinkler plan, which they expounded at much length and with a profusion of optimistic detail, was to search for and find a school in the neighbourhood for the daughters of gentlemen, and go to it for three months, or six months, or whatever time Mrs. Dellogg wanted to recover in.

Up to this point the harmony was complete, and Mr. Twist could only nod approval. Beyond it all was confusion, for it appeared that the twins didn't dream of entering a school in any capacity except as teachers. Professors, they said; professors of languages and literatures. They could speak German, as they pointed out, very much better than most people, and had, as Mr. Twist had sometimes himself remarked, an extensive vocabulary in English. They would give lessons in English and German literature. They would be able to teach quite a lot about Heine, for instance, the whole of whose poetry they knew by heart and whose sad life in Paris—

"It's no good running on like that," interrupted Mr. Twist. "You're not old enough."

Not old enough? The Twinklers, from their separate rocks, looked at each other in surprised indignation.

"Not old enough?" repeated Anna-Rose. "We're grown up. And I don't see how one can be more than grown up. One either is or isn't grown up. And there can be no doubt as to which we are."

And this the very man who so respectfully had been holding their chairs for them only a few minutes before! As if people did things like that for children.

"You're not old enough I say," said Mr. Twist again, bringing his hand down with a slap on the rock to emphasize his words. "Nobody would take you. Why, you've got perambulator faces, the pair of you—"

"Perambulator—?"

"And what school is going to want two teachers both teaching the same thing, anyway?"

And he then quickly got out his plan, and the conversation became so heated that for a time it was molten.

The Twinklers were shocked by his plan. More; they were outraged. Go to school? To a place they had never been to even in their suitable years? They, two independent grown-ups with £200 in the bank and nobody with any right to stop their doing anything they wanted to? Go to school now, like a couple of little suck-a-thumbs?

It was Anna-Rose, very flushed and bright of eye, who flung this expression at Mr. Twist from her rock. He might think they had perambulator faces if he liked—they didn't care, but they did desire him to bear in mind that if it hadn't been for the war they would be now taking their proper place in society, that they had already done a course of nursing in a hospital, an activity not open to any but adults, and that Uncle Arthur had certainly not given them all that money to fritter away on paying for belated schooling.

"We would be anachronisms," said Anna-Felicitas, winding up the discussion with a firmness so unusual in her that it showed how completely she had been stirred.

"Are you aware that we are marriageable?" inquired Anna-Rose icily.

"And don't you think it's bad enough for us to be aliens and undesirables," asked Anna-Felicitas, "without getting chronologically confused as well?"

Mr. Twist was quiet for a bit. He couldn't compete with the Twinklers when it came to sheer language. He sat hunched on his rock, his face supported by his two fists, staring out to sea while the twins watched him indignantly. School indeed! Then presently he pushed his hat back and began slowly to rub his ear.

"Well, I'm blest if I know what to do with you, then," he said, continuing to rub his ear and stare out to sea.

The twins opened their mouths simultaneously at this to protest against any necessity for such knowledge on his part, but he interrupted them. "If you don't mind," he said, "I'd like to resume this discussion when you're both a little more composed."

"We're perfectly composed," said Anna-Felicitas.

"Less ruffled, then."

"We're quite unruffled," said Anna-Rose.

"Well, you don't look it, and you don't sound like it. But as this is important I'd be glad to resume the discussion, say, to-morrow. I suggest we spend to-day exploring the neighbourhood and steadying our minds—"

"Our minds are perfectly steady, thank you."

"—and to-morrow we'll have another go at this question. I haven't told you all my plan yet"—Mr. Twist hadn't had time to inform them of his wish to become their guardian, owing to the swiftness with which he had been engulfed in their indignation,—"but whether you approve of it or not, what is quite certain is that we can't stay on at the hotel much longer."

"Because it's so dear?"

"Oh, it isn't so much *that*,—the proprietor is a friend of mine, or anyhow he very well might be—"

"It looks very dear," said Anna-Rose, visions of their splendid bedroom and bathroom rising before her. They too had slept in silken beds, and the taps in their bathroom they had judged to be pure gold.

"And it's because we can't afford to be in a dear place spending money," said Anna-Felicitas, "that it's so important we should find a salaried position in a school without loss of time."

"And it's because we can't afford reckless squandering that we ought to start looking for such a situation at once" said Anna-Rose.

"Not to-day," said Mr. Twist firmly, for he wouldn't give up the hope of getting them, once they were used to it, to come round to his plan. "To-day, this one day, we'll give ourselves up to enjoyment. It'll do us all good. Besides, we don't often get to a place like this, do we. And it has taken some getting to, hasn't it."

He rose from his rock and offered his hand to help them off theirs.

"To-day enjoyment," he said, "to-morrow business. I'm crazy," he added artfully, "to see what the country is like away up in those hills."

And so it was that about five o'clock that afternoon, having spent the whole day exploring the charming environs of Acapulco,—having been seen at different periods going over the Old Mission in tow of a monk who wouldn't look at them but kept his eyes carefully fixed on the ground, sitting on high stools eating strange and enchanting ices at the shop in the town that has the best ices, bathing deliciously in the warm sea at the foot of a cliff along the top of which a great hedge of rose-coloured geraniums flared against the sky, lunching under a grove of ilexes on the contents of a basket produced by Mr. Twist from somewhere in the car he had hired, wandering afterwards up through eucalyptus woods across the fields towards the foot of the mountains,—they came about five o'clock, thirsty and thinking of tea, to a delightful group of flowery cottages clustering round a restaurant and forming collectively, as Mr. Twist explained, one of the many American forms of hotel. "To which," he said, "people not living in the cottages can come and have meals at the restaurant, so we'll go right in and have tea."

And it was just because they couldn't get tea—any other meal, the proprietress said, but no teas were served, owing to the Domestic Help Eight Hours Bill which obliged her to do without domestics during the afternoon hours—that Anna-Felicitas came by her great idea.

CHAPTER XXI

But she didn't come by it at once.

They got into the car first, which was waiting for them in the scented road at the bottom of the field they had walked across, and they got into it in silence and were driven back to their hotel for tea, and her brain was still unvisited by inspiration.

They were all tired and thirsty, and were disappointed at being thwarted in their desire to sit at a little green table under whispering trees and rest, and drink tea, and had no sort of wish to have it at the Cosmopolitan. But both Mr. Twist, who had been corrupted by Europe, and the twins, who had the habits of their mother, couldn't imagine doing without it in the afternoon, and they would have it in the hotel sooner than not have it at all. It was brought to them after a long time of waiting. Nobody else was having any at that hour, and the waiter, when at last one was found, had difficulty apparently in believing that they were serious. When at last he did bring it, it was toast and marmalade and table-napkins, for all the world as though it had been breakfast.

Then it was that, contemplating this with discomfort and distaste, as well as the place they were sitting in and its rocking-chairs and marble and rugs, Anna-Felicitas was suddenly smitten by her idea.

It fell upon her like a blow. It struck her fairly, as it were, between the eyes. She wasn't used to ideas, and she stopped dead in the middle of a piece of toast and looked at the others. They stopped too in their eating and locked at her.

"What's the matter?" asked Anna-Rose. "Has another button come off?"

At this Mr. Twist considered it wisest to turn his head away, for experience had taught him that Anna-Felicitas easily came undone.

"I've thought of something," said Anna-Felicitas.

Mr. Twist turned his head back again. "You don't say," he said, mildly sarcastic.

"*Ich gratuliere*," said Anna-Rose, also mildly sarcastic.

"I've got an idea," said Anna-Felicitas. "But it's so luminous," she said, looking from one to the other in a kind of surprise. "Of course. That's what we'll do. Ridiculous to waste time bothering about schools."

There was a new expression on her face that silenced the comments rising to Anna-Rose's and Mr. Twist's tongues, both of whom had tired feet and were therefore disposed to sarcasm.

Anna-Felicitas looked at them, and they looked at her, and her face continued to become visibly more and more illuminated, just as if a curtain were being pulled up. Animation and interest shone in her usually dreamy eyes. Her drooping body sat up quite straight. She reminded Anna-Rose, who had a biblically well-furnished mind, of Moses when he came down from receiving the Law on the mountain.

"Well, tell us," said Anna-Rose. "But not," she added, thinking of Moses, "if it's only more commandments."

Anna-Felicitas dropped the piece of toast she was still holding in her fingers, and pushed back her cup. "Come out on to the rocks," she said getting up—"where we sat this morning." And she marched out, followed by the other two with the odd submissiveness people show towards any one who is thoroughly determined.

It was dark and dinner-time before they got back to the hotel. Throughout the sunset Anna-Felicitas sat on her rock, the same rock she had sat on so unsatisfactorily eight hours earlier, and expounded her idea. She couldn't talk fast enough. She, so slow and listless, for once was shaken into burning activity. She threw off her hat directly she got on to the sands, climbed up the rock as if it were a pulpit, and with her hands clasped round her knees poured out her plan, the long shafts of the setting sun bathing her in bright flames and making her more like Moses than ever,—if, that is, one could imagine Moses as beautiful as Anna-F., thought Anna-Rose, and as felicitously without his nose and beard.

It was wonderful how complete Anna-Felicitas's inspiration was. It reminded Mr. Twist of his own about the teapot. It was, of course, a far more complicated matter than that little device of his, and would have to be thought out very carefully and approached very judiciously, but the wealth of detail she was already ready with immensely impressed him. She even had a name for the thing; and it was when he heard this name, when it flashed into her talk with the unpremeditatedness of an inspiration, that Mr. Twist became definitely enthusiastic.

He had an American eye for advertisement. Respect for it was in his blood. He instantly saw the possibilities contained in the name. He saw what could be done with it, properly worked. He saw it on hoarding-on signposts, in a thousand contrivances for catching the public attention and sticking there.

The idea, of course, was fantastic, unconventional, definitely outside what his mother and that man Uncle Arthur would consider proper, but it was outside the standards of such people that life and fruitfulness and interest and joy began. He had escaped from the death-like grip of his mother, and Uncle Arthur had himself forcibly expulsed the Annas from his, and now that they were all so far away, instead of still timorously trying to go on living up to those distant sterile ideas why shouldn't they boldly go out into the light and colour that was waiting everywhere for the free of spirit?

Mr. Twist had often observed how perplexingly much there is to be said for the opposite sides of a question. He was now, but with no perplexity, for Anna-Felicitas had roused his enthusiasm, himself taking the very opposite view as to the proper thing for the twins to do from the one he had taken in the night and on the rocks that morning. School? Nonsense. Absurd to bury these bright shoots of everlastingness—this is what they looked like to him, afire with enthusiasm and the setting sun—in such a place of ink. If the plan, owing to the extreme youth of the Annas, were unconventional, conventionality could be secured by giving a big enough salary to a middle-aged lady to come and preside. He himself would hover beneficently in the background over the undertaking.

Anna-Felicitas's idea was to use Uncle Arthur's £200 in renting one of the little wooden cottages that seemed to be plentiful, preferably one about five miles out in the country, make it look inside like an English cottage, all pewter and chintz and valances, make it look outside like the more innocent type of German wayside inn, with green tables and spreading trees, get a cook who would concentrate on cakes, real lovely ones, various, poetic, wonderful cakes, and start an inn for tea alone that should become the fashion. It ought to be so arranged that it became the fashion. She and Anna-Rose would do the waiting. The prices would be very high, indeed exorbitant—this Mr. Twist regarded as another inspiration,—so that it should be a distinction, give people a *cachet*, to have had tea at their cottage; and in a prominent position in the road in front of it, where every motor-car would be bound to see it, there would be a real wayside inn signboard, such as inns in England always have, with its name on it.

"If people here were really neutral you might have the Imperial arms of Germany and England emblazoned on it," interrupted Mr. Twist, "just to show your own extreme and peculiar neutrality."

"We might call it The Christopher and Columbus," interrupted Anna-Rose, who had been sitting open-mouthed hanging on Anna-Felicitas's words.

"Or you might call it The Cup and Saucer," said Mr. Twist, "and have a big cup brimming with tea and cream painted on it—"

"No," said Anna-Felicitas. "It is The Open Arms. That is its name."

And Mr. Twist, inclined to smile and criticise up to this, bowed his head in instantaneous recognition and acceptance.

He became definitely enthusiastic. Of course he would see to it that not a shadow of ambiguousness was allowed to rest on such a name. The whole thing as he saw it, his mind working rapidly while Anna-Felicitas still talked, would be a happy joke, a joyous, gay little assault on the purses of millionaires, in whom the district abounded judging from the beautiful houses and gardens he had passed that day,—but a joke and a gay assault that would at the same time employ and support the Annas; solve them, in fact, saw Mr. Twist, who all day long had been regarding them much as one does a difficult mathematical problem.

It was Mr. Twist who added the final inspiration to Anna-Felicitas's many, when at last she paused for want of breath. The inn, he said, should be run as a war philanthropy. All that was over after the expenses were paid and a proper percentage reserved by the Annas as interest on their invested capital—they listened with eager respect to these business-like expressions— would be handed over to the American Red Cross. "That," explained Mr. Twist, "would seal the inn as both respectable and fashionable, which is exactly what we would want to make it."

And he then announced, and they accepted without argument or questioning in the general excitement, that he would have himself appointed their legal guardian.

They didn't go back to the Cosmopolitan till dinnertime, there was so much to say, and after dinner, a meal at which Mr. Twist had to suppress them a good deal because The Open Arms kept on bursting through into their talk and, as at breakfast, the people at the tables round them were obviously trying to hear, they went out once again on to the sea-front and walked up and down till late continuing the discussion, mostly simultaneously as regards the twins, while Mr. Twist chimed in with practical suggestions whenever they stopped to take breath.

He had to drive them indoors to bed at last, for the lights were going out one by one in the Cosmopolitan bedroom windows, where the virtuous rich, exhausted by their day of virtue, were subsiding, prostrate with boredom and respectability, into their various legitimate lairs, and he stayed alone out by the sea rapidly sketching out his activities for the next day.

There was the guardianship to be arranged, the cottage to be found, and the middle-aged lady to be advertised for. She, indeed, must be secured at once; got to come at once to the Cosmopolitan and preside over the twins until they all proceeded in due season to The Open Arms. She must be a motherly middle-aged lady, decided Mr. Twist, affectionate, skilled in managing a cook, business-like, intellectual, and obedient. Her feminine tact would enable her to appear to preside while she was in reality obeying. She must understand that she was there for the Annas, and that the Annas were not there for her. She must approach the situation in the spirit of the enlightened king of a democratic country, who receives its honours, accepts its respect, but does not lose sight of the fact that he is merely the Chief Servant of the people. Mr. Twist didn't want a female Uncle Arthur let loose upon those blessed little girls; besides, they would have the dangerous weapon in their hands of being able to give her notice, and it would considerably dim the reputation of The Open Arms if there were a too frequent departure from it of middle-aged ladies.

Mr. Twist felt himself very responsible and full of anxieties as he paced up and down alone, but he was really enjoying himself. That youthful side of him, so usual in the artistic temperament, which leaped about at the least pleasant provocation like a happy lamb when the sunshine tickles it, was feeling that this was great fun; and the business side of him was feeling that it was not only great fun but probably an extraordinarily productive piece of money-making.

The ignorant Annas—bless their little hearts, he thought, he who only the night before on that very spot had been calling them accursed—believed that their £200 was easily going to do everything. This was lucky, for otherwise there would have been some thorny paths of argument and convincing to be got through before they would have allowed him to help finance the undertaking; probably they never would have, in their scrupulous independence. Mr. Twist reflected with satisfaction on the usefulness of his teapot. At last he was going to be able to do something, thanks to it, that gave him real gladness. His ambulance to France—that was duty. His lavishness to his mother—that again was duty. But here was delight, here at last was what his lonely heart had always longed for,—a chance to help and make happy, and be with and watch being made happy, dear women-things, dear soft sweet kind women-things, dear sister-things, dear children-things....

It has been said somewhere before that Mr. Twist was meant by Nature to be a mother; but Nature, when she was half-way through him, forgot and turned him into a man.

CHAPTER XXII

The very next morning they set out house-hunting, and two days later they had found what they wanted. Not exactly what they wanted of course, for the reason, as Anna-Felicitas explained that nothing ever is *exactly*, but full of possibilities to the eye of imagination, and there were six of this sort of eye gazing at the little house.

It stood at right angles to a road much used by motorists because of its beauty, and hidden from it by trees on the top of a slope of green fields scattered over with live oaks that gently descended down towards the sea. Its back windows, and those parts of it that a house is ashamed of, were close up to a thick grove of eucalyptus which continued to the foot of the mountains. It had an overrun little garden in front, separated from the fields by a riotous hedge of sweetbriar. It had a few orange, and lemon, and peach trees on its west side, the survivors of what had once been intended for an orchard, and a line of pepper trees on the other, between it and the road. Neglected roses and a huge wistaria clambered over its dilapidated face. Somebody had once planted syringas, and snowballs, and lilacs along the inside of the line of pepper trees, and they had grown extravagantly and were an impenetrable screen, even without the sweeping pepper trees from the road.

It hadn't been lived in for years, and it was well on in decay, being made of wood, but the situation was perfect for The Open Arms. Every motorist coming up that road would see the signboard outside the pepper trees, and would certainly want to stop at the neat little gate, and pass through the flowery tunnel that would be cut through the syringas, and see what was inside. Other houses were offered of a far higher class, for this one had never been lived in by gentry, said the house-agent endeavouring to put them off a thing so broken down. A farmer had had it years back, he told them, and instead of confining himself to drinking the milk from his own cows, which was the only appropriate drink for a farmer the agent maintained—he was the president of the local Anti-Vice-In-All-Its-Forms League—he put his money as he earned it into gin, and the gin into himself, and so after a bit was done for.

The other houses the agent pressed on them were superior in every way except situation; but situation being the first consideration, Mr. Twist agreed with the twins, who had fallen in love with the neglected little house whose shabbiness was being so industriously hidden by roses, that this was the place, and a week later it and its garden had been bought—Mr. Twist didn't tell the twins he had bought it, in order to avoid argument, but it was manifestly the simple thing to do—and over and round and through it swarmed workmen all day long, like so many diligent and determined ants. Also, before the week was out, the middle-aged lady had been found and engaged, and a cook of gifts in the matter of cakes. This is the way you do things in America. You decide what it is that you really want, and you start right away and get it. "And everything so cheap too!" exclaimed the twins gleefully, whose £200 was behaving, it appeared, very like the widow's cruse.

This belief, however, received a blow when they went without Mr. Twist, who was too busy now for any extra expeditions, to choose and buy chintzes, and it was finally shattered when the various middle-aged ladies who responded to Mr. Twist's cry for help in the advertising columns of the Acapulco and Los Angeles press one and all demanded as salary more than the whole Twinkler capital.

The twins had a bad moment of chill fear and misgiving, and then once more were saved by an inspiration,—this time Anna-Rose's.

"I know," she exclaimed, her face clearing. "We'll make it Co-operative."

Mr. Twist, whose brow too had been puckered in the effort to think out a way of persuading the twins to let him help them openly with his money, for in spite of his going to be their guardian they remained difficult on this point, jumped at the idea. He couldn't, of course, tell what in Anna-Rose's mind the word co-operative stood for, but felt confident that whatever it stood for he could manipulate it into covering his difficulties.

"What is co-operative?" asked Anna-Felicitas, with a new respect for a sister who could suddenly produce a business word like that and seem to know all about it. She had heard the word herself, but it sat very loosely in her head, at no point touching anything else.

"Haven't you heard of Co-operative Stores?" inquired Anna-Rose.

. "Yes but—"

"Well, then."

"Yes, but what would a co-operative inn be?" persisted Anna-Felicitas.

"One run on co-operative lines, of course," said Anna-Rose grandly. "Everybody pays for everything, so that nobody particular pays for anything."

"Oh," said Anna-Felicitas.

"I mean," said Anna-Rose, who felt herself that this might be clearer, "it's when you pay the servants and the rent and the cakes and things out of what you get."

"Oh," said Anna-Felicitas. "And will they wait quite quietly till we've got it?"

"Of course, if we're all co-operative."

"I see," said Anna-Felicitas, who saw as little as before, but knew of old that Anna-Rose grew irascible when pressed.

"See here now," said Mr. Twist weightily, "if that isn't an idea. Only you've got hold of the wrong word. The word you want is profit-sharing. And as this undertaking is going to be a big success there will be big profits, and any amount of cakes and salaries will be paid for as glibly and easily as you can say your ABC."

And he explained that till they were fairly started he was going to stay in California, and that he intended during this time to be book-keeper, secretary, and treasurer to The Open Arms, besides Advertiser-in-Chief, which was, he said, the most important post of all; and if they would be so good as to leave this side of it unquestioningly to him, who had had a business training, he would undertake that the Red Cross, American or British, whichever they decided to support, should profit handsomely.

Thus did Mr. Twist artfully obtain a free hand as financial backer of The Open Arms. The profit-sharing system seemed to the twins admirable. It cleared away every scruple and every difficulty, they now bought chintzes and pewter pots in the faith of it without a qualm, and even ceased to blench at the salary of the lady engaged to be their background,—indeed her very expensiveness pleased them, for it gave them confidence that she must at such a price be the right one, because nobody, they agreed, who knew herself not to be the right one would have the face to demand so much.

This lady, the widow of Bruce D. Bilton of Chicago of whom of course, she said, the Miss Twinklers had heard—the Miss Twinklers blushed and felt ashamed of themselves because they hadn't, and indistinctly murmured something about having heard of Cornelius K. Vanderbilt, though, and wouldn't he do—had a great deal of very beautiful snow-white hair, while at the same time she was only middle-aged. She firmly announced, when she perceived Mr. Twist's spectacles dwelling on her hair, that she wasn't yet forty, and her one fear was that she mightn't be middle-aged enough. The advertisement had particularly mentioned middle-aged; and though she was aware that her brains and fingers and feet couldn't possibly be described as coming under that heading, she said her hair, on the other hand, might well be regarded as having overshot the mark. But its turning white had nothing to do with age. It had done that when Mr. Bilton passed over. No hair could have stood such grief as hers when Mr. Bilton took that final step. She had been considering the question of age, she informed Mr. Twist, from every aspect before coming to the interview, for she didn't want to make a mistake herself nor allow the Miss Twinklers to make a mistake; and she had arrived at the conclusion that what with her hair being too old and the rest of her being too young, taken altogether she struck an absolute average and perfectly fulfilled the condition required; and as she wished to live in the country, town life disturbing her psychically too much, she was willing to give up her home and her circle—it was a real sacrifice—and accept the position offered by the Miss Twinklers. She was, she said, very quiet, and yet at the same time she was very active. She liked to fly round among duties, and she liked to retire into her own mentality and think. She was all for equilibrium, for the right balancing of body and mind in a proper alternation of suitable action. Thus she attained poise,—she was one of the most poised women her friends knew, they told her. Also she had a warm heart, and liked both philanthropy and orphans. Especially if they were war ones.

Mrs. Bilton talked so quickly and so profusely that it took quite a long time to engage her. There never seemed to be a pause in which one could do it. It was in Los Angeles, in an hotel to which Mr. Twist had motored the twins, starting at daybreak that morning in order to see this lady, that the personal interview took place, and by lunch-time they had been personally interviewing her for three hours without stopping. It seemed years. The twins longed to engage her, if only to keep her quiet; but Mrs. Bilton's spirited description of life as she saw it and of the way it affected something she called her psyche, was without punctuation and without even the tiny gap of a comma in it through which one might have dexterously slipped a definite offer. She had to be interrupted at last, in spite of the discomfort this gave to the Twinkler and Twist politeness, because a cook was coming to be interviewed directly after lunch, and they were dying for some food.

The moment Mr. Twist saw Mrs. Bilton's beautiful white hair he knew she was the one. That hair was what The Open Arms wanted and must have; that hair, with a well-made black dress to go with it, would be a shield through which no breath of misunderstanding as to the singleness of purpose with which the inn was run would ever penetrate. He would have settled it with her in five minutes if she could have been got to listen, but Mrs. Bilton couldn't be got to listen; and when it became clear that no amount of patient waiting would bring him any nearer the end of what she had to say Mr. Twist was forced to take off his coat, as it were, and plunge abruptly into the very middle of her flow of words and convey to her as quickly as possible, as one swimming for his life against the stream, that she was engaged. "Engaged, Mrs. Bilton,"—he called out, raising his voice above the sound of Mrs. Bilton's rushing words, "engaged." She would be expected at the Cosmopolitan, swiftly continued Mr. Twist, who was as particularly anxious to have her at the Cosmopolitan as the twins were particularly anxious not to,—for for the life of them they couldn't see why Mrs. Bilton should be stirred up before they started inhabiting the cottage,—within three days—

"Mr. Twist, it can't be done," broke in Mrs. Bilton a fresh and mountainous wave of speech gathering above Mr. Twist's head. "It absolutely—"

"Within a week, then," he called out quickly, holding up the breaking of the wave for an instant while he hastened to and opened the door. "And goodmorning Mrs. Bilton—my apologies, my sincere apologies, but we have to hurry away—"

The cook was engaged that afternoon. Mr. Twist appeared to have mixed up the answers to his advertisement, for when, after paying the luncheon-bill, he went to join the twins in the sitting-room, he found them waiting for him in the passage outside the door looking excited.

"The cook's come," whispered Anna-Rose, jerking her head towards the shut door. "She's a man."

"She's a Chinaman," whispered Anna-Felicitas.

Mr. Twist was surprised. He thought he had an appointment with a woman,—a coloured lady from South Carolina who was a specialist in pastries and had immaculate references, but the Chinaman assured him that he hadn't, and that his appointment was with him alone, with him, Li Koo. In proof of it, he said, spreading out his hands, here he was. "We make cakies—li'l cakies—many, lovely li'l cakies," said Li Koo, observing doubt on the gentleman's face; and from somewhere on his person he whipped out a paper bag of them as a conjurer whips a rabbit out of a hat, and offered them to the twins.

They ate. He was engaged. It took five minutes.

After he had gone, and punctually to the minute of her appointment, an over-flowing Negress appeared and announced that she was the coloured lady from South Carolina to whom the gentleman had written.

Mr. Twist uncomfortably felt that Li Koo had somehow been clever. Impossible, however, to go back on him, having eaten his cakes. Besides, they were perfect cakes, blown together apparently out of flowers and honey and cream,—cakes which, combined with Mrs. Bilton's hair, would make the fortune of The Open Arms.

The coloured lady, therefore, was sent away, disappointed in spite of the *douceur* and fair words Mr. Twist gave her; and she was so much disappointed that they could hear her being it out loud all the way along the passage and down the stairs, and the nature of her expression of her disappointment was such that Mr. Twist, as he tried by animated conversation to prevent it reaching the twins' ears, could only be thankful after all that Li Koo had been so clever. It did, however, reach the twins' ears, but they didn't turn a hair because of Uncle Arthur. They merely expressed surprise at its redness, seeing that it came out of somebody so black.

Directly after this trip to Los Angeles advertisements began to creep over the countryside. They crept along the roads where motorists were frequent and peeped at passing cars round corners and over hedges. They were taciturn advertisements, and just said three words in big, straight, plain white letters on a sea-blue ground:

THE OPEN ARMS

People passing in their cars saw them, and vaguely thought it must be the name of a book. They had better get it. Other people would have got it. It couldn't be a medicine nor anything to eat, and was probably a religious novel. Novels about feet or arms were usually religious. A few considered it sounded a little improper, and as though the book, far from being religious, would not be altogether nice; but only very proper people who distrusted everything, even arms took this view.

After a week the same advertisements appeared with three lines added:

THE OPEN ARMS
YES
BUT
WHY? WHERE? WHAT?

and then ten days after that came fresh ones:

THE OPEN ARMS
WILL OPEN
WIDE

On November 20th at Four P.M.

N.B. WATCH THE SIGNPOSTS.

And while the countryside—an idle countryside, engaged almost wholly in holiday-making and glad of any new distraction—began to be interested and asked questions, Mr. Twist was working day and night at getting the thing ready.

All day long he was in Acapulco or out at the cottage, urging, hurrying, criticizing, encouraging, praising and admonishing. His heart and soul and brain was in this, his business instincts and his soft domestic side. His brain, after working at top speed during the day with the architect, the painter and decorator, the furnisher, the garden expert, the plumbing expert, the electric-light expert, the lawyer, the estate agent, and numberless other persons, during the night meditated and evolved advertisements. There was to be a continual stream week by week after the inn was opened of ingenious advertisements. Altogether Mr. Twist had his hands full.

The inn was to look artless and simple and small, while actually being the last word in roomy and sophisticated comfort. It was to be as like an old English inn to look at as it could possibly be got to be going on his own and the twins' recollections and the sensationally coloured Elizabethan pictures in the architect's portfolio. It didn't disturb Mr. Twist's unprejudiced American mind that an English inn embowered in heliotrope and arum lilies and eucalyptus trees would be odd and unnatural, and it wouldn't disturb anybody else there either. Were not Swiss mountain chalets to be found in the fertile plains along the Pacific, complete with fir trees specially imported and uprooted in their maturity and brought down with tons of their own earth attached to their roots and replanted among carefully disposed, apparently Swiss rocks, so that what one day had been a place smiling with orange-groves was the next a bit of frowning northern landscape? And were there not Italian villas dotted about also? But these looked happier and more at home than the chalets. And there were buildings too, like small Gothic cathedrals, looking as uncomfortable and depressed as a woman who has come to a party in the wrong clothes. But no matter. Nobody minded. So that an English inn added to this company, with a little German beer-garden—only there wasn't to be any beer—wouldn't cause the least surprise or discomfort to anybody.

In the end, the sole resemblance the cottage had to an English inn was the signboard out in the road. With the best will in the world, and the liveliest financial encouragement from Mr. Twist, the architect couldn't in three weeks turn a wooden Californian cottage into an ancient red-brick Elizabethan pothouse. He got a thatched roof on to it by a miracle of hustle, but the wooden walls remained; he also found a real antique heavy oak front door studded with big rusty nailheads in a San Francisco curiosity shop, that would serve, he said, as a basis for any wished-for hark-back later on when there was more time to the old girl's epoch—thus did he refer to Great Eliza and her spacious days—and meanwhile it gave the building, he alleged, a considerable air; but as this door in that fine climate was hooked open all day long it didn't disturb the gay, the almost jocose appearance of the place when everything was finished.

Houses have their expressions, their distinctive faces, very much as people have, meditated Mr. Twist the morning of the opening, as he sat astride a green chair at the bottom of the little garden, where a hedge of sweetbriar beautifully separated the Twinkler domain from the rolling fields that lay between it and the Pacific, and stared at his handiwork; and the conclusion was forced upon him—reluctantly, for it was the last thing he had wanted The Open Arms to do—that the thing looked as if it were winking at him.

Positively, thought Mr. Twist, his hat on the back of his head, staring, that was what it seemed to be doing. How was that? He studied it profoundly, his head on one side. Was it that it was so very gay? He hadn't meant it to be gay like that. He had intended a restrained and disciplined simplicity, a Puritan unpretentiousness, with those sweet maidens, the Twinkler twins, flitting like modest doves in and out among its tea-tables; but one small thing had been added to another small thing at their suggestion, each small thing taken separately apparently not mattering at all and here it was almost—he hoped it was only his imagination—winking at him. It looked a familiar little house; jocular; very open indeed about the arms.

CHAPTER XXIII

Various things had happened, however, before this morning of the great day was reached, and Mr. Twist had had some harassing experiences.

One of the first things he had done after the visit to Los Angeles was to take steps in the matter of the guardianship. He had written to Mrs. Bilton that he was the Miss Twinklers' guardian, though it was not at that moment true. It was clear, he thought, that it should be made true as quickly as possible, and he therefore sought out a lawyer in Acapulco the morning after the interview. This was not the same lawyer who did his estate business for him; Mr. Twist thought it best to have a separate one for more personal affairs.

On hearing Mr. Twist's name announced, the lawyer greeted him as an old friend. He knew, of course, all about the teapot, for the Non-Trickler was as frequent in American families as the Bible and much more regularly used; but he also knew about the cottage at the foot of the hills, what it had cost—which was little—and what it would cost—which was enormous— before it was fit to live in. The only thing he didn't know was that it was to be used for anything except an ordinary *pied-à-terre*. He had heard, too, of the presence at the Cosmopolitan of the twins, and on this point, like the rest of Acapulco, was a little curious.

The social column of the Acapulco daily paper hadn't been able to give any accurate description of the relationship of the Twinklers to Mr. Twist. Its paragraph announcing his arrival had been obliged merely to say, while awaiting more detailed information, that Mr. Edward A. Twist, the well-known Breakfast Table Benefactor and gifted inventor of the famous Non-Trickler Teapot, had arrived from New York and was staying at the Cosmopolitan Hotel with *entourage*; and the day after this the lawyer, who got about a bit, as everybody else did in that encouraging climate, happening to look in at the Cosmopolitan to have a talk with a friend, had seen the *entourage*.

It was in the act of passing through the hall on its way upstairs, followed by a boy carrying a canary in a cage. Even without the boy and the canary it was a conspicuous object. The lawyer asked his friend who the cute little girls were, and was interested to hear he was beholding Mr. Edward A.

Twist's *entourage*. His friend told him that opinion in the hotel was divided about the precise nature of this *entourage* and its relationship to Mr. Twist, but it finally came to be generally supposed that the Miss Twinklers had been placed in his charge by parents living far away in order that he might safely see them put to one of the young ladies' finishing schools in that agreeable district. The house Mr. Twist was taking was not connected in the Cosmopolitan mind with the Twinklers. Houses were always being taken in that paradise by wealthy persons from unkinder climates. He would live in it three months in the year, thought the Cosmopolitan, bring his mother, and keep in this way an occasional eye on his charges. The hotel guests regarded the Twinklers at this stage with nothing but benevolence and goodwill, for they had up to then only been seen and not heard; and as one of their leading characteristics was a desire to explain, especially if anybody looked a little surprised, which everybody usually did quite early in conversation with them, this was at that moment, the delicate moment before Mrs. Bilton's arrival, fortunate.

The lawyer, then, who appreciated the young and pretty as much as other honest men, began the interview with Mr. Twist by warmly congratulating him, when he heard what he had come for, on his taste in wards.

Mr. Twist received this a little coldly, and said it was not a matter of taste but of necessity. The Miss Twinklers were orphans, and he had been asked—he cleared his throat—asked by their relatives, by, in fact, their uncle in England, to take over their guardianship and see that they came to no harm.

The lawyer nodded intelligently, and said that if a man had wards at all they might as well be cute wards.

Mr. Twist didn't like this either, and said briefly that he had had no choice.

The lawyer said, "Quite so. Quite so," and continued to look at him intelligently.

Mr. Twist then explained that he had come to him rather than, as might have been more natural, to the solicitor who had arranged the purchase of the cottage because this was a private and personal matter—

"Quite so. Quite so," interrupted the lawyer, with really almost too much intelligence.

Mr. Twist felt the excess of it, and tried to look dignified, but the lawyer was bent on being friendly and frank. Friendliness was natural to him when visited for the first time by a new client, and that there should be frankness between lawyers and clients he considered essential. If, he held, the client wouldn't be frank, then the lawyer must be; and he must go on being so till the client came out of his reserve.

Mr. Twist, however, was so obstinate in his reserve that the lawyer cheerfully and unhesitatingly jumped to the conclusion that the *entourage* must have some very weak spots about it somewhere.

"There's another way out of it of course, Mr. Twist," he said, when he had done rapidly describing the different steps to be taken. There were not many steps. The process of turning oneself into a guardian was surprisingly simple and swift.

"Out of it?" said Mr. Twist, his spectacles looking very big and astonished. "Out of what?"

"Out of your little difficulty. I wonder it hasn't occurred to you. Upon my word now, I do wonder."

"But I'm not in any little diff—" began Mr. Twist.

"The elder of these two girls, now—"

"There isn't an elder," said Mr. Twist.

"Come, come," said the lawyer patiently, waiting for him to be sensible.

"There isn't an elder," repeated Mr. Twist, "They're twins."

"Twins, are they? Well I must say we manage to match up our twins better than that over here. But come now—hasn't it occurred to you you might marry one of them, and so become quite naturally related to them both?"

Mr. Twist's spectacles seemed to grow gigantic.

"Marry one of them?" he repeated, his mouth helplessly opening.

"Yep," said the lawyer, giving him a lead in free-and-easiness.

"Look here," said Mr. Twist suddenly gathering his mouth together, "cut that line of joke out. I'm here on serious business. I haven't come to be facetious. Least of all about those children—"

"Quite so, quite so," interrupted the lawyer pleasantly. "Children, you call them. How old are they? Seventeen? My wife was sixteen when we married. Oh quite so, quite so. Certainly. By all means. Well then, they're to be your wards. And you don't want it known how recently they've become your wards—"

"I didn't say that," said Mr. Twist.

"Quite so, quite so. But it's your wish, isn't it. The relationship is to look as grass-grown as possible. Well, I shall be dumb of course, but most things get into the press here. Let me see—" He pulled a sheet of paper towards him and took up his fountain pen. "Just oblige me with particulars. Date of birth. Place of birth. Parentage—"

He looked up ready to write, waiting for the answers.

None came.

"I can't tell you off hand," said Mr. Twist presently, his forehead puckered.

"Ah," said the lawyer, laying down his pen. "Quite so. Not known your young friends long enough yet."

"I've known them quite long enough," said Mr. Twist stiffly, "but we happen to have found more alive topics of conversation than dates and parents."

"Ah. Parents not alive."

"Unfortunately they are not. If they were, these poor children wouldn't be knocking about in a strange country."

"Where would they be?" asked the lawyer, balancing his pen across his forefinger.

Mr. Twist looked at him very straight. Vividly he remembered his mother's peculiar horror when he told her the girls he was throwing away his home life for and breaking her heart over were Germans. It had acted upon her like the last straw. And since then he had felt everywhere, with every one he talked to, in every newspaper he read, the same strong hostility to Germans, so much stronger than when he left America the year before.

Mr. Twist began to perceive that he had been impetuous in this matter of the guardianship. He hadn't considered it enough. He suddenly saw innumerable difficulties for the twins and for The Open Arms if it was known it was run by Germans. Better abandon the guardianship idea than that such difficulties should arise. He hadn't thought; he hadn't had time properly to think; he had been so hustled and busy the last few days....

"They come from England," he said, looking at the lawyer very straight.

"Ah," said the lawyer.

Mr. Twist wasn't going to lie about the twins, but merely, by evading, he hoped to put off the day when their nationality would be known. Perhaps it never would be known; or if known, known later on when everybody, as everybody must who knew them, loved them for themselves and accordingly wouldn't care.

"Quite so," said the lawyer again, nodding. "I asked because I overheard them talking the other day as they passed through the hall of your hotel. They were talking about a canary. The r in the word seemed a little rough. Not quite English, Mr. Twist? Not quite American?"

"Not quite," agreed Mr. Twist. "They've been a good deal abroad."

"Quite so. At school, no doubt."

He was silent a moment, intelligently balancing his pen on his forefinger.

"Then these particulars," he went on, looking up at Mr. Twist, —"could you let me have them soon? I tell you what. You're in a hurry to fix this. I'll call round to-night at the hotel, and get them direct from your young friends. Save time. And make me acquainted with a pair of charming girls."

"No," said Mr. Twist. He got on to his feet and held out his hand. "Not to-night. We're engaged to-night. To-morrow will be soon enough. I'll send round. I'll let you know. I believe I'm going to think it over a bit. There isn't any such terrible hurry, anyhow."

"There isn't? I understood —"

"I mean, a day or two more or less don't figure out at much in the long run."

"Quite so, quite so," said the lawyer, getting up too. "Well, I'm always at your service, at any time." And he shook hands heartily with Mr. Twist and politely opened the door for him.

Then he went back to his writing-table more convinced than ever that there was something very weak somewhere about the *entourage*.

As for Mr. Twist, he perceived he had been a fool. Why had he gone to the lawyer at all? Why not simply have announced to the world that he was the Twinkler guardian? The twins themselves would have believed it if he had come in one day and said it was settled, and nobody outside would ever have dreamed of questioning it. After all, you couldn't see if a man was a guardian or not just by looking at him. Well, he would do no more about it, it was much too difficult. Bother it. Let Mrs. Bilton go on supposing he was the legal guardian of her charges. Anyway he had all the intentions of a guardian. What a fool he had been to go to the lawyer. Curse that lawyer. Now he knew, however distinctly and frequently he, Mr. Twist, might say he was the Twinkler guardian, that he wasn't.

It harassed Mr. Twist to perceive, as he did perceive with clearness, that he had been a fool; but the twins, when he told them that evening that owing to technical difficulties, with the details of which he wouldn't trouble them, the guardianship was off, were pleased.

"We want to be bound to you," said Anna-Felicitas her eyes very soft and her voice very gentle, "only by ties of affection and gratitude."

And Anna-Rose, turning red, opened her mouth as though she were going to say something handsome like that too, but seemed unable after all to get it out, and only said, rather inaudibly, "Yes."

CHAPTER XXIV

Yet another harassing experience awaited Mr. Twist before the end of that week.

It had been from the first his anxious concern that nothing should occur at the Cosmopolitan to get his party under a cloud; yet it did get under a cloud, and on the very last afternoon, too, before Mrs. Bilton's arrival. Only twenty-four hours more and her snowy-haired respectability would have spread over the twins like a white whig. They would have been safe. His party would have been unassailable. But no; those Twinklers, in spite of his exhortation whenever he had a minute left to exhort in, couldn't, it seemed, refrain from twinkling,—the word in Mr. Twist's mind covered the whole of their easy friendliness, their flow of language, their affable desire to explain.

He had kept them with him as much as he could, and luckily the excited interest they took in the progress of the inn made them happy to hang about it most of the time of the delicate and dangerous week before Mrs. Bilton came; but they too had things to do,—shopping in Acapulco choosing the sea-blue linen frocks and muslin caps and aprons in which they were to wait at tea, and buying the cushions and flower-pots and canary that came under the general heading, in Anna-Rose's speech, of feminine touches. So they sometimes left him; and he never saw them go without a qualm.

"Mind and not say anything to anybody about this, won't you," he would say hastily, making a comprehensive gesture towards the cottage as they went.

"Of course we won't."

"I meant, nobody is to know what it's really going to be. They're to think it's just a *pied-à-terre.* It would most ruin my advertisement scheme if they—"

"But of *course* we won't. Have we ever?" the twins would answer, looking very smug and sure of themselves.

"No. Not yet. But—"

And the hustled man would plunge again into technicalities with whichever expert was at that moment with him, leaving the twins, as he needs must, to God and their own discretion.

Discretion, he already amply knew, was not a Twinkler characteristic. But the week passed, Mrs. Bilton's arrival grew near, and nothing had happened. It was plain to the watchful Mr. Twist, from the pleasant looks of the other guests when the twins went in and out of the restaurant to meals, that nothing had happened. His heart grew lighter. On the last afternoon, when Mrs. Bilton was actually due next day, his heart was quite light, and he saw them leave him to go back and rest at the hotel, because they were tired by the accumulated standing about of the week, altogether unconcernedly.

The attitude of the Cosmopolitan guests towards the twins was, indeed, one of complete benevolence. They didn't even mind the canary. Who would not be indulgent towards two such sweet little girls and their pet bird, even if it did sing all day and most of the night without stopping? The Twinkler girls were like two little bits of snapped-off sunlight, or bits of white blossom blowing in and out of the hotel in their shining youth and it was impossible not to regard them indulgently. But if the guests were indulgent, they were also inquisitive. Everybody knew who Mr. Twist was; who, however, were the Twinklers? Were they relations of his? *Protégées*? Charges?

The social column of the Acapulco daily paper, from which information as to new arrivals was usually got, had, as we know, in its embarrassment at being ignorant to take refuge in French, because French may so easily be supposed to mean something. The paper had little knowledge of, but much confidence in, French. *Entourage* had seemed to it as good a word as any other, as indeed did *clientèle*. It had hesitated between the two, but finally chose *entourage* because there happened to be no accent in its stock of type. The Cosmopolitan guests were amused at the word, and though inquisitive were altogether amiable; and, until the last afternoon, only the manager didn't like the Twinklers. He didn't like them because of the canary. His sympathies had been alienated from the Miss Twinklers the moment he heard through the chambermaid that they had tied the heavy canary cage on to the hanging electric light in their bedroom. He said nothing, of course. One doesn't say anything if one is an hotel manager, until the unique and final moment when one says everything.

On the last afternoon before Mrs. Bilton's advent the twins, tired of standing about for days at the cottage and in shops, appeared in the hall of the hotel and sat down to rest. They didn't go to their room to rest because they didn't feel inclined for the canary, and they sat down very happily in the comfortable rocking-chairs with which the big hall abounded, and, propping their dusty feet on the lower bar of a small table, with friendly and interested eyes they observed the other guests.

The other guests also observed them.

It was the first time the *entourage* had appeared without its companion, and the other guests were dying to know details about it. It hadn't been sitting in the hall five minutes before a genial old gentleman caught Anna-Felicitas's friendly eye and instantly drew up his chair.

"Uncle gone off by himself to-day?" he asked; for he was of the party in the hotel which inclined, in spite of the marked difference in profiles, to the relationship theory, and he made a shot at the relationship being that of uncle.

"We haven't got an uncle nearer than England," said Anna-Felicitas affably.

"And we only got him by accident," said Anna-Rose, equally affably.

"It was an unfortunate accident," said Anna-Felicitas, considering her memories.

"Indeed," said the old gentleman. "Indeed. How was that?"

"By the usual method, if an uncle isn't a blood uncle," said Anna-Rose. "We happened to have a marriageable aunt, and he married her. So we have to have him."

"It was sheer bad luck," said Anna-Felicitas, again brooding on that distant image.

"Yes," said Anna-Rose. "Just bad luck. He might so easily have married some one else's aunt. But no. His roving glance must needs go and fall on ours."

"Indeed," said the old gentleman. "Indeed." And he ruminated on this, with an affectionate eye—he was affectionate—resting in turn on each Anna.

"Then Mr. Twist," he went on presently—"we all know him of course—a public benefactor—"

"Yes, *isn't* he," said Anna-Rose radiantly.

"A boon to the breakfast-table—"

"Yes, *isn't* he," said Anna-Rose again, all asparkle. "He *is* so pleasant at breakfast."

"Then he—Mr. Twist—Teapot Twist we call him where I live—"

"Teapot Twist?" said Anna-Rose. "I think that's irreverent."

"Not at all. It's a pet name. A sign of our affection and gratitude. Then he isn't your uncle?"

"We haven't got a real uncle nearer than heaven," said Anna-Felicitas, her cheek on her hand, dreamily reconstructing the image of Onkel Col.

"Indeed," said the old gentleman. "Indeed." And he ruminated, on this too, his thirsty heart—he had a thirsty heart, and found difficulty in slaking it because of his wife—very indulgent toward the twins.

Then he said: "That's a long way off."

"What is?" asked Anna-Rose.

"The place your uncle's in."

"Not too far really," said Anna-Felicitas softly. "He's safe there. He was very old, and was difficult to look after. Why, he got there at last through his own carelessness."

"Indeed," said the old gentleman.

"Sheer carelessness," said Anna-Rose.

"Indeed," said the old gentleman. "How was that?"

"Well, you see where we lived they didn't have electric light," began Anna-Rose, "and one night—the the night he went to heaven—he put the petroleum lamp—"

And she was about to relate that dreadful story of Onkle Col's end which has already been described in these pages as unfit for anywhere but an appendix for time had blunted her feelings, when Anna-Felicitas put out a beseeching hand and stopped her. Even after all these years Anna-Felicitas couldn't bear to remember Onkle Col's end. It had haunted her childhood. It had licked about her dreams in leaping tongues of flame. And it wasn't only tongues of flame. There were circumstances connected with it.... Only quite recently, since the war had damped down lesser horrors, had she got rid of it. She could at least now talk of him calmly, and also speculate with pleasure on the probable aspect of Onkle Col in glory, but she still couldn't bear to hear the details of his end.

At this point an elderly lady of the spare and active type, very upright and much wrinkled, that America seems so freely to produce, came down the stairs; and seeing the twins talking to the old gentleman, crossed straight over and sat down briskly next to them smiling benevolently.

"Well, if Mr. Ridding can talk to you I guess so can I," she said, pulling her knitting out of a brocaded bag and nodding and smiling at the group.

She was knitting socks for the Allied armies in France the next winter, but it being warm just then in California they were cotton socks because wool made her hands too hot.

The twins were all polite, reciprocal smiles.

"I'm just crazy to hear about you," said the brisk lady, knitting with incredible energy, while her smiles flicked over everybody. "You're fresh from Europe, aren't you? What say? Quite fresh? My, aren't you cute little things. Thinking of making a long stay in the States? What say? For the rest of your lives? Why now, I call that just splendid. Parents coming out West soon too? What say? Prevented? Well, I guess they won't let themselves be prevented long. Mr. Twist looking after you meanwhile? What say? There isn't any meanwhile? Well, I don't quite—Mr. Twist your uncle, or cousin? What say? No relation at all? H'm, h'm. No relation at all, is he. Well, I guess he's an old friend of your parents, then. What say? They didn't know him? H'm, h'm. They didn't know him, didn't they. Well, I don't quite—What say? But you know him? Yes, yes, so I see. H'm, h'm. I don't quite—" Her needles flew in and out, and her ball of cotton rolled on to the floor in her surprise.

Anna-Rose got up and fetched it for her before the old gentleman, who was gazing with thirsty appreciation at Anna-Felicitas, could struggle out of his chair.

"You see," explained Anna-Felicitas, taking advantage of the silence that had fallen on the lady, "Mr. Twist, regarded as a man, is old, but regarded as a friend he is new."

"Brand new," said Anna-Rose.

"H'm, h'm," said the lady, knitting faster than ever, and looking first at one twin and then at the other. "H'm, h'm, h'm. Brand new, is he. Well, I don't quite—" Her smiles had now to struggle with the uncertainty and doubt, and were weakening visibly.

"Say now, where did you meet Teapot Twist?" asked the old gentleman, who was surprised too, but remained quite benevolent owing to his affectionate heart and his not being a lady.

"We met Mr. Twist," said Anna-Rose, who objected to this way of alluding to him, "on the steamer."

"Not before? You didn't meet Mr. Twist before the steamer?" exclaimed the lady, the last of her smiles flickering out. "Not before the steamer, didn't you. Just a steamship acquaintance. Parents never seen him. H'm, h'm, h'm."

"We would have met him before if we could," said Anna-Felicitas earnestly.

"I should think so," said Anna-Rose. "It has been the great retrospective loss of our lives meeting him so late in them."

"Why now," said the old gentleman smiling, "I shouldn't call it so particularly late in them."

But the knitting lady didn't smile at all, and sat up very straight and said "H'm, h'm, h'm" to her flashing needles as they flew in and out; for not only was she in doubt now about the cute little things, but she also regretted, on behalf of the old gentleman's wife who was a friend of hers, the alert interest of his manner. He sat there so very much awake. With his wife he never seemed awake at all. Up to now she had not seen him except with his wife.

"You mustn't run away with the idea that we're younger than we really are," Anna-Rose said to the old gentleman.

"Why no, I won't," he answered with a liveliness that deepened the knitting lady's regret on behalf of his wife. "When I run away you bet it won't be with an idea."

And he chuckled. He was quite rosy in the face, and chuckled; he whom she knew only as a quiet man with no chuckle in him. And wasn't what he had just said very like what the French call a *double entendre?* She hadn't a husband herself, but if she had she would wish him to be at least as quiet when away from her as when with her, and at least as free from *double entendres.* At least. Really more. "H'm, h'm, h'm," she said, clicking her needles and looking first at the twins and then at the old gentleman.

"Do you mean to say you crossed the Atlantic quite alone, you two?" she asked, in order to prevent his continuing on these remarkable and unusual lines of *badinage.*

"Quite," said Anna-Felicitas.

"That is to say, we had Mr. Twist of course," said Anna-Rose.

"Once we had got him," amended Anna-Felicitas.

"Yes, yes," said the knitting lady, "so you say. H'm, h'm, h'm. Once you had got him. I don't quite—"

"Well, I call you a pair of fine high-spirited girls," said the old gentleman heartily, interrupting in his turn, "and all I can say is I wish I had been on that boat."

"Here's Mrs. Ridding," said the knitting lady quickly, relief in her voice; whereupon he suddenly grew quiet. "My, Mrs. Ridding," she added when the lady drew within speaking distance, "you do look as though you needed a rest."

Mrs. Ridding, the wife of the old gentleman, Mr. Ridding, had been approaching slowly for some time from behind. She had been out on the verandah since lunch, trying to recover from it. That was the one drawback to meals, she considered, that they required so much recovering from; and the nicer they were the longer it took. The meals at the Cosmopolitan were particularly nice, and really all one's time was taken up getting over them.

She was a lady whose figure seemed to be all meals. The old gentleman had married her in her youth, when she hadn't had time to have had so many. He and she were then the same age, and unfortunately hadn't gone on being the same age since. It had wrecked his life this inability of his wife to stay as young and new as himself. He wanted a young wife, and the older he got in years—his heart very awkwardly retained its early freshness—the younger he wanted her; and, instead, the older he got the older his wife got too. Also the less new. The old gentleman felt the whole thing was a dreadful mistake. Why should he have to be married to this old lady? Never in his life had he wanted to marry old ladies; and he thought it very hard that at an age when he most appreciated bright youth he should be forced to spend his precious years, his crowning years when his mind had attained wisdom while his heart retained freshness, stranded with an old lady of costly habits and inordinate bulk just because years ago he had fallen in love with a chance pretty girl.

He struggled politely out of his chair on seeing her. The twins, impressed by such venerable abundance, got up too.

"Albert, if you try to move too quick you'll crick your back again," said Mrs. Ridding in a monotonous voice, letting herself down carefully and a little breathlessly on to the edge of a chair that didn't rock, and fanning herself with a small fan she carried on the end of a massive gold chain. Her fatigued eyes explored the twins while she spoke.

"I can't get Mr. Ridding to remember that we're neither of us as young as we were," she went on, addressing the knitting lady but with her eyes continuing to explore the twins.

They naturally thought she was speaking to them, and Anna-Felicitas said politely, "Really?" and Anna-Rose, feeling she too ought to make some comment, said, "Isn't that very unusual?"

Aunt Alice always said, "Isn't that very unusual?" when she didn't know what else to say, and it worked beautifully, because then the other person launched into affirmations or denials with the reasons for them, and was quite happy.

But Mrs. Ridding only stared at the twins heavily and in silence.

"Because," explained Anna-Rose, who thought the old lady didn't quite follow, "nobody ever is. So that it must be difficult not to remember it."

Mr. Ridding too was silent, but that was because of his wife. It was quite untrue to say that he forgot, seeing that she was constantly reminding him. "Old stranger," he thought resentfully, as he carefully arranged a cushion behind her back. He didn't like her back. Why should he have to pay bills for putting expensive clothes on it? He didn't want to. It was all a dreadful mistake.

"You're the Twinkler girls," said the old lady abruptly.

They made polite gestures of agreement.

The knitting lady knitted vigorously, sitting up very straight and saying nothing, with a look on her face of disclaiming every responsibility.

"Where does your family come from?" was the next question.

This was unexpected. The twins had no desire to talk of Pomerania. They hadn't wanted to talk about Pomerania once since the war began; and they felt very distinctly in their bones that America, though she was a neutral, didn't like Germany any more than the belligerents did. It had been their intention to arrange together the line they would take if asked questions of this sort, but life had been so full and so exciting since their arrival that they had forgotten to.

Anna-Rose found herself unable to say anything at all. Anna-Felicitas, therefore, observing that Christopher was unnerved, plunged in.

"Our family," she said gently, "can hardly be said to come so much as to have been."

The old lady thought this over, her lustreless eyes on Anna-Felicitas's face.

The knitting lady clicked away very fast, content to leave the management of the Twinklers in more competent hands.

"How's that?" asked the old lady, finally deciding that she hadn't understood.

"It's extinct," said Anna-Felicitas. "Except us. That is, in the direct line."

The old lady was a little impressed by this, direct lines not being so numerous or so clear in America as in some other countries.

"You mean you two are the only Twinklers left?" she asked.

"The only ones left that matter," said Anna-Felicitas. "There are branches of Twinklers still existing, I believe, but they're so unimportant that we don't know them."

"Mere twigs," said Anna-Rose, recovering her nerves on seeing Anna-Felicitas handle the situation so skilfully; and her nose unconsciously gave a slight Junker lift.

"Haven't you got any parents?" asked the old lady.

"We used to have," said Anna-Felicitas flushing, afraid that her darling mother was going to be asked about.

The old gentleman gave a sudden chuckle. "Why yes," he said, forgetting his wife's presence for an instant, "I guess you had them once, or I don't see how—"

"Albert," said his wife.

"We are the sole surviving examples of the direct line of Twinklers," said Anna-Rose, now quite herself and ready to give Columbus a hand. "There's just us. And we—" she paused a moment, and then plunged—"we come from England."

"Do you?" said the old lady. "Now I shouldn't have said that. I can't say just why, but I shouldn't. Should you, Miss Heap?"

"I shouldn't say a good many things, Mrs. Ridding," said Miss Heap enigmatically, her needles flying.

"It's because we've been abroad a great deal with our parents, I expect," said Anna-Rose rather quickly. "I daresay it has left its mark on us."

"Everything leaves its mark on one," observed Anna-Felicitas pleasantly.

"Ah," said the old lady. "I know what it is now. It's the foreign r. You've picked it up. Haven't they, Miss Heap."

"I shouldn't like to say what they haven't picked up, Mrs. Ridding," said Miss Heap, again enigmatically.

"I'm afraid we have," said Anna-Rose, turning red. "We've been told that before. It seems to stick, once one has picked it up."

And the old gentleman muttered that everything stuck once one had picked it up, and looked resentfully at his wife.

She moved her slow eyes round, and let them rest on him a moment.

"Albert, if you talk so much you won't be able to sleep to-night," she said. "I can't get Mr. Ridding to remember we've got to be careful at our age," she added to the knitting lady.

"You seem to be bothered by your memory," said Anna-Rose politely, addressing the old gentleman "Have you ever tried making notes on little bits of paper of the things you have to remember? I think you would probably be all right then. Uncle Arthur used to do that. Or rather he made Aunt Alice do it for him, and put them where he would see them."

"Uncle Arthur," explained Anna-Felicitas to the old lady, "is an uncle of ours. The one," she said turning to the old gentleman, "we were just telling you about, who so unfortunately insisted on marrying our aunt. Uncle, that is, by courtesy," she added, turning to the old lady, "not by blood."

The old lady's eyes moved from one twin to the other as each one spoke, but she said nothing.

"But Aunt Alice," said Anna-Rose, "is our genuine aunt. Well, I was going to tell you," she continued briskly, addressing the old gentleman. "There used to be things Uncle Arthur had to do every day and every week, but still he had to be reminded of them each time, and Aunt Alice had a whole set of the regular ones written out on bits of cardboard, and brought them out in turn. The Monday morning one was: Wind the Clock, and the Sunday morning one was: Take your Hot Bath, and the Saturday evening one was: Remember your Pill. And there was one brought in regularly every morning with his shaving water and stuck in his looking-glass: Put on your Abdominable Belt."

The knitting needles paused an instant.

"Yes," Anna-Felicitas joined in, interested by these recollections, her long limbs sunk in her chair in a position of great ease and comfort, "and it seemed to us so funny for him to have to be reminded to put on what was really a part of his clothes every day, that once we wrote a slip of our own for him and left it on his dressing-table: Don't forget your Trousers."

The knitting needles paused again.

"But the results of that were dreadful," added Anna-Felicitas, her face sobering at the thought of them.

"Yes," said Anna-Rose. "You see, he supposed Aunt Alice had done it, in a fit of high spirits, though she never had high spirits—"

"And wouldn't have been allowed to if she had," explained Anna-Felicitas.

"And he thought she was laughing at him," said Anna-Rose, "though we have never seen her laugh—"

"And I don't believe he has either," said Anna-Felicitas.

"So there was trouble, because he couldn't bear the idea of her laughing at him, and we had to confess."

"But that didn't make it any better for Aunt Alice."

"No, because then he said it was her fault anyhow for not keeping us stricter."

"So," said Anna-Felicitas, "after the house had been steeped in a sulphurous gloom for over a week, and we all felt as though we were being slowly and steadily gassed, we tried to make it up by writing a final one—a nice one—and leaving it on his plate at breakfast: Kiss your Wife. But instead of kissing her he—" She broke off, and then finished a little vaguely: "Oh well, he didn't."

"Still," remarked Anna-Rose, "it must be pleasant not to be kissed by a husband. Aunt Alice always wanted him to, strange to say, which is why we reminded him of it. He used to forget that more regularly than almost anything. And the people who lived in the house nearest us were just the opposite—the husband was for ever trying to kiss the person who was his wife, and she was for ever dodging him."

"Yes," said Anna-Felicitas. "Like the people on Keats's Grecian Urn."

"Yes," said Anna-Rose. "And that sort of husband, must be even worse.

"Oh, much worse," agreed Anna-Felicitas.

She looked round amiably at the three quiet figures in the chairs. "I shall refrain altogether from husbands," she said placidly. "I shall take something that doesn't kiss."

And she fell into an abstraction, wondering, with her cheek resting on her hand, what he, or it, would look like.

There was a pause. Anna-Rose was wondering too what sort of a creature Columbus had in her mind, and how many, if any, legs it would have; and the other three were, as before, silent.

Then the old lady said, "Albert," and put out her hand to be helped on to her feet.

The old gentleman struggled out of his chair, and helped her up. His face had a congested look, as if he were with difficulty keeping back things he wanted to say.

Miss Heap got up too, stuffing her knitting as she did so into her brocaded bag.

"Go on ahead and ring the elevator bell, Albert," said the old lady. "It's time we went and had our nap."

"I ain't going to," said the old gentleman suddenly.

"What say? What ain't you going to, Albert?" said the old lady, turning her slow eyes round to him.

"Nap," said the old gentleman, his face very red.

It was intolerable to have to go and nap. He wished to stay where he was and talk to the twins. Why should he have to nap because somebody else wanted to? Why should he have to nap with an old lady, anyway? Never in his life had he wanted to nap with old ladies. It was all a dreadful mistake.

"Albert," said his wife looking at him.

He went on ahead and rang the lift-bell.

"You're quite right to see that he rests, Mrs. Ridding," said Miss Heap, walking away with her and slowing her steps to suit hers. "I should say it was essential that he should be kept quiet in the afternoons. You should see that Mr. Ridding rests more than he does. *Much* more," she added significantly.

"I can't get Mr. Ridding to remember that we're neither of us—"

This was the last the twins heard.

They too had politely got out of their chairs when the old lady began to heave into activity, and they stood watching the three departing figures. They were a little surprised. Surely they had all been in the middle of an interesting conversation?

"Perhaps it's American to go away in the middle," remarked Anna-Rose, following the group with her eyes as it moved toward the lift.

"Perhaps it is," said Anna-Felicitas, also gazing after it.

The old gentleman, in the brief moment during which the two ladies had their backs to him while preceding him into the lift, turned quickly round on his heels and waved his hand before he himself went in.

The twins laughed, and waved back; and they waved with such goodwill that the old gentleman couldn't resist giving one more wave. He was seen doing it by the two ladies as they faced round, and his wife, as she let herself down on to the edge of the seat, remarked that he mustn't exert himself like that or he would have to begin taking his drops again.

That was all she said in the lift; but in their room, when she had got her breath again, she said, "Albert, there's just one thing in the world I hate worse than a fool, and that's an old fool."

CHAPTER XXV

That evening, while the twins were undressing, a message came up from the office that the manager would be obliged if the Miss Twinklers' canary wouldn't sing.

"But it can't help it," said Anna-Felicitas through the crack of door she held open; she was already in her nightgown. "You wouldn't either if you were a canary," she added, reasoning with the messenger.

"It's just got to help it," said he.

"But why shouldn't it sing?"

"Complaints."

"But it always has sung."

"That is so. And it has sung once too often. It's unpopular in this hotel, that canary of yours. It's just got to rest a while. Take it easy. Sit quiet on its perch and think."

"But it won't sit quiet and think."

"Well, I've told you," he said, going away.

This was the bird that had been seen arriving at the Cosmopolitan about a week before by the lawyer, and it had piercingly sung ever since. It sang, that is, as long as there was any light, real or artificial, to sing by. The boy who carried it from the shop for the twins said its cage was to be hung in a window in the sun, or it couldn't do itself justice. But electric light also enabled it to do itself justice, the twins discovered, and if they sat up late the canary sat up late too, singing as loudly and as mechanically as if it hadn't been a real canary at all, but something clever and American with a machine inside it.

Secretly the twins didn't like it. Shocked at its loud behaviour, they had very soon agreed that it was no lady, but Anna-Rose was determined to have it at The Open Arms because of her conviction that no house showing the trail of a woman's hand was without a canary. That, and a workbag. She bought them both the same day. The workbag didn't matter, because it kept quiet; but the canary was a very big, very yellow bird, much bigger and yellower than the frailer canaries of a more exhausted civilization, and quite incapable, unless it was pitch dark, of keeping quiet for a minute. Evidently, as Anna-Felicitas said, it had a great many lungs. Her idea of lungs, in spite of her time among them and similar objects at a hospital, was what it had always been: that they were things like pink macaroni strung across a frame of bones on the principle of a lyre or harp, and producing noises. She thought the canary had unusual numbers of these pink strings, and all of them of the biggest and dearest kind of macaroni.

The other guests at the Cosmopolitan had been rather restive from the first on account of this bird, but felt so indulgent toward its owners, those cute little relations or charges or whatever they were of Teapot Twist's, that they bore its singing without complaint. But on the evening of the day the Annas had the interesting conversation with Mr. and Mrs. Ridding and Miss Heap, two definite complaints were lodged in the office, and one was from Mrs. Ridding and the other was from Miss Heap.

The manager, as has been said, was already sensitive about the canary. Its cage was straining his electric light cord, and its food, assiduously administered in quantities exceeding its capacity, littered the expensive pink pile carpet. He therefore lent a ready ear and sent up a peremptory message; and while the message was going up, Miss Heap, who had come herself with her complaint, stayed on discussing the Twist and Twinkler party.

She said nothing really; she merely asked questions; and not one of the questions, now they were put to him, did the manager find he could answer. No doubt everything was all right. Everybody knew about Mr. Twist, and it wasn't likely he would choose an hotel of so high a class to stay in if his relations to the Miss Twinklers were anything but regular. And a lady companion, he understood, was joining the party shortly; and besides, there was the house being got ready, a permanent place of residence he gathered, in which the party would settle down, and experience had taught him that genuine illicitness was never permanent. Still, the manager himself hadn't really cared about the Twinklers since the canary came. He could fill the hotel very easily, and there was no need to accommodate people who spoilt carpets. Also, the moment the least doubt or question arose among his guests, all of whom he knew and most of whom came back regularly every year, as to the social or moral status of any new arrivals, then those arrivals must go. Miss Heap evidently had doubts. Her standard, it is true, was the almost impossibly high one of the unmarried lady of riper years, but Mrs. Ridding, he understood, had doubts too; and once doubts started in an hotel he knew from experience that they ran through it like measles. The time had come for him to act.

Next morning, therefore, he briskly appeared in Mr. Twist's room as he was pulling on his boots, and cheerfully hoped he was bearing in mind what he had been told the day he took the rooms, that they were engaged for the date of the month now arrived at.

Mr. Twist paused with a boot half on. "I'm not bearing it in mind," he said, "because you didn't tell me."

"Oh yes I did, Mr. Twist," said the manager briskly. "It isn't likely I'd make a mistake about that. The rooms are taken every year for this date by the same people. Mrs. Hart of Boston has this one, and Mr. and Mrs.—"

Mr. Twist heard no more. He finished lacing his boots in silence. What he had been so much afraid of had happened: he and the twins had got under a cloud.

The twins had been saying things. Last night they told him they had made some friends. He had been uneasy at that, and questioned them. But it appeared they had talked chiefly of their Uncle Arthur. Well, damnable as Uncle Arthur was as a man he was safe enough as a topic of conversation. He was English. He was known to people in America like the Delloggs and the Sacks. But it was now clear they must have said things besides that. Probably they had expatiated on Uncle Arthur from some point of view undesirable to American ears. The American ear was very susceptible. He hadn't been born in New England without becoming aware of that.

Mr. Twist tied his bootlaces with such annoyance that he got them into knots. He ought never to have come with the Annas to a big hotel. Yet lodgings would have been worse. Why hadn't that white-haired gasbag, Mrs. Bilton—Mr. Twist's thoughts were sometimes unjust—joined them sooner? Why had that shirker Dellogg died? He got his bootlaces hopelessly into knots.

"I'd like to start right in getting the rooms fixed up, Mr. Twist," said the manager pleasantly. "Mrs. Hart of Boston is very—"

"See here," said Mr. Twist, straightening himself and turning the full light of his big spectacles on to him, "I don't care a curse for Mrs. Hart of Boston."

The manager expressed regret that Mr. Twist should connect a curse with a lady. It wasn't American to do that. Mrs. Hart—

"Damn Mrs. Hart," said Mr. Twist, who had become full-bodied of speech while in France, and when he was goaded let it all out.

The manager went away. And so, two hours later, did Mr. Twist and the twins.

"I don't know what you've been saying," he said in an extremely exasperated voice, as he sat opposite them in the taxi with their grips, considerably added to and crowned by the canary who was singing, piled up round him.

"Saying?" echoed the twins, their eyes very round.

"But whatever it was you'd have done better to say something else. Confound that bird. Doesn't it ever stop screeching?"

It was the twins, however, who were confounded. So much confounded by what they considered his unjust severity that they didn't attempt to defend themselves, but sat looking at him with proud hurt eyes.

By this time they both had become very fond of Mr. Twist, and accordingly he was able to hurt them. Anna-Rose, indeed, was so fond of him that she actually thought him handsome. She had boldly said so to the astonished Anna-Felicitas about a week before; and when Anna-Felicitas was silent, being unable to agree, Anna-Rose had heatedly explained that there was handsomeness, and there was the higher handsomeness, and that that was the one Mr. Twist had. It was infinitely better than mere handsomeness, said Anna-Rose—curly hair and a straight nose and the rest of the silly stuff—because it was real and lasting; and it was real and lasting because it lay in the play of the features and not in their exact position and shape.

Anna-Felicitas couldn't see that Mr. Twist's features played. She looked at him now in the taxi while he angrily stared out of the window, and even though he was evidently greatly stirred his features weren't playing. She didn't particularly want them to play. She was fond of and trusted Mr. Twist, and would never even have thought whether he had features or not ii Anna-Rose hadn't taken lately to talking so much about them. And she couldn't help remembering how this very Christopher, so voluble now on the higher handsomeness, had said on board the *St. Luke* when first commenting on Mr. Twist that God must have got tired of making him by the time his head was reached. Well, Christopher had always been an idealist. When she was eleven she had violently loved the coachman. Anna-Felicitas hadn't ever violently loved anybody yet, and seeing Anna-Rose like this now about Mr. Twist made her wonder when she too was going to begin. Surely it was time. She hoped her inability to begin wasn't perhaps because she had no heart. Still, she couldn't begin if she didn't see anybody to begin on.

She sat silent in the taxi, with Christopher equally silent beside her, both of them observing Mr. Twist through lowered eyelashes. Anna-Rose watched him with hurt and anxious eyes like a devoted dog who has been kicked without cause. Anna-Felicitas watched him in a more detached spirit. She had a real affection for him, but it was not, she was sure and rather regretted, an affection that would ever be likely to get the better of her reason. It wasn't because he was so old, of course, she thought, for one could love the oldest people, beginning with that standard example of age, the *liebe Gott*; it was because she liked him so much.

How could one get sentimental over and love somebody one so thoroughly liked? The two things on reflection didn't seem to combine well. She was sure, for instance, that Aunt Alice had loved Uncle Arthur, amazing as it seemed, but she was equally sure she hadn't liked him. And look at the *liebe Gott*. One loves the *liebe Gott*, but it would be going too far, she thought, to say that one likes him.

These were the reflections of Anna-Felicitas in the taxi, as she observed through her eyelashes the object of Anna-Rose's idealization. She envied Anna-Rose; for here she had been steadily expanding every day more and more like a flower under the influence of her own power of idealization. She used to sparkle and grow rosy like that for the coachman. Perhaps after all it didn't much matter what you loved, so long as you loved immensely. It was, perhaps, thought Anna-Felicitas approaching this subject with some caution and diffidence, the quantity of one's love that mattered rather than the quality of its object. Not that Mr. Twist wasn't of the very first quality, except to look at; but what after all were faces? The coachman had been, as it were, nothing else but face, so handsome was he and so without any other recommendation. He couldn't even drive; and her father had very soon kicked him out with the vigour and absence of hesitation peculiar to Junkers when it comes to kicking and Anna-Rose had wept all over her bread and butter at tea that day, and was understood to say that she knew at last what it must be like to be a widow.

Mr. Twist, for all that he was looking out of the taxi window with an angry and worried face, his attention irritably concentrated, so it seemed, on the objects passing in the road, very well knew he was being observed. He wouldn't, however, allow his eye to be caught. He wasn't going to become entangled at this juncture in argument with the Annas. He was hastily making up his mind, and there wasn't much time to do it in. He had had no explanation with the twins since the manager's visit to his room, and he didn't want to have any. He had issued brief orders to them, told them to pack, declined to answer questions, and had got them safely into the taxi with a minimum waste of time and words. They were now on their way to the station to meet Mrs. Bilton. Her train from Los Angeles was not due till that evening at six. Never mind. The station was a secure place to deposit the twins and the baggage in till she came. He wished he could deposit the twins in the parcel-room as easily as he could their grips—neatly labelled, put away safely on a shelf till called for.

Rapidly, as he stared out of the window, he arrived at decisions. He would leave the twins in the waiting room at the station till Mrs. Bilton was due, and meanwhile go out and find lodgings for them and her. He himself would get a room in another and less critical hotel, and stay in it till the cottage was habitable. So would unassailable respectability once more descend like a white garment upon the party and cover it up.

But he was nettled; nettled; nettled by the *contretemps* that had occurred on the very last day, when Mrs. Bilton was so nearly there; nettled and exasperated. So immensely did he want the twins to be happy, to float serenely in the unclouded sunshine and sweetness he felt was their due, that he was furious with them for doing anything to make it difficult. And, jerkily, his angry thoughts pounced, as they so often did, on Uncle Arthur. Fancy kicking two little things like that out into the world, two little breakable things like that, made to be cherished and watched over. Mr. Twist was pure American in his instinct to regard the female as an object to be taken care of, to be placed securely in a charming setting and kept brightly free from dust. If Uncle Arthur had had a shred of humanity in him, he angrily reflected, the Annas would have stayed under his roof throughout the war, whatever the feeling was against aliens. Never would a decent man have chucked them out.

He turned involuntarily from the window and looked at the twins. Their eyes were fixed, affectionate and anxious, on his face. With the quick change of mood of those whose chins are weak and whose hearts are warm, a flood of love for them gushed up within him and put out his anger. After all, if Uncle Arthur had been decent he, Edward A. Twist, never would have met these blessed children. He would now have been at Clark; leading lightless days; hopelessly involved with his mother.

His loose, unsteady mouth broke into a big smile. Instantly the two faces opposite cleared into something shining.

"Oh dear," said Anna-Felicitas with a sigh of relief, "it *is* refreshing when you leave off being cross."

"We're fearfully sorry if we've said anything we oughtn't to have," said Anna-Rose, "and if you tell us what it is we won't say it again."

"I can't tell you, because I don't know what it was," said Mr. Twist, in his usual kind voice. "I only see the results. And the results are that the Cosmopolitan is tired of us, and we've got to find lodgings."

"Lodgings?"

"Till we can move into the cottage. I'm going to put you and Mrs. Bilton in an apartment in Acapulco, and go myself to some hotel."

The twins stared at him a moment in silence. Then Anna-Rose said with sudden passion, "You're not."

"How's that?" asked Mr. Twist; but she was prevented answering by the arrival of the taxi at the station.

There followed ten minutes' tangle and confusion, at the end of which the twins found themselves free of their grips and being piloted into the waiting-room by Mr. Twist.

"There," he said. "You sit here quiet and good. I'll come back about one o'clock with sandwiches and candy for your dinner, and maybe a story-book or two. You mustn't leave this, do you hear? I'm going to hunt for those lodgings."

And he was in the act of taking off his hat valedictorily when Anna-Rose again said with the same passion, "You're not."

"Not what?" inquired Mr. Twist, pausing with his hat in mid-air.

"Going to hunt for lodgings. We won't go to them."

"Of course we won't," said Anna-Felicitas, with no passion but with an infinitely rock-like determination.

"And pray—" began Mr. Twist.

"Go into lodgings alone with Mrs. Bilton?" interrupted Anna-Rose her face scarlet, her whole small body giving the impression of indignant feathers standing up on end. "While you're somewhere else? Away from us? We won't."

"Of course we won't," said Anna-Felicitas again, an almost placid quality in her determination, it was so final and so unshakable. "Would you?"

"See here—" began Mr. Twist.

"We won't see anywhere," said Anna-Rose.

"Would you," inquired Anna-Felicitas, again reasoning with him, "like being alone in lodgings with Mrs. Bilton?"

"This is no time for conversation," said Mr. Twist, making for the door. "You've got to do what I think best on this occasion. And that's all about it."

"We won't," repeated Anna-Rose, on the verge of those tears which always with her so quickly followed any sort of emotion.

Mr. Twist paused on his way to the door. "Well now what the devil's the matter with lodgings?" he asked angrily.

"It isn't the devil, it's Mrs. Bilton," said Anna-Felicitas. "Would you yourself like—"

'But you've got to have Mrs. Bilton with you anyhow from to-day on."

"But not unadulterated Mrs. Bilton. You were to have been with us too. We can't be drowned all by ourselves in Mrs. Bilton. *You* wouldn't like it."

"Of course I wouldn't. But it's only for a few days anyhow," said Mr. Twist, who had been quite unprepared for opposition to his very sensible arrangement.

"I shouldn't wonder if it's only a few days now before we can all squeeze into some part of the cottage. If you don't mind dust and noise and workmen about all day long."

A light pierced the gloom that had gathered round Anna-Felicitas's soul.

"We'll go into it to-day," she said firmly, "Why not? We can camp out. We can live in those little rooms at the back over the kitchen,—the ones you got ready for Li Koo. We'd be on the spot. We wouldn't mind anything. It would just be a picnic."

"And we—we wouldn't be—sep—separated," said Anna-Rose, getting it out with a gasp.

Mr. Twist stood looking at them.

"Well, of all the—" he began, pushing his hat back. "Are you aware," he went on more calmly, "that there are only two rooms over that kitchen, and that you and Mrs. Bilton will have to be all together in one of them?"

"We don't mind that as long as you're in the other one," said Anna-Rose.

"Of course," suggested Anna-Felicitas, "if you were to happen to marry Mrs. Bilton it would make a fairer division."

Mr. Twist's spectacles stared enormously at her.

"No, no," said Anna-Rose quickly. "Marriage is a sacred thing, and you can't just marry so as to be more comfortable."

"I guess if I married Mrs. Bilton I'd be more uncomfortable," remarked Mr. Twist with considerable dryness.

He seemed however to be quieted by the bare suggestion, for he fixed his hat properly on his head and said, sobriety in his voice and manner, "Come along, then. We'll get a taxi and anyway go out and have a look at the rooms. But I shouldn't be surprised," he added, "if before I've done with you you'll have driven me sheer out of my wits."

"Oh, *don't* say that," said the twins together, with all and more of their usual urbanity.

CHAPTER XXVI

By superhuman exertions and a lavish expenditure of money, the rooms Li Koo was later on to inhabit were ready to be slept in by the time Mrs. Bilton arrived. They were in an outbuilding at the back of the house, and consisted of a living-room with a cooking-stove in it, a bedroom behind it, and up a narrow and curly staircase a larger room running the whole length and width of the shanty. This sounds spacious, but it wasn't. The amount of length and width was small, and it was only just possible to get three camp-beds into it and a washstand. The beds nearly touched each other. Anna-Felicitas thought she and Anna-Rose were going to be regrettably close to Mrs. Bilton in them, and again urged on Mr. Twist's consideration the question of removing Mrs. Bilton from the room by marriage; but Anna-Rose said it was all perfect, and that there was lots of room, and she was sure Mrs. Bilton, used to the camp life so extensively practised in America, would thoroughly enjoy herself.

They worked without stopping all the rest of the day at making the little place habitable, nailing up some of the curtains intended for the other house, unpacking cushions, and fetching in great bunches of the pale pink and mauve geraniums that scrambled about everywhere in the garden and hiding the worst places in the rooms with them. Mr. Twist was in Acapulco most of the time, getting together the necessary temporary furniture and cooking utensils, but the twins didn't miss him, for they were helped with zeal by the architect, the electrical expert, the garden expert and the chief plumber.

These young men—they were all young, and very go-ahead— abandoned the main building that day to the undirected labours of the workmen they were supposed to control, and turned to on the shanty as soon as they realized what it was to be used for with a joyous energy that delighted the twins. They swept and they garnished. They cleaned the dust off the windows and the rust off the stove. They fetched out the parcels with the curtains and cushions in them from the barn where all parcels and packages had been put till the house was ready, and extracted various other comforts from the piled up packing-cases,—a rug or two, an easy chair for Mrs. Bilton, a looking-glass. They screwed in hooks behind the doors for clothes to be hung on, and they tied the canary to a neighbouring eucalyptus tree where it could be seen and hardly heard. The chief plumber found buckets and filled them with water, and the electrical expert rigged up a series of lanterns inside the shanty, even illuminating its tortuous staircase. There was much *badinage*, but as it was all in American, a language of which the twins were not yet able to apprehend the full flavour, they responded only with pleasant smiles. But their smiles were so pleasant and the family dimple so engaging that the hours flew, and the young men were sorry indeed when Mr. Twist came back.

He came back laden, among other things, with food for the twins, whom he had left in his hurry high and dry at the cottage with nothing at all to eat; and he found them looking particularly comfortable and well-nourished, having eaten, as they explained when they refused his sandwiches and fruit, the chief plumber's dinner.

They were sitting on the stump of an oak tree when he arrived, resting from their labours, and the grass at their feet was dotted with the four experts. It was the twins now who were talking, and the experts who were smiling. Mr. Twist wondered uneasily what they were saying. It wouldn't have added to his comfort if he had heard, for they were giving the experts an account of their attempt to go and live with the Sacks, and interweaving with it some general reflections of a philosophical nature suggested by the Sack *ménage*. The experts were keenly interested, and everybody looked very happy, and Mr. Twist was annoyed; for clearly if the experts were sitting there on the grass they weren't directing the workmen placed under their orders. Mr. Twist perceived a drawback to the twins living on the spot while the place was being finished; another drawback. He had perceived several already, but not this one. Well, Mrs. Bilton would soon be there. He now counted the hours to Mrs. Bilton. He positively longed for her.

When they saw him coming, the experts moved away. "Here's the boss," they said, nodding and winking at the twins as they got up quickly and departed. Winking was not within the traditions of the Twinkler family, but no doubt, they thought, it was the custom of the country to wink, and they wondered whether they ought to have winked back. The young men were certainly deserving of every friendliness in return for all they had done. They decided they would ask Mrs. Bilton, and then they could wink at them if necessary the first thing to-morrow morning.

Mr. Twist took them with him when he went down to the station to meet the Los Angeles train. It was dark at six, and the workmen had gone home by then, but the experts still seemed to be busy. He had been astonished at the amount the twins had accomplished in his absence in the town till they explained to him how very active the experts had been, whereupon he said,

"Now isn't that nice," and briefly informed them they would go with him to the station.

"That's waste of time," said Anna-Felicitas. "We could be giving finishing touches if we stayed here."

"You will come with me to the station," said Mr. Twist.

Mrs. Bilton arrived in a thick cloud of conversation. She supposed she was going to the Cosmopolitan Hotel, as indeed she originally was, and all the way back in the taxi Mr. Twist was trying to tell her she wasn't; but Mrs. Bilton had so much to say about her journey, and her last days among her friends, and all the pleasant new acquaintances she had made on the train, and her speech was so very close-knit, that he felt he was like a rabbit on the wrong side of a thick-set hedge running desperately up and down searching for a gap to get through. It was nothing short of amazing how Mrs. Bilton talked; positively, there wasn't at any moment the smallest pause in the flow.

"It's a disease," thought Anna-Rose, who had several things she wanted to say herself, and found herself hopelessly muzzled.

"No wonder Mr. Bilton preferred heaven," thought Anna-Felicitas, also a little restless at the completeness of her muzzling.

"Anyhow she'll never hear the Annas saying anything," thought Mr. Twist, consoling himself.

"This hotel we're going to seems to be located at some distance from the station," said Mrs. Bilton presently, in the middle of several pages of rapid unpunctuated monologue. "Isolated, surely—" and off she went again to other matters, just as Mr. Twist had got his mouth open to explain at last.

She arrived therefore at the cottage unconscious of the change in her fate.

Now Mrs. Bilton was as fond of comfort as any other woman who has been deprived for some years of that substitute for comfort, a husband. She had looked forward to the enveloping joys of the Cosmopolitan, its bath, its soft bed and good food, with frank satisfaction. She thought it admirable that before embarking on active duties she should for a space rest luxuriously in an excellent hotel, with no care in regard to expense, and exchange ideas while she rested with the interesting people she would be sure to meet in it. Before the interview in Los Angeles, Mr. Twist had explained to her by letter and under the seal of confidence the philanthropic nature of the project he and the Miss Twinklers were engaged upon, and she was prepared, in return for the very considerable salary she had accepted, to do her duty loyally and unremittingly; but after the stress and hard work of her last days in Los Angeles she had certainly looked forward with a particular pleasure to two or three weeks' delicious wallowing in flesh-pots for which she had not to pay. She was also, however, a lady of grit; and she possessed, as she said her friends often told her, a redoubtable psyche, a genuine American free and fearless psyche; so that when, talking ceaselessly, her thoughts eagerly jostling each other as they streamed through her brain to get first to the exit of her tongue, she caught her foot in some builder's débris carelessly left on the path up to the cottage and received in this way positively her first intimation that this couldn't be the Cosmopolitan, she did not, as a more timid female soul well might have, become alarmed and suppose that Mr. Twist, whom after all she didn't know, had brought her to this solitary place for purposes of assassination, but stopped firmly just where she was, and turning her head in the darkness toward him said, "Now Mr. Twist, I'll stand right here till you're able to apply some sort of illumination to what's at my feet. I can't say what it is I've walked against but I'm not going any further with this promenade till I can say. And when you've thrown light on the subject perhaps you'll oblige me with information as to where that hotel is I was told I was coming to."

"Information?" cried Mr. Twist. "Haven't I been trying to give it you ever since I met you? Haven't I been trying to stop your getting out of the taxi till I'd fetched a lantern? Haven't I been trying to offer you my arm along the path—"

"Then why didn't you say so, Mr. Twist?" asked Mrs. Bilton.

"Say so!" cried Mr. Twist.

At that moment the flash of an electric torch was seen jerking up and down as the person carrying it ran toward them. It was the electrical expert who, most fortunately, happened still to be about.

Mrs. Bilton welcomed him warmly, and taking his torch from him first examined what she called the location of her feet, then gave it back to him and put her hand through his arm. "Now guide me to whatever it is has been substituted without my knowledge for that hotel," she said; and while Mr. Twist went back to the taxi to deal with her grips, she walked carefully toward the shanty on the expert's arm, expressing, in an immense number of words, the astonishment she felt at Mr. Twist's not having told her of the disappearance of the Cosmopolitan from her itinerary.

The electrical expert tried to speak, but was drowned without further struggle. Anna-Rose, unable to listen any longer without answering to the insistent inquiries as to why Mr. Twist had kept her in the dark, raised her voice at last and called out, "But he wanted to—he wanted to all the time—you wouldn't listen—you wouldn't stop—"

Mrs. Bilton did stop however when she got inside the shanty. Her tongue and her feet stopped dead together. The electrical expert had lit all the lanterns, and coming upon it in the darkness its lighted windows gave it a cheerful, welcoming look. But inside no amount of light and bunches of pink geraniums could conceal its discomforts, its dreadful smallness; besides, pink geraniums, which the twins were accustomed to regard as precious, as things brought up lovingly in pots, were nothing but weeds to Mrs. Bilton's experienced Californian eye.

She stared round her in silence. Her sudden quiet fell on the twins with a great sense of refreshment. Standing in the doorway—for Mrs. Bilton and the electrical expert between them filled up most of the kitchen—they heaved a deep sigh. "And see how beautiful the stars are," whispered Anna-Felicitas in Anna-Rose's ear; she hadn't been able to see them before somehow, Mrs. Bilton's voice had so much ruffled the night.

"Do you think she talks in her sleep?" Anna-Rose anxiously whispered back.

But Mr. Twist, arriving with his hands full, was staggered to find Mrs. Bilton not talking. An icy fear seized his heart. She was going to refuse to stay with them. And she would be within her rights if she did, for certainly what she called her itinerary had promised her a first-rate hotel, in which she was to continue till a finished and comfortable house was stepped into.

"I wish you'd say something," he said, plumping down the bags he was carrying on the kitchen floor.

The twins from the doorway looked at him and then at each other in great surprise. Fancy *asking* Mrs. Bilton to say something.

"They would come," said Mr. Twist, resentfully, jerking his head toward the Annas in the doorway.

"It's worse upstairs," he went on desperately as Mrs. Bilton still was dumb.

"Worse upstairs?" cried the twins, as one woman.

"It's perfect upstairs," said Anna-Felicitas.

"It's like camping out without *being* out," said Anna-Rose.

"The only drawback is that there are rather a lot of beds in our room," said Anna-Felicitas, "but that of course"—she turned to Mr. Twist—"might easily be arranged—"

"I wish you'd *say* something, Mrs. Bilton," he interrupted quickly and loud.

Mrs. Bilton drew a deep breath and looked round her. She looked round the room, and she looked up at the ceiling, which the upright feather in her hat was tickling, and she looked at the faces of the twins, lit flickeringly by the uncertain light of the lanterns. Then, woman of grit, wife who had never failed him of Bruce D. Bilton, widow who had remained poised and indomitable on a small income in a circle of well-off friends, she spoke; and she said:

"Mr. Twist, I can't say what this means, and you'll furnish me no doubt with information, but whatever it is I'm not the woman to put my hand to a plough and then turn back again. That type of behaviour may have been good enough for Pharisees and Sadducees, who if I remember rightly had to be specially warned against the practice, but it isn't good enough for me. You've conducted me to a shack instead of the hotel I was promised, and I await your explanation. Meanwhile, is there any supper?"

CHAPTER XXVII

It was only a fortnight after this that the inn was ready to be opened, and it was only during the first days of this fortnight that the party in the shanty had to endure any serious discomfort. The twins didn't mind the physical discomfort at all; what they minded, and began to mind almost immediately, was the spiritual discomfort of being at such close quarters with Mrs. Bilton. They hardly noticed the physical side of that close association in such a lovely climate, where the whole of out-of-doors can be used as one's living-room; and their morning dressing, a difficult business in the shanty for anybody less young and more needing to be careful, was rather like the getting up of a dog after its night's sleep—they seemed just to shake themselves, and there they were.

They got up before Mrs. Bilton, who was, however, always awake and talking to them while they dressed, and they went to bed before she did, though she came up with them after the first night and read aloud to them while they undressed; so that as regarded the mysteries of Mrs. Bilton's toilette they were not, after all, much in her way. It was like caravaning or camping out: you managed your movements and moments skilfully, and if you were Mrs. Bilton you had a curtain slung across your part of the room, in case your younger charges shouldn't always be asleep when they looked as if they were.

Gradually one alleviation was added to another, and Mrs. Bilton forgot the rigours of the beginning. Li Koo arrived, for instance, fetched by a telegram, and under a tent in the eucalyptus grove at the back of the house set up an old iron stove and produced, with no apparent exertion, extraordinarily interesting and amusing food. He went into Acapulco at daylight every morning and did the marketing. He began almost immediately to do everything else in the way of housekeeping. He was exquisitely clean, and saw to it that the shanty matched him in cleanliness. To the surprise and gratification of the twins, who had supposed it would be their lot to go on doing the housework of the shanty, he took it over as a matter of course, dusting, sweeping, and tidying like a practised and very excellent housemaid. The only thing he refused to do was to touch the three beds in the upper chamber. "Me no make lady-beds," he said briefly.

Li Koo's salary was enormous, but Mr. Twist, with a sound instinct, cared nothing what he paid so long as he got the right man. He was, indeed, much satisfied with his two employees, and congratulated himself on his luck. It is true in regard to Mrs. Bilton his satisfaction was rather of the sorrowful sort that a fresh ache in a different part of one's body from the first ache gives: it relieved him from one by substituting another. Mrs. Bilton overwhelmed him; but so had the Annas begun to. Her overwhelming, however, was different, and freed him from that other worse one. He felt safe now about the Annas, and after all there were parts of the building in which Mrs. Bilton wasn't. There was his bedroom, for instance. Thank God for bedrooms, thought Mr. Twist. He grew to love his. What a haven that poky and silent place was; what a blessing the conventions were, and the proprieties. Supposing civilization were so far advanced that people could no longer see the harm there is in a bedroom, what would have become of him? Mr. Twist could perfectly account for Bruce D. Bilton's death. It wasn't diabetes, as Mrs. Bilton said; it was just bedroom.

Still, Mrs. Bilton was an undoubted find, and did immediately in those rushed days take the Annas off his mind. He could leave them with her in the comfortable certitude that whatever else they did to Mrs. Bilton they couldn't talk to her. Never would she know the peculiar ease of the Twinkler attitude toward subjects Americans approach with care. Never would they be able to tell her things about Uncle Arthur, the kind of things that had caused the Cosmopolitan to grow so suddenly cool. There was, most happily for this particular case, no arguing with Mrs. Bilton. The twins couldn't draw her out because she was already, as it were, so completely out. This was a great thing, Mr. Twist felt, and made up for any personal suffocation he had to bear; and when on the afternoon of Mrs. Bilton's first day the twins appeared without her in the main building in search of him, having obviously given her the slip, and said they were sorry to disturb him but they wanted his advice, for though they had been trying hard all day, remembering they were ladies and practically hostesses, they hadn't yet succeeded in saying anything at all to Mrs. Bilton and doubted whether they ever would, he merely smiled happily at them and said to Anna-Rose, "See how good comes out of evil" — a remark that they didn't like when they had had time to think over it.

But they went on struggling. It seemed so unnatural to be all alone all day long with someone and only listen. Mrs. Bilton never left their side, regarding it as proper and merely fulfilling her part of the bargain, in these first confused days when there was nothing for ladies to do but look on while perspiring workmen laboured at apparently producing more and more chaos, to become thoroughly acquainted with her young charges. This she did by imparting to them intimate and meticulous information about her own life, with the whole of the various uplifts, as she put it, her psyche had during its unfolding experienced. There was so much to tell about herself that she never got to inquiring about the twins. She knew they were orphans, and that this was a good work, and for the moment had no time for more.

The twins were profoundly bored by her psyche, chiefly because they didn't know what part of her it was, and it was no use asking for she didn't answer; but they listened with real interest to her concrete experiences, and especially to the experiences connected with Mr. Bilton. They particularly wished to ask questions about Mr. Bilton, and find out what he had thought of things. Mrs. Bilton was lavish in her details of what she had thought herself, but Mr. Bilton's thoughts remained impenetrable. It seemed to the twins that he must have thought a lot, and have come to the conclusion that there was much to be said for death.

The Biltons, it appeared, had been the opposite of the Clouston-Sacks, and had never been separated for a single day during the whole of their married life. This seemed to the twins very strange, and needing a great deal of explanation. In order to get light thrown on it the first thing they wanted to find out was how long the marriage had lasted; but Mrs. Bilton was deaf to their inquiries, and having described Mr. Bilton's last moments and obsequies—obsequies scheduled by her, she said, with so tender a regard for his memory that she insisted on a horse-drawn hearse instead of the more fashionable automobile conveyance, on the ground that a motor hearse didn't seem sorry enough even on first speed—she washed along with an easy flow to descriptions of the dreadfulness of the early days of widowhood, when one's crepe veil keeps on catching in everything—chairs, overhanging branches, and passers-by, including it appeared on one occasion a policeman. She inquired of the twins whether they had ever seen a new-made widow in a wind. Chicago, she said, was a windy place, and Mr. Bilton passed in its windiest month. Her long veil, as she proceeded down the streets on the daily constitutional she considered it her duty toward the living to take, for one owes it to one's friends to keep oneself fit and not give way, was blown hither and thither in the buffeting cross-currents of that uneasy climate, and her walk in the busier streets was a series of entanglements. Embarrassing entanglements, said Mrs. Bilton. Fortunately the persons she got caught in were delicacy and sympathy itself; often, indeed, seeming quite overcome by the peculiar poignancy of the situation, covered with confusion, profuse in apologies. Sometimes the wind would cause her veil for a few moments to rear straight up above her head in a monstrous black column of woe. Sometimes, if she stopped a moment waiting to cross the street, it would whip round the body of any one who happened to be near, like a cord. It did this once about the body of the policeman directing the traffic, by whose side she had paused, and she had to walk round him backwards before it could be unwound. The Chicago evening papers, prompt on the track of a sensation, had caused her friends much painful if only short-lived amazement by coming out with huge equivocal headlines:

WELL-KNOWN SOCIETY WIDOW AND POLICEMAN CAUGHT TOGETHER

and beginning their description of the occurrence by printing her name in full. So that for the first sentence or two her friends were a prey to horror and distress, which turned to indignation on discovering there was nothing in it after all.

The twins, their eyes on Mrs. Bilton's face, their hands clasped round their knees, their bodies sitting on the grass at her feet, occasionally felt as they followed her narrative that they were somehow out of their depth and didn't quite understand. It was extraordinarily exasperating to them to be so completely muzzled. They were accustomed to elucidate points they didn't understand by immediate inquiry; they had a habit of asking for information, and then delivering comments on it.

This condition of repression made them most uncomfortable. The ilex tree in the field below the house, to which Mrs. Bilton shepherded them each morning and afternoon for the first three days, became to them, in spite of its beauty with the view from under its dark shade across the sunny fields to the sea and the delicate distant islands, a painful spot. The beauty all round them was under these conditions exasperating. Only once did Mrs. Bilton leave them, and that was the first afternoon, when they instantly fled to seek out Mr. Twist; and she only left them then—for it wasn't just her sense of duty that was strong, but also her dislike of being alone—because something unexpectedly gave way in the upper part of her dress, she being of a tight well-held-in figure, depending much on its buttons; and she had very hastily to go in search of a needle.

After that they didn't see Mr. Twist alone for several days. They hardly indeed saw him at all. The only meal he shared with them was supper, and on finding the first evening that Mrs. Bilton read aloud to people after supper, he made the excuse of accounts to go through and went into his bedroom, repeating this each night.

The twins watched him go with agonized eyes. They considered themselves deserted; shamefully abandoned to a miserable fate.

"And it isn't as if he didn't *like* reading aloud," whispered Anna-Rose, bewildered and indignant as she remembered the "Ode to Dooty."

"Perhaps he's one of those people who only like it if they do it themselves," Anna-Felicitas whispered back, trying to explain his base behaviour.

And while they whispered, Mrs. Bilton with great enjoyment declaimed—she had had a course of elocution lessons during Mr. Bilton's life so as to be able to place the best literature advantageously before him—the diary of a young girl written in prison. The young girl had been wrongfully incarcerated, Mrs. Bilton explained, and her pure soul only found release by the demise of her body. The twins hated the young girl from the first paragraph. She wrote her diary every day till her demise stopped her. As nothing happens in prisons that hasn't happened the day before, she could only write her reflections; and the twins hated her reflections, because they were so very like what in their secret moments of slush they were apt to reflect themselves. Their mother had had a horror of slush. There had been none anywhere about her; but it is in the air in Germany, in people's blood, everywhere; and though the twins, owing to the English part of them, had a horror of it too, there it was in them, and they knew it,—genuine German slush.

They felt uncomfortably sure that if they were in prison they would write a diary very much on these lines. For three evenings they had to listen to it, their eyes on Mr. Twist's door. Why didn't he come out and save them? What happy, what glorious evenings they used to have at the Cosmopolitan, spent in intelligent conversation, in a decent give and take—not this button-holing business, this being got into a corner and held down; and alas, how little they had appreciated them! They used to get sleepy and break them off and go to bed. If only he would come out now and talk to them they would sit up all night. They wriggled with impatience in their seats beneath the *épanchements* of the young girl, the strangely and distressingly familiar *épanchements*. The diary was published in a magazine, and after the second evening, when Mrs. Bilton on laying it down announced she would go on with it while they were dressing next morning, they got up very early before Mrs. Bilton was awake and crept out and hid it.

But Li Koo found it and restored it.

Li Koo found everything. He found Mrs. Bilton's outdoor shoes the third morning, although the twins had hidden them most carefully. Their idea was that while she, rendered immobile, waited indoors, they would zealously look for them in all the places where they well knew that they weren't, and perhaps get some conversation with Mr. Twist.

But Li Koo found everything. He found the twins themselves the fourth morning, when, unable any longer to bear Mrs. Bilton's voice, they ran into the woods instead of coming in to breakfast. He seemed to find them at once, to walk unswervingly to their remote and bramble-filled ditch.

In order to save their dignity they said as they scrambled out that they were picking flowers for Mrs. Bilton's breakfast, though the ditch had nothing in it but stones and thorns. Li Koo made no comment. He never did make comments; and his silence and his ubiquitous efficiency made the twins as fidgety with him as they were with Mrs. Bilton for the opposite reason. They had an uncomfortable feeling that he was rather like the *liebe Gott*, —he saw everything, knew everything, and said nothing. In vain they tried, on that walk back as at other times, to pierce his impassivity with genialities. Li Koo—again, they silently reflected, like the *liebe Gott*—had a different sense of geniality from theirs; he couldn't apparently smile; they doubted if he even ever wanted to. Their genialities faltered and froze on their lips.

Besides, they were deeply humiliated by having been found hiding, and were ashamed to find themselves trying anxiously in this manner to conciliate Li Koo. Their dignity on the walk back to the shanty seemed painfully shrunk. They ought never to have condescended to do the childish things they had been doing during the last three days. If they hadn't been found out it would, of course, have remained a private matter between them and their Maker, and then one doesn't mind so much; but they had been found out, and by Li Koo, their own servant. It was intolerable. All the blood of all the Twinklers, Junkers from time immemorial and properly sensitive to humiliation, surged within them. They hadn't felt so naughty and so young for years. They were sure Li Koo didn't believe them about the ditch. They had a dreadful sensation of being led back to Mrs. Bilton by the ear.

If only they could sack Mrs. Bilton!

This thought, immense and startling, came to Anna-Rose, who far more than Anna-Felicitas resented being cut off from Mr. Twist, besides being more naturally impetuous; and as they walked in silence side by side, with Li Koo a little ahead of them, she turned her head and looked at Anna-Felicitas. "Let's give her notice," she murmured, under her breath.

Anna-Felicitas was so much taken aback that she stopped in her walk and stared at Anna-Rose's flushed face.

She too hardly breathed it. The suggestion seemed fantastic in its monstrousness. How could they give anybody so old, so sure of herself, so determined as Mrs. Bilton, notice?

"Give her notice?" she repeated.

A chill ran down Anna-Felicitas's spine. Give Mrs. Bilton notice! It was a great, a breath-taking idea, magnificent in its assertion of independence, of rights; but it needed, she felt, to be approached with caution. They had never given anybody notice in their lives, and they had always thought it must be a most painful thing to do—far, far worse than tipping. Uncle Arthur usedn't to mind it a bit; did it, indeed, with gusto. But Aunt Alice hadn't liked it at all, and came out in a cold perspiration and bewailed her lot to them and wished that people would behave and not place her in such a painful position.

Mrs. Bilton couldn't be said not to have behaved. Quite the contrary. She had behaved too persistently; and they had to endure it the whole twenty-four hours. For Mrs. Bilton had no turn, it appeared, in spite of what she had said at Los Angeles, for solitary contemplation, and after the confusion of the first night, when once she had had time to envisage the situation thoroughly, as she said, she had found that to sit alone downstairs in the uncertain light of the lanterns while the twins went to bed and Mr. Twist wouldn't come out of his room, was not good for her psyche; so she had followed the twins upstairs, and continued to read the young girl's diary to them during their undressing and till the noises coming from their beds convinced her that it was useless to go on any longer. And that morning, the morning they hid in the ditch, she had even done this while they were getting up.

"It isn't to be borne," said Anna-Rose under her breath, one eye on Li Koo's ear which, a little in front of her, seemed slightly slanted backward and sideways in the direction of her voice. "And why should it be? We're not in her power."

"No," said Anna-Felicitas, also under her breath and also watching Li Koo's ear, "but it feels extraordinarily as if we were."

"Yes. And that's intolerable. And it forces us to do silly baby things, wholly unsuited either to our age or our position. Who would have thought we'd ever hide from somebody in a ditch again!" Anna-Rose's voice was almost a sob at the humiliation.

"It all comes from sleeping in the same room," said Anna-Felicitas. "Nobody can stand a thing that doesn't end at night either."

"Of course they can't," said Anna-Rose. "It isn't fair. If you have to have a person all day you oughtn't to have to have the same person all night. Some one else should step in and relieve you then. Just as they do in hospitals."

"Yes," said Anna-Felicitas. "Mr. Twist ought to. He ought to remove her forcibly from our room by marriage."

"No he oughtn't," said Anna-Rose hastily, "because we can remove her ourselves by the simple process of giving her notice."

"I don't believe it's simple," said Anna-Felicia again feeling a chill trickling down her spine.

"Of course it is. We just go to her very politely and inform her that the engagement is terminated on a basis of mutual esteem but inflexible determination."

"And suppose she doesn't stop talking enough to hear?"

"Then we'll hand it to her in writing."

The rest of the way they walked in silence, Anna-Rose with her chin thrust out in defiance, Anna-Felicitas dragging her feet along with a certain reluctance and doubt.

Mrs. Bilton had finished her breakfast when they got back, having seen no sense in letting good food get cold, and was ready to sit and chat to them while they had theirs. She was so busy telling them what she had supposed they were probably doing, that she was unable to listen to their attempted account of what they had done. Thus they were saved from telling humiliating and youthful fibs; but they were also prevented, as by a wall of rock, from getting the speech through to her ear that Anna-Rose, trembling in spite of her defiance, had ready to launch at her. It was impossible to shout at Mrs. Bilton in the way Mr. Twist, when in extremity of necessity, had done. Ladies didn't shout; especially not when they were giving other ladies notice. Anna-Rose, who was quite cold and clammy at the prospect of her speech, couldn't help feeling relieved when breakfast was over and no opportunity for it had been given.

"We'll write it," she whispered to Anna-Felicitas beneath the cover of a lively account Mrs. Bilton was giving them, à propos of their being late for breakfast, of the time it took her, after Mr. Bilton's passing, to get used to his unpunctuality at meals.

That Mr. Bilton, who had breakfasted and dined with her steadily for years, should suddenly leave off being punctual freshly astonished her every day, she said. The clock struck, yet Mr. Bilton continued late. It was poignant, said Mrs. Bilton, this way of being reminded of her loss. Each day she would instinctively expect; each day would come the stab of recollection. The vacancy these non-appearances had made in her life was beyond any words of hers. In fact she didn't possess such words, and doubted if the completest dictionary did either. Everything went just vacant, she said. No need any more to hurry down in the morning, so as to be behind the coffee pot half a minute before the gong went and Mr. Bilton simultaneously appeared. No need any more to think of him when ordering meals. No need any more to eat the dish he had been so fond of and she had found so difficult to digest, Boston baked beans and bacon; yet she found herself ordering it continually after his departure, and choking memorially over the mouthfuls—"And people in Europe," cried Mrs Bilton, herself struck as she talked by this extreme devotion, "say that American women are incapable of passion!"

"We'll write it," whispered Anna-Rose to Anna-Felicitas.

"Write what?" asked Anna-Felicitas abstractedly, who as usual when Mrs. Bilton narrated her reminiscences was absorbed in listening to them and trying to get some clear image of Mr. Bilton.

But she remembered the next moment, and it was like waking up to the recollection that this is the day you have to have a tooth pulled out. The idea of not having the tooth any more, of being free from it charmed and thrilled her, but how painful, how alarming was the prospect of pulling it out!

There was one good thing to be said for Mrs. Bilton's talk, and that was that under its voluminous cover they could themselves whisper occasionally to each other. Anna-Rose decided that if Mrs. Bilton didn't notice that they whispered neither probably would she notice if she wrote. She therefore under Mrs. Bilton's very nose got a pencil and a piece of paper, and with many pauses and an unsteady hand wrote the following:

DEAR MRS. BILTON—For some time past my sister and I have felt that we aren't suited to you, and if you don't mind would you mind regarding the engagement as terminated? We hope you won't think this abrupt, because it isn't really, for we seem to have lived ages since you came, and we've been thinking this over ripely ever since. And we hope you won't take it as anything personal either, because it isn't really. It's only that we feel we're unsuitable, and we're sure we'll go on getting more and more unsuitable. Nobody can help being unsuitable, and we're fearfully sorry. But on the other hand we're inflexible.—Yours affectionately,

ANNA-ROSE and ANNA-FELICITAS TWINKLER

With a beating heart she cautiously pushed the letter across the table under cover of the breakfast *débris* to Anna-Felicitas, who read it with a beating heart and cautiously pushed it back.

Anna-Felicitas felt sure Christopher was being terribly impetuous, and she felt sure she ought to stop her. But what a joy to be without Mrs. Bilton!

The thought of going to bed in the placid sluggishness dear to her heart, without having to listen, to be attentive, to remember to be tidy because if she weren't there would be no room for Mrs. Bilton's things, was too much for her. Authority pursuing her into her bedroom was what she had found most difficult to bear. There must be respite. There must be intervals in every activity or endurance. Even the *liebe Gott*, otherwise so indefatigable, had felt this and arranged for the relaxation of Sundays.

She pushed the letter back with a beating heart, and told herself that she couldn't and never had been able to stop Christopher when she was in this mood of her chin sticking out. What could she do in face of such a chin? And besides, Mrs. Bilton's friends must be missing her very much and ought to have her back. One should always live only with one's own sort of people. Every other way of living, Anna-Felicitas was sure even at this early stage of her existence, was bound to come to a bad end. One could be fond of almost anybody, she held, if they were somewhere else. Even of Uncle Arthur. Even he somehow seemed softened by distance. But for living-together purposes there was only one kind of people possible, and that was one's own kind. Unexpected and various were the exteriors of one's own kind and the places one found them in, but one always knew them. One felt comfortable with them at once; comfortable and placid. Whatever else Mrs. Bilton might be feeling she wasn't feeling placid. That was evident; and it was because she too wasn't with her own kind. With her eyes fixed nervously on Mrs. Bilton who was talking on happily, Anna-Felicitas reasoned with herself in the above manner as she pushed back the letter, instead of, as at the back of her mind she felt she ought to have done, tearing it up.

Anna-Rose folded it and addressed it to Mrs. Bilton. Then she got up and held it out to her.

Anna-Felicitas got up too, her inside feeling strangely unsteady and stirred round and round.

"Would you mind reading this?" said Anna-Rose faintly to Mrs. Bilton, who took the letter mechanically and held it in her hand without apparently noticing it, so much engaged was she by what she was saying.

"We're going out a moment to speak to Mr. Twist," Anna-Rose then said, making for the door and beckoning to Anna-Felicitas, who still stood hesitating.

She slipped out; and Anna-Felicitas, suddenly panic-stricken lest she should be buttonholed all by herself fled after her.

CHAPTER XXVIII

Mr. Twist, his mind at ease, was in the charming room that was to be the tea-room. It was full of scattered fittings and the noise of hammering, but even so anybody could see what a delightful place it would presently turn into.

The Open Arms was to make a specialty of wet days. Those were the days, those consecutive days of downpour that came in the winter and lasted without interruption for a fortnight at a time, when visitors in the hotels were bored beyond expression and ready to welcome anything that could distract them for an hour from the dripping of the rain on the windows. Bridge was their one solace, and they played it from after breakfast till bedtime; but on the fourth or fifth day of doing this, just the mere steady sitting became grievous to them. They ached with weariness. They wilted with boredom. All their natural kindness got damped out of them, and they were cross. Even when they won they were cross, and when they lost it was really distressing. They wouldn't, of course, have been in California at all at such a time if it were possible to know beforehand when the rains would begin, but one never did know, and often it was glorious weather right up to and beyond Christmas. And then how glorious! What a golden place of light and warmth to be in, while in the East one's friends were being battered by blizzards.

Mr. Twist intended to provide a break in the day each afternoon for these victims of the rain. He would come to their rescue. He made up his mind, clear and firm on such matters, that it should become the habit of these unhappy people during the bad weather to motor out to The Open Arms for tea; and, full of forethought, he had had a covered way made, by which one could get out of a car and into the house without being touched by a drop of rain, and he had had a huge open fireplace made across the end of the tea-room, which would crackle and blaze a welcome that would cheer the most dispirited arrival. The cakes, at all times wonderful were on wet days to be more than wonderful. Li Koo had a secret receipt, given him, he said, by his mother for cakes of a quite peculiar and original charm, and these were to be reserved for the rainy season only, and be made its specialty. They were to become known and endeared to the public under the brief designation of Wet Day Cakes. Mr. Twist felt there was something thoroughly American about this name—plain and business-like, and attractively in contrast to the subtle, the almost immoral exquisiteness of the article itself. This cake had been one of those produced by Li Koo from the folds of his garments the day in Los Angeles, and Mr. Twist had happened to be the one of his party who ate it. He therefore knew what he was doing when he decided to call it and its like simply Wet Day Cakes.

The twins found him experimenting with a fire in the fireplace so as to be sure it didn't smoke, and the architect and he were in their shirt sleeves, deftly manipulating wood shavings and logs. There was such a hammering being made by the workmen fixing in the latticed windows, and such a crackling being made by the logs Mr. Twist and the architect kept on throwing on the fire, that only from the sudden broad smile on the architect's face as he turned to pick up another log did Mr. Twist realize that something that hadn't to do with work was happening behind his back.

He looked round and saw the Annas picking their way toward him. They seemed in a hurry.

"Hello," he called out.

They made no reply to this, but continued hurriedly to pick their way among the obstacles in their path. They appeared to be much perturbed. What, he wondered, had they done with Mrs. Bilton? He soon knew.

"We've given Mrs. Bilton notice," panted Anna-Rose as soon as she got near enough to his ear for him to hear her in the prevailing noise.

Her face, as usual when she was moved and excited, was scarlet, her eyes looking bluer and brighter than ever by contrast.

"We simply can't stand it any longer," she went on as Mr. Twist only stared at her.

"And you wouldn't either if you were us," she continued, the more passionately as he still didn't say anything.

"Of course," said Anna-Felicitas, taking a high line, though her heart was full of doubt, "it's your fault really. We could have borne it if we hadn't had to have her at night."

"Come outside," said Mr. Twist, walking toward the door that led on to the verandah.

They followed him, Anna-Rose shaking with excitement, Anna-Felicitas trying to persuade herself that they had acted in the only way consistent with real wisdom.

The architect stood with a log in each hand looking after them and smiling all by himself. There was something about the Twinklers that lightened his heart whenever he caught sight of them. He and his fellow experts had deplored the absence of opportunities since Mrs. Bilton came of developing the friendship begun the first day, and talked of them on their way home in the afternoons with affectionate and respectful familiarity as The Cutes.

"Now," said Mr. Twist, having passed through the verandah and led the twins to the bottom of the garden where he turned and faced them, "perhaps you'll tell me exactly what you've done."

"You should rather inquire what Mrs. Bilton has done," said Anna-Felicitas, pulling herself up as straight and tall as she would go. She couldn't but perceive that the excess of Christopher's emotion was putting her at a disadvantage in the matter of dignity.

"I can guess pretty much what she has done," said Mr. Twist.

"You can't—you can't," burst out Anna-Rose. "Nobody could—nobody ever could—who hadn't been with her day and night."

"She's just been Mrs. Bilton," said Mr. Twist, lighting a cigarette to give himself an appearance of calm.

"Exactly," said Anna-Felicitas. "So you won't be surprised at our having just been Twinklers."

"Oh Lord," groaned Mr. Twist, in spite of his cigarette, "oh, Lord."

"We've given Mrs. Bilton notice," continued Anna-Felicitas, making a gesture of great dignity with her hand, "because we find with regret that she and we are incompatible."

"Was she aware that you were giving it her?" asked Mr. Twist, endeavouring to keep calm.

"We wrote it."

"Has she read it?"

"We put it into her hand, and then came away so that she should have an opportunity of quietly considering it."

"You shouldn't have left us alone with her like this," burst out Anna-Rose again, "you shouldn't really. It was cruel, it was wrong, leaving us high and dry—never seeing you—leaving us to be talked to day and night—to be read to—would *you* like to be read to while you're undressing by somebody still in all their clothes? We've never been able to open our mouths. We've been taken into the field for our airing and brought in again as if we were newborns, or people in prams, or flocks and herds, or prisoners suspected of wanting to escape. We haven't had a minute to ourselves day or night.

There hasn't been a single exchange of ideas, not a shred of recognition that we're grown up. We've been followed, watched, talked to—oh, oh, how awful it has been! Oh, oh, how awful! Forced to be dumb for days—losing our power of speech—"

"Anna-Rose Twinkler," interrupted Mr. Twist sternly, "you haven't lost it. And you not only haven't, but that power of yours has increased tenfold during its days of rest."

He spoke with the exasperation in his voice that they had already heard several times since they landed in America. Each time it took them aback, for Mr. Twist was firmly fixed in their minds as the kindest and gentlest of creatures, and these sudden kickings of his each time astonished them.

On this occasion, however, only Anna-Rose was astonished. Anna-Felicitas all along had had an uncomfortable conviction in the depth of her heart that Mr. Twist wouldn't like what they had done. He would be upset, she felt, as her reluctant feet followed Anna-Rose in search of him. He would be, she was afraid very much upset. And so he was. He was appalled by what had happened. Lose Mrs. Bilton? Lose the very foundation of the party's respectability? And how could he find somebody else at the eleventh hour and where and how could the twins and he live, unchaperoned as they would be, till he had? What a peculiar talent these Annas had for getting themselves and him into impossible situations! Of course at their age they ought to be safe under the wing of a wise and unusually determined mother. Well, poor little wretches, they couldn't help not being under it; but that aunt of theirs ought to have stuck to them—faced up to her husband, and stuck to them.

"I suppose," he said angrily, "being you and not being able to see farther than the ends of your noses, you haven't got any sort of an idea of what you've done."

"We—"

"She—"

"And I don't suppose it's much use my trying to explain, either. Hasn't it ever occurred to you, though I'd be real grateful if you'd give me information on this point—that maybe you don't know everything?"

"She—"

"We—"

"And that till you do know everything, which I take it won't be for some time yet, judging from the samples I've had of your perspicacity, you'd do well not to act without first asking some one's advice? Mine, for instance?"

"She—" began Anna-Rose again; but her voice was trembling, for she couldn't bear Mr. Twist's anger. She was too fond of him. When he looked at her like that her own anger was blown out as if by an icy draught and she could only look back at him piteously.

But Anna-Felicitas, being free from the weaknesses inherent in adoration, besides continuing to perceive how Christopher's feelings put her at a disadvantage, drew Mr. Twist's attention from her by saying with gentleness, "But why add to the general discomfort by being bitter?"

"Bitter!" cried Mr. Twist, still glaring at Anna-Rose.

"Do you dispute that God made us?" inquired Anna-Felicitas, placing herself as it were like a shield between Mr. Twist's wrathful concentration on Christopher and that unfortunate young person's emotion.

"See here," said Mr. Twist turning on her, "I'm not going to argue with you—not about *anything*. Least of all about God."

"I only wanted to point out to you," said Anna-Felicitas mildly, "that that being so, and we not able to help it, there seems little use in being bitter with us because we're not different. In regard to anything fundamental about us that you deplore I'm afraid we must refer you to Providence."

"Say," said Mr. Twist, not in the least appeased by this reasoning but, as Anna-Felicitas couldn't but notice, quite the contrary, "used you to talk like this to that Uncle Arthur of yours? Because if you did, upon my word I don't wonder—"

But what Mr. Twist didn't wonder was fortunately concealed from the twins by the appearance at that moment of Mrs. Bilton, who, emerging from the shades of the verandah and looking about her, caught sight of them and came rapidly down the garden.

There was no escape.

They watched her bearing down on them without a word. It was a most unpleasant moment. Mr. Twist re-lit his cigarette to give himself a countenance, but the thought of all that Mrs. Bilton would probably say was dreadful to him, and his hand couldn't help shaking a little. Anna-Rose showed a guilty tendency to slink behind him. Anna-Felicitas stood motionless, awaiting the deluge. All Mr. Twist's sympathies were with Mrs. Bilton, and he was ashamed that she should have been treated so. He felt that nothing she could say would be severe enough, and he was extraordinarily angry with the Annas. Yet when he saw the injured lady bearing down on them, if he only could he would have picked up an Anna under each arm, guilty as they were, and run and run; so much did he prefer them to Mrs.

Bilton and so terribly did he want, at this moment, to be somewhere where that lady wasn't.

There they stood then, anxiously watching the approaching figure, and the letter in Mrs. Bilton's hand bobbed up and down as she walked, white and conspicuous in the sun against her black dress. What was their amazement to see as she drew nearer that she was looking just as pleasant as ever. They stared at her with mouths falling open. Was it possible, thought the twins, that she was longing to leave but hadn't liked to say so, and the letter had come as a release? Was it possible, thought Mr. Twist with a leap of hope in his heart, that she was taking the letter from a non-serious point of view?

And Mr. Twist, to his infinite relief, was right. For Mrs. Bilton, woman of grit and tenacity, was not in the habit of allowing herself to be dislodged or even discouraged. This was the opening sentence of her remarks when she had arrived, smiling, in their midst. Had she not explained the first night that she was one who, having put her hand to the plough, held on to it however lively the movements of the plough might be? She would not conceal from them, she said, that even Mr Bilton had not, especially, at first, been entirely without such movements. He had settled down, however on finding he could trust her to know better than he did what he wanted. Don't wise wives always? she inquired. And the result had been that no man ever had a more devoted wife while he was alive, or a more devoted widow after he wasn't. She had told him one day, when he was drawing near the latter condition and she was conversing with him, as was only right, on the subject of wills, and he said that his affairs had gone wrong and as far as he could see she would be left a widow and that was about all she would be left—she had told him that if it was any comfort to him to know it, he might rely on it that he would have the most devoted widow any man had ever had, and he said—Mr. Bilton had odd fancies, especially toward the end— that a widow was the one thing a man never could have because he wasn't there by the time he had got her. Yes, Mr. Bilton had odd fancies. And if she had managed, as she did manage, to steer successfully among them, he being a man of ripe parts and character, was it likely that encountering odd fancies in two very young and unformed girls—oh, it wasn't their fault that they were unformed, it was merely because they hadn't had time enough yet—she would be unable, experienced as she was, to steer among them too? Besides, she had a heart for orphans; orphans and dumb animals always had had a special appeal for her. "No, no, Mr. Twist," Mrs. Bilton wound up, putting a hand affectionately on Anna-Rose's shoulder as a more convenient one than Anna-Felicitas's, "my young charges aren't going to be left in the lurch, you may rely on that. I don't undertake a duty without carrying it out. Why, I feel a lasting affection for them already. We've made real progress these few days in intimacy. And I just love to sit and listen to all their fresh young chatter."

CHAPTER XXIX

This was the last of Mr. Twist's worries before the opening day.

Remorseful that he should have shirked helping the Annas to bear Mrs. Bilton, besides having had a severe fright on perceiving how near his shirking had brought the party to disaster, he now had his meals with the others and spent the evenings with them as well. He was immensely grateful to Mrs. Bilton. Her grit had saved them. He esteemed and respected her. Indeed, he shook hands with her then and there at the end of her speech, and told her he did, and the least he could do after that was to come to dinner. But this very genuine appreciation didn't prevent his finding her at close quarters what Anna-Rose, greatly chastened, now only called temperately "a little much," and the result was a really frantic hurrying on of the work. He had rather taken, those first four days of being relieved of responsibility in regard to the twins, to finnicking with details, to dwelling lovingly on them with a sense of having a margin to his time, and things accordingly had considerably slowed down; but after twenty-four hours of Mrs. Bilton they hurried up again, and after forty-eight of her the speed was headlong. At the end of forty-eight hours it seemed to Mr. Twist more urgent than anything he had ever known that he should get out of the shanty, get into somewhere with space in it, and sound-proof walls—lots of walls—and long passages between people's doors; and before the rooms in the inn were anything like finished he insisted on moving in.

"You must turn to on this last lap and help fix them up," he said to the twins. "It'll be a bit uncomfortable at first, but you must just take off your coats to it and not mind."

Mind? Turn to? It was what they were languishing for. It was what, in the arid hours under the ilex tree, collected so ignominiously round Mrs. Bilton's knee they had been panting for, like thirsty dogs with their tongues out. And such is the peculiar blessedness of work that instantly, the moment there was any to be done, everything that was tangled and irritating fell quite naturally into its proper place. Magically life straightened itself out smooth, and left off being difficult. *Arbeit und Liebe*, as their mother used to say, dropping into German whenever a sentence seemed to her to sound better that way—*Arbeit und Liebe*: these were the two great things of life;

the two great angels, as she assured them, under whose spread-out wings lay happiness.

With a hungry zeal, with the violent energy of reaction, the Annas fell upon work. They started unpacking. All the things they had bought in Acapulco, the linen, the china, the teaspoons, the feminine touches that had been piled up waiting in the barn, were pulled out and undone and carried indoors. They sorted, and they counted, and they arranged on shelves. Anna-Rose flew in and out with her arms full. Anna-Felicitas slouched zealously after her, her arms full too when she started, but not nearly so full when she got there owing to the way things had of slipping through them and dropping on to the floor. They were in a blissful, busy confusion. Their faces shone with heat and happiness. Here was liberty; here was freedom; here was true dignity—*Arbeit und Liebe....*

When Mr. Twist, as he did whenever he could, came and looked on for a moment in his shirt sleeves, with his hat on the back of his head and his big, benevolent spectacles so kind, Anna-Rose's cup seemed full. Her dimple never disappeared for a moment. It was there all day long now; and even when she was asleep it still lurked in the corner of her mouth. *Arbeit und Liebe.*

Immense was the reaction of self-respect that took hold of the twins. They couldn't believe they were the people who had been so crude and ill-conditioned as to hide Mrs. Bilton's belongings, and actually finally to hide themselves. How absurd. How like children. How unpardonably undignified. Anna-Rose held forth volubly to this effect while she arranged the china, and Anna-Felicitas listened assentingly, with a kind of grave, ashamed sheepishness.

The result of this reaction was that Mrs. Bilton, whose pressure on them was relieved by the necessity of her too being in several places at once, and who was displaying her customary grit, now became the definite object of their courtesy. They were the mistresses of a house, they began to realize, and as such owed her every consideration. This bland attitude was greatly helped by their not having to sleep with her any more, and they found that the mere coming fresh to her each morning made them feel polite and well-disposed. Besides, they were thoroughly and finally grown-up now, Anna-Rose declared—never, never to lapse again. They had had their lesson, she said, gone through a crisis, and done that which Aunt Alice used to say people did after severe trials, aged considerably.

Anna-Felicitas wasn't quite so sure. Her own recent behaviour had shaken and shocked her too much. Who would have thought she would have gone like that? Gone all to pieces, back to sheer naughtiness, on the first provocation? It was quite easy, she reflected while she worked, and cups kept on detaching themselves mysteriously from her fingers, and tables tumbling over at her approach, to be polite and considerate to somebody you saw very little of, and even, as she found herself doing, to get fond of the person; but suppose circumstances threw one again into the person's continual society, made one again have to sleep in the same room? Anna-Felicitas doubted whether it would be possible for her to stand such a test, in spite of her earnest desire to behave; she doubted, indeed, whether anybody ever did stand that test successfully. Look at husbands.

Meanwhile there seemed no likelihood of its being applied again. Each of them had now a separate bedroom, and Mrs. Bilton had, in the lavish American fashion, her own bathroom, so that even at that point there was no collision. The twins' rooms were connected by a bathroom all to themselves, with no other door into it except the doors from their bedrooms, and Mr. Twist, who dwelt discreetly at the other end of the house, also had a bathroom of his own. It seemed as natural for American architects to drop bathrooms about, thought Anna-Rose, as for the little clouds in the psalms to drop fatness. They shed them just as easily, and the results were just as refreshing. To persons hailing from Pomerania, a place arid of bathrooms, it was the last word of luxury and comfort to have one's own. Their pride in theirs amused Mr. Twist, used from childhood to these civilized arrangements; but then, as they pointed out to him, he hadn't lived in Pomerania, where nothing stood between you and being dirty except the pump.

But it wasn't only the bathrooms that made the inn as planned by Mr. Twist and the architect seem to the twins the most perfect, the most wonderful magic little house in the world: the intelligent American spirit was in every corner, and it was full of clever, simple devices for saving labour—so full that it almost seemed to the Annas as if it would get up quite unaided at six every morning and do itself; and they were sure that if the smallest encouragement were given to the kitchen-stove it would cook and dish up a dinner all alone. Everything in the house was on these lines. The arrangements for serving innumerable teas with ease were admirable. They were marvels of economy and clever thinking-out. The architect was surprised at the attention and thought Mr. Twist concentrated on this particular part of the future housekeeping. "You seem sheer crazy on teas," he remarked; to which Mr. Twist merely replied that he was.

The last few days before the opening were as full of present joy and promise of yet greater joys to come as the last few days of a happy betrothal. They reminded Anna-Felicitas of those days in April, those enchanting days she had always loved the best, when the bees get busy for the first time, and suddenly there are wallflowers and a flowering currant bush and the sound of the lawn being mown and the smell of cut grass. How one's heart leaps up to greet them, she thought. What a thrill of delight rushes through one's body, of new hope, of delicious expectation.

Even Li Koo, the wooden-faced, the brief and rare of speech seemed to feel the prevailing satisfaction and harmony and could be heard in the evenings singing strange songs among his pots. And what he was singing, only nobody knew it, were soft Chinese hymns of praise of the two white-lily girls, whose hair was woven sunlight, and whose eyes were deep and blue even as the waters that washed about the shores of his father's dwelling-place. For Li Koo, the impassive and inarticulate, in secret seethed with passion. Which was why his cakes were so wonderful. He had to express himself somehow.

But while up on their sun-lit, eucalyptus-crowned slopes Mr. Twist and his party—he always thought of them as his party—were innocently and happily busy full of hopefulness and mutual goodwill, down in the town and in the houses scattered over the lovely country round the town, people were talking. Everybody knew about the house Teapot Twist was doing up, for the daily paper had told them that Mr. Edward A. Twist had bought the long uninhabited farmhouse in Pepper Lane known as Batt's, and was converting it into a little *ventre-à-terre* for his widowed mother—launching once more into French, as though there were something about Mr. Twist magnetic to that language. Everybody knew this, and it was perfectly natural for a well-off Easterner to have a little place out West, even if the choice of the little place was whimsical. But what about the Miss Twinklers? Who and what were they? And also, Why?

There were three weeks between the departure of the Twist party from the Cosmopolitan and the opening of the inn, and in that time much had been done in the way of conjecture. The first waves of it flowed out from the Cosmopolitan, and were met almost at once by waves flowing in from the town. Good-natured curiosity gave place to excited curiosity when the rumour got about that the Cosmopolitan had been obliged to ask Mr. Twist to take his *entourage* somewhere else. Was it possible the cute little girls, so well known by sight on Main Street going from shop to shop, were secretly scandalous? It seemed almost unbelievable, but luckily nothing was really unbelievable.

The manager of the hotel, dropped in upon casually by one guest after the other, and interviewed as well by determined gentlemen from the local press, was not to be drawn. His reserve was most interesting. Miss Heap knitted and knitted and was persistently enigmatic. Her silence was most exciting. On the other hand, Mrs. Ridding's attitude was merely one of contempt, dismissing the Twinklers with a heavy gesture. Why think or trouble about a pair of chits like that? They had gone; Albert was quiet again; and wasn't that the gong for dinner?

But doubts as to the private morals of the Twist *entourage* presently were superseded by much graver and more perturbing doubts. Nobody knew when exactly this development took place. Acapulco had been enjoying the first set of doubts. There was no denying that doubts about somebody else's morals were not unpleasant. They did give one, if one examined one's sensations carefully, a distinct agreeable tickle; they did add the kick to lives which, if they had been virtuous for a very long time like the lives of the Riddings, or virgin for a very long time like the life of Miss Heap, were apt to be flat. But from the doubts that presently appeared and overshadowed the earlier ones, one got nothing but genuine discomfort and uneasiness. Nobody knew how or when they started. Quite suddenly they were there.

This was in the November before America's coming into the war. The feeling in Acapulco was violently anti-German. The great majority of the inhabitants, permanent and temporary, were deeply concerned at the conduct of their country in not having, immediately after the torpedoing of the *Lusitania*, joined the Allies. They found it difficult to understand, and were puzzled and suspicious, as well as humiliated in their national pride. Germans who lived in the neighbourhood, or who came across from the East for the winter, were politely tolerated, but the attitude toward them was one of growing watchfulness and distrust; and week by week the whispered stories of spies and gun-emplacements and secret stores of arms in these people's cellars or back gardens, grew more insistent and detailed. There certainly had been at least one spy, a real authentic one, afterward shot in England, who had stayed near-by, and the nerves of the inhabitants had that jumpiness on this subject with which the inhabitants of other countries have long been familiar. All the customary inexplicable lights were seen; all the customary mysterious big motor cars rushed at forbidden and yet unhindered speeds along unusual roads at unaccountable hours; all the customary signalling out to sea was observed and passionately sworn to by otherwise calm people. It was possible, the inhabitants found, to believe with ease things about Germans—those who were having difficulty with religion wished it were equally easy to believe things about God. There was nothing Germans wouldn't think of in the way of plotting, and nothing they wouldn't, having thought of it, carry out with deadly thoroughness and patience.

And into this uneasy hotbed of readiness to believe the worst, arrived the Twinkler twins, rolling their r's about.

It needed but a few inquiries to discover that none of the young ladies' schools in the neighbourhood had been approached on their behalf; hardly inquiries,—mere casual talk was sufficient, ordinary chatting with the principals of these establishments when one met them at the lectures and instructive evenings the more serious members of the community organized and supported. Not many of the winter visitors went to these meetings, but Miss Heap did. Miss Heap had a restless soul. It was restless because it was worried by perpetual thirst,—she couldn't herself tell after what; it wasn't righteousness, for she knew she was still worldly, so perhaps it was culture. Anyhow she would give culture a chance, and accordingly she went to the instructive evenings. Here she met that other side of Acapulco which doesn't play bridge and is proud to know nothing of polo, which believes in education, and goes in for mind training and welfare work; which isn't, that is, well off.

Nobody here had been asked to educate the Twinklers. No classes had been joined by them.

Miss Heap was so enigmatic, she who was naturally of an unquiet and exercise-loving tongue, that this graver, more occupied section of the inhabitants was instantly as much pervaded by suspicions as the idlest of the visitors in the hotels and country houses. It waved aside the innocent appearance and obvious extreme youth of the suspects. Useless to look like cherubs if it were German cherubs you looked like. Useless being very nearly children if it were German children you very nearly were. Why, precisely these qualities would be selected by those terribly clever Germans for the furtherance of their nefarious schemes. It would be quite in keeping with the German national character, that character of bottomless artfulness, to pick out two such young girls with just that type of empty, baby face, and send them over to help weave the gigantic invisible web with which America was presently to be choked dead.

The serious section of Acapulco, the section that thought, hit on this explanation of the Twinklers with no difficulty whatever once its suspicions were roused because it was used to being able to explain everything instantly. It was proud of its explanation, and presented it to the town with much the same air of deprecating but conscious achievement with which one presents drinking-fountains.

Then there was the lawyer to whom Mr. Twist had gone about the guardianship. He said nothing, but he was clear in his mind that the girls were German and that Mr. Twist wanted to hide it. He had thought more highly of Mr. Twist's intelligence than this. Why hide it? America was a neutral country; technically she was neutral, and Germans could come and go as they pleased. Why unnecessarily set tongues wagging? He did not, being of a continuous shrewd alertness himself, a continuous wide-awakeness and minute consideration of consequences, realize, and if he had he wouldn't have believed, the affectionate simplicity and unworldliness of Mr. Twist. If it had been pointed out to him he would have dismissed it as a pose; for a man who makes money in any quantity worth handling isn't affectionately simple and unworldly—he is calculating and steely.

The lawyer was puzzled. How did Mr. Twist manage to have a forehead and a fortune like that, and yet be a fool? True, he had a funny sort of face on him once you got down to the nose part and what came after,—a family sort of face, thought the lawyer; a sort of rice pudding, wet-nurse face. The lawyer listened intently to all the talk and rumours, while himself saying nothing. In spite of being a married man, his scruples about honour hadn't been blunted by the urge to personal freedom and the necessity for daily self-defence that sometimes afflicts those who have wives. He remained honourably silent, as he had said he would, but he listened; and he came to the conclusion that either there was a quite incredible amount of stupidity about the Twist party, or that there was something queer.

What he didn't know, and what nobody knew, was that the house being got ready with such haste was to be an inn. He, like the rest of the world, took the newspapers *ventre-à-terre* theory of the house for granted, and it was only the expectation of the arrival of that respectable lady, the widowed Mrs. Twist, which kept the suspicions a little damped down. They smouldered, hesitating, beneath this expectation; for Teapot Twist's family life had been voluminously described in the entire American press when first his invention caught on, and it was known to be pure. There had been snapshots of the home at Clark where he had been born, of the home at Clark (west aspect) where he would die—Mr. Twist read with mild surprise that his liveliest wish was to die in the old home—of the corner in the Clark churchyard where he would probably be entombed, with an inset showing his father's gravestone on which would clearly be read the announcement that he was the Resurrection and the Life. And there was an inset of his mother, swathed in the black symbols of ungluttable grief,—a most creditable mother. And there were accounts of the activities of another near relative, that Uncle Charles who presided over the Church of Heavenly Refreshment in New York, and a snapshot of his macerated and unrefreshed body in a cassock,—a most creditable uncle.

These articles hadn't appeared so very long ago, and the impression survived and was general that Mr. Twist's antecedents were unimpeachable. If it were true that the house was for his mother and she was shortly arriving, then, although still very odd and unintelligible, it was probable that his being there now with the two Germans was after all capable of explanation. Not much of an explanation, though. Even the moderates who took this view felt this. One wasn't with Germans these days if one could help it. There was no getting away from that simple fact. The inevitable deduction was that Mr. Twist couldn't help it. Why couldn't he help it? Was he enslaved by a scandalous passion for them, a passion cold-bloodedly planned for him by the German Government, which was known to have lists of the notable citizens of the United States with photographs and details of their probable weaknesses, and was exactly informed of their movements? He had met the Twinklers, so it was reported, on a steamer coming over from England. Of course. All arranged by the German Government. That was the peculiar evil greatness of this dangerous people, announced the serious section of Acapulco, again with the drinking-fountain-presentation air, that nothing was too private or too petty to escape their attention, to be turned to their own wicked uses. They were as economical of the smallest scraps of possible usefulness as a French cook of the smallest scraps and leavings of food. Everything was turned to account. Nothing was wasted. Even the mosquitoes in Germany were not wasted. They contained juices, Germans had discovered, especially after having been in contact with human beings, and with these juices the talented but unscrupulous Germans made explosives. Could one sufficiently distrust a nation that did things like that? asked the serious section of Acapulco.

CHAPTER XXX

People were so much preoccupied by the Twinkler problem that they were less interested than they otherwise would have been in the sea-blue advertisements, and when the one appeared announcing that The Open Arms would open wide on the 29th of the month and exhorting the public to watch the signposts, they merely remarked that it wasn't, then, the title of a book after all. Mr. Twist would have been surprised and nettled if he had known how little curiosity his advertisements were exciting; he would have been horrified if he had known the reason. As it was, he didn't know anything. He was too busy, too deeply absorbed, to be vulnerable to rumour; he, and the twins, and Mrs. Bilton were safe from it inside their magic circle of *Arbeit und Liebe*.

Sometimes he was seen in Main Street, that street in Acapulco through which everybody passes at certain hours of the morning, looking as though he had a great deal to do and very little time to do it in; and once or twice the Twinklers were seen there, also apparently very busy, but they didn't now come alone. Mrs. Bilton, the lady from Los Angeles—Acapulco knew all about her and admitted she was a lady of strictest integrity and unimpeachable character, but this only made the Twinkler problem more obscure—came too, and seemed, judging from the animation of her talk, to be on the best of terms with her charges.

But once an idea has got into people's heads, remarked the lawyer, who was nudged by the friend he was walking with as the attractive trio were seen approaching,—Mrs. Bilton with her black dress and her snowy hair setting off, as they in their turn set her off, the twins in their clean white frocks and shining youth,—once an idea has got into people's heads it sticks. It is slow to get in, and impossible to get out. Yet on the face of it, was it likely that Mrs. Bilton—

"Say," interrupted his friend, "since when have you joined up with the water-blooded believe-nothing-but-good-ites?"

And only his personal affection for the lawyer restrained him from using the terrible word pro-German; but it had been in his mind.

The day before the opening, Miss Heap heard from an acquaintance in the East to whom she had written in her uneasiness, and who was staying with some people living in Clark. Miss Heap wrote soon after the departure—she didn't see why she shouldn't call it by its proper name and say right out expulsion—of the Twist party from the Cosmopolitan, but letters take a long time to get East and answers take the same long time to come back in, and messages are sometimes slow in being delivered if the other person doesn't realize, as one does oneself, the tremendous interests that are at stake. What could be a more tremendous interest, and one more adapted to the American genius, than safe-guarding public morals? Miss Heap wrote before the sinister rumours of German machinations had got about; she was still merely at the stage of uneasiness in regard to the morals of the Twist party; she couldn't sleep at night for thinking of them. Of course if it were true that his mother was coming out ... but was she? Miss Heap somehow felt unable to believe it. "Do tell your friends in Clark," she wrote, "how *delighted* we all are to hear that Mrs. Twist is going to be one of us in our sunny refuge here this winter. A real warm welcome awaits her. Her son is working day and night getting the house ready for her, helped indefatigably by the two Miss Twinklers."

She had to wait over a fortnight for the answer, and by the time she got it those other more terrible doubts had arisen, the doubts as to the exact position occupied by the Twinklers and Mr. Twist in the German secret plans for, first, the pervasion, and, second, the invasion of America; and on reading the opening lines of the letter Miss Heap found she had to sit down, for her legs gave way beneath her.

It appeared that Mrs. Twist hadn't known where her son was till Miss Heap's letter came. He had left Clark in company of the two girls mentioned, and about whom his mother knew nothing, the very morning after his arrival home from his long absence in Europe. That was all his mother knew. She was quite broken. Coming on the top of all her other sorrow her only son's behaviour had been a fearful, perhaps a finishing blow, but she was such a good woman that she still prayed for him. Clark was horrified. His mother had decided at first she would try to shield him and say nothing, but when she found that nobody had the least idea of what he had done she felt she owed it to her friends to be open and have no secrets from them. Whatever it cost her in suffering and humiliation she would be frank. Anything was better than keeping up false appearances to friends who believed in you. She was a brave woman, a splendid woman. The girls—poor Mrs. Twist— were Germans.

On reading this Miss Heap was all of a tingle. Her worst suspicions hadn't been half bad enough. Here was everything just about as black as it could be; and Mr Twist, a well-known and universally respected American citizen, had been turned, by means of those girls playing upon weaknesses she shuddered to think of but that she had reason to believe, from books she had studied and conversations she had reluctantly taken part in, were not altogether uncommon, into a cat's-paw of the German Government.

What should she do? What should she say? To whom should she go? Which was the proper line of warning for her to take? It seemed to her that the presence of these people on the Pacific coast was a real menace to its safety, moral and physical; but how get rid of them? And if they were got rid of wouldn't it only be exposing some other part of America, less watchful, less perhaps able to take care of itself, to the ripening and furtherance of their schemes, whatever their schemes might be? Even at that moment. Miss Heap unconsciously felt that to let the Twinklers go would be to lose thrills. And she was really thrilled. She prickled with excitement and horror. Her circulation hadn't been so good for years. She wasn't one to dissect her feelings, so she had no idea of how thoroughly she was enjoying herself. And it was while she sat alone in her bedroom, her fingers clasping and unclasping the arms of her chair, her feet nervously nibbing up and down on the thick soft carpet, hesitating as to the best course for her to take, holding her knowledge meanwhile tight, hugging it for a little altogether to herself, her very own, shared as yet by no one,—it was while she sat there, that people out of doors in Acapulco itself, along the main roads, out in the country towards Zamora on the north and San Blas on the south, became suddenly aware of new signposts.

They hadn't been there the day before. They all turned towards the spot at the foot of the mountains where Pepper Lane was. They all pointed, with a long white finger, in that direction. And on them all was written in plain, sea-blue letters, beneath which the distance in miles or fractions of a mile was clearly marked, *To The Open Arms.*

Curiosity was roused at last. People meeting each other in Main Street stopped to talk about these Arms wondered where and what they were, and decided to follow the signposts that afternoon in their cars and track them down. They made up parties to go and track together. It would be a relief to have something a little different to do. What on earth could The Open Arms be? Hopes were expressed that they weren't something religious. Awful to follow signposts out into the country only to find they landed you in a meeting-house.

At lunch in the hotels, and everywhere where people were together, the signposts were discussed. Miss Heap heard them being discussed from her solitary table, but was so much taken up with her own exciting thoughts that she hardly noticed. After lunch, however, as she was passing out of the restaurant, still full of her unshared news and still uncertain as to whom she should tell it first, Mr. Ridding called out from his table and said he supposed she was going too.

They had been a little chilly to each other since the afternoon of the conversation with the Twinklers, but he would have called out to any one at that moment He was sitting waiting while Mrs. Ridding finished her lunch, his own lunch finished long ago, and was in the condition of muffled but extreme exasperation which the unoccupied watching of Mrs. Ridding at meals produced. Every day three times this happened, that Mr. Ridding got through his meal first by at least twenty minutes and then sat trying not to mind Mrs. Ridding. She wasn't aware of these efforts. They would greatly have shocked her; for to try not to mind one's wife surely isn't what decent, loving husbands ever have to do.

"Going where?" asked Miss Heap, stopping by the table; whereupon Mr. Ridding had the slight relief of getting up.

Mrs. Ridding continued to eat impassively.

"Following these new signposts that are all over the place," said Mr. Ridding. "Sort of paper-chase business."

"Yes. I'd like to. Were you thinking of going, Mrs. Ridding?"

"After our nap," said Mrs. Ridding, steadily eating. "I'll take you. Car at four o'clock, Albert."

She didn't raise her eyes from her plate, and as Miss Heap well knew that Mrs. Ridding was not open to conversation during meals and as she had nothing to say to Mr. Ridding, she expressed her thanks and pleasure, and temporarily left them.

This was a day of shocks and thrills. When the big limousine—symbol of Mrs. Ridding's power, for Mr. Ridding couldn't for the life of him see why he should have to provide a strange old lady with cars, and yet did so on an increasing scale of splendour—arrived at the turn on the main road to San Blas which leads into Pepper Lane and was confronted by the final signpost pointing up it, for the first time The Open Arms and the Twist and Twinkler party entered Miss Heap's mind in company. So too did they enter Mr. Ridding's mind; and they only remained outside Mrs. Ridding's because of her profound uninterest. Her thoughts were merged in aspic. That was the worst of aspic when it was as good as it was at the Cosmopolitan; one wasn't able to leave off eating it quite in time, and then, unfortunately, had to go on thinking of it afterwards.

The Twist house, remembered her companions simultaneously, was in Pepper Lane. Odd that this other thing, whatever it was, should happen to be there too. Miss Heap said nothing, but sat very straight and alert, her eyes everywhere. Mr. Ridding of course said nothing either. Not for worlds would he have mentioned the word Twist, which so instantly and inevitably suggested that other and highly controversial word Twinkler. But he too sat all eyes; for anyhow he might in passing get a glimpse of the place containing those cunning little bits of youngness, the Twinkler sisters, and even with any luck a glimpse of their very selves.

Up the lane went the limousine, slowly because of the cars in front of it. It was one of a string of cars, for the day was lovely, there was no polo, and nobody happened to be giving a party. All the way out from Acapulco they had only had to follow other cars. Cars were going, and cars were coming back. The cars going were full of solemn people, pathetically anxious to be interested. The cars coming back were full of animated people who evidently had achieved interest.

Miss Heap became more and more alert as they approached the bend in the lane round which the Twist house was situated. She had been there before, making a point of getting a friend to motor her past it in order to see what she could for herself, but Mr. Ridding, in spite of his desire to go and have a look too, had always, each time he tried to, found Mrs. Ridding barring the way. So that he didn't exactly know where it was; and when on turning the corner the car suddenly stopped, and putting his head out—he was sitting backwards—- he saw a great, old-fashioned signboard, such as he was accustomed to in pictures of ancient English village greens, with

The Open Arms

in medieval letters painted on it, all he said was, "Guess we've run it to earth."

Miss Heap sat with her hands in her lap, staring. Mrs. Ridding, her mind blocked by aspic, wasn't receiving impressions. She gazed with heavy eyes straight in front of her. There she saw cars. Many cars. All stopped at this particular spot. With a dull sensation of fathomless fatigue she dimly wondered at them.

"Looks as though it's a hostelry," said Mr. Ridding, who remembered his Dickens; and he blinked up, craning his head out, at the signboard, on which through a gap in the branches of the pepper trees a shaft of brilliant late afternoon sun was striking. "Don't see one, though."

He jerked his thumb. "Up back of the trees there, I reckon," he said.

Then he prepared to open the door and go and have a look.

A hand shot out of Miss Heap's lap at him. "Don't," she said quickly. "Don't, Mr. Ridding."

There was a little green gate in the thick hedge that grew behind the pepper trees, and some people he knew, who had been in the car in front, were walking up to it. Some other people he knew had already got to it, and were standing talking together with what looked like leaflets in their hands. These leaflets came out of a green wooden box fastened on to one of the gate-posts, with the words *Won't you take one?* painted on it.

Mr. Ridding naturally wanted to go and take one, and here was Miss Heap laying hold of him and saying "Don't."

"Don't what?" he asked looking down at her, his hand on the door.

"Hello Ridding," called out one of the people he knew. "No good getting out. Show doesn't open till to-morrow at four. Can't get in to-day. Gate's bolted. Nothing doing."

And then the man detached himself from the group at the gate and came over to the car with a leaflet in his hand.

"Say—" he said,—"how are you to-day, Miss Heap? Mrs. Ridding, your humble servant—say, look at this. Teapot Twist wasn't born yesterday when it comes to keeping things dark. No mention of his name on this book of words, but it's the house he was doing up all right, and it is to be used as an inn. Afternoon-tea inn. Profits to go to the American Red Cross. Price per head five dollars. Bit stiff, five dollars for tea. Wonder where those Twinkler girls come in. Here—you have this, Ridding, and study it. I'll get another." And taking off his hat a second time to the ladies he went back to his friends.

In great agitation Miss Heap turned to Mrs. Ridding, whose mind, galvanized by the magic words Twist and Twinkler, was slowly heaving itself free of aspic. "Perhaps we had best go back to the hotel, Mrs Ridding," said Miss Heap, her voice shaking. "There's something I wish particularly to tell you. I ought to have done so this morning, directly I knew, but I had no idea of course that this...." She waved a hand at the signboard, and collapsed into speechlessness.

"Albert—hotel," directed Mrs. Ridding.

And Mr. Ridding, clutching the leaflet, his face congested with suppressed emotions, obediently handed on the order through the speaking-tube to the chauffeur.

CHAPTER XXXI

"It's *perfect*," said the twins, looking round the tea-room.

This was next day, at a quarter to four. They had been looking round saying it was perfect at intervals since the morning. Each time they finished getting another of the little tables ready, each time they brought in and set down another bowl of flowers they stood back and gazed a moment in silence, and then said with one voice, "It's *perfect*."

Mr. Twist, though the house was not, as we have seen, quite as sober, quite as restrained in its effect as he had intended, was obliged to admit that it did look very pretty. And so did the Annas. Especially the Annas. They looked so pretty in the sea-blue frocks and little Dutch caps and big muslin aprons that he took off his spectacles and cleaned them carefully so as to have a thoroughly uninterrupted view; and as they stood at a quarter to four gazing round the room, he stood gazing at them, and when they said "It's *perfect*," he said, indicating them with his thumb, "Same here," and then they all laughed for they were all very happy, and Mrs. Bilton, arrayed exactly as Mr. Twist had pictured her when he engaged her in handsome black, her white hair beautifully brushed and neat, crossed over to the Annas and gave each of them a hearty kiss—for luck, she said—which Mr. Twist watched with an odd feeling of jealousy.

"I'd like to do that," he thought, filled with a sudden desire to hug. Then he said it out loud. "I'd like to do that," he said boldly. And added, "As it's the opening day."

"I don't think it would afford you any permanent satisfaction," said Anna-Felicitas placidly. "There's nothing really to be gained, we think, by kissing. Of course," she added politely to Mrs. Bilton, "we like it very much as an expression of esteem."

"Then why not in that spirit—" began Mr. Twist.

"We don't hold with kissing," said Anna-Rose quickly, turning very red. Intolerable to be kissed *en famille*. If it had to be done at all, kissing should be done quietly, she thought. But she and Anna-Felicitas didn't hold with it anyhow. Never. Never. To her amazement she found tears in her eyes. Well, of all the liquid idiots.... It must be that she was so happy. She had never been so happy. Where on earth had her handkerchief got to....

"Hello," said Mr. Twist, staring at her.

Anna-Felicitas looked at her quickly.

"It's merely bliss," she said, taking the corner of her beautiful new muslin apron to Christopher's eyes. "Excess of it. We are, you know," she said, smiling over her shoulder at Mr. Twist, so that the corner of her apron, being undirected, began dabbing at Christopher's perfectly tearless ears, "quite extraordinarily happy, and all through you. Nevertheless Anna-R." she continued, addressing her with firmness while she finished her eyes and began her nose, "You may like to be reminded that there's only ten minutes left now before all those cars that were here yesterday come again, and you wouldn't wish to embark on your career as a waitress hampered by an ugly face, would you?"

But half an hour later no cars had come. Pepper Lane was still empty. The long shadows lay across it in a beautiful quiet, and the crickets in the grass chirruped undisturbed. Twice sounds were heard as if something was coming up it, and everybody flew to their posts—Li Koo to the boiling water, Mrs. Bilton to her raised desk at the end of the room, and the twins to the door—but the sounds passed on along the road and died away round the next corner.

At half-past four the *personnel* of The Open Arms was sitting about silently in a state of increasing uneasiness, when Mr. Ridding walked in.

There had been no noise of a car to announce him; he just walked in mopping his forehead, for he had come in the jitney omnibus to the nearest point and had done the last mile on his own out-of-condition feet. Mrs. Ridding thought he was writing letters in the smoking-room. She herself was in a big chair on the verandah, and with Miss Heap and most of the other guests was discussing The Open Arms in all its probable significance. He hadn't been able to get away sooner because of the nap. He had gone through with the nap from start to finish so as not to rouse suspicion. He arrived very hot, but with a feeling of dare-devil running of risks that gave him great satisfaction. He knew that he would cool down again presently and that then the consequences of his behaviour would be unpleasant to reflect upon, but meanwhile his blood was up.

He walked in feeling not a day older than thirty,—most gratifying sensation. The *personnel*, after a moment's open-mouthed surprise, rushed to greet him. Never was a man more welcome. Never had Mr. Ridding been so warmly welcomed anywhere in his life.

"Now isn't this real homey," he said, beaming at Anna-Rose who took his stick. "Wish I'd known you were going to do it, for then I'd have had something to look forward to."

"Will you have tea or coffee?" asked Anna-Felicitas, trying to look very solemn and like a family butler but her voice quivering with eagerness. "Or perhaps you would prefer frothed chocolate? Each of these beverages can be provided either hot or iced—"

"There's ice-cream as well," said Anna-Rose, tumultuously in spite of also trying to look like a family butler. "*I'd* have ice-cream if I were you. There's more body in it. Cold, delicious body. And you look so hot. Hot things should always as soon as possible be united to cold things, so as to restore the proper balance—"

"And there's some heavenly stuff called cinnamon-toast—hot, you know, but if you have ice-cream at the same time it won't matter," said Anna-Felicitas, hanging up his hat for him. "I don't know whether you've studied the leaflets," she continued, "but in case you haven't I feel I oughtn't to conceal from you that the price is five dollars whatever you have."

"So that," said Anna-Rose, "you needn't bother about trying to save, for you can't."

"Then I'll have tea to start with and see how I get on," said Mr. Ridding, sitting down in the chair Anna-Felicitas held for him and beaming up at her.

She flicked an imaginary grain of dust off the cloth with the corner of her apron to convey to him that she knew her business, and hurried away to give the order. Indeed, they both hurried away to give the order.

"Say—" called out Mr. Ridding, for he thought one Anna would have been enough for this and he was pining to talk to them; but the twins weren't to be stopped from both giving the very first order, and they disappeared together into the pantry.

Mrs. Bilton sat in the farthest corner at her desk, apparently absorbed in an enormous ledger. In this ledger she was to keep accounts and to enter the number of teas, and from this high seat she was to preside over the activities of the *personnel*. She had retired hastily to it on the unexpected entrance of Mr. Ridding, and pen in hand was endeavouring to look as if she were totting up figures. As the pages were blank this was a little difficult. And it was difficult to sit there quiet. She wanted to get down and go and chat with the guest; she felt she had quite a good deal she could say to him; she had a great itch to go and talk, but Mr. Twist had been particular that to begin with, till the room was fairly full, he and she should leave the guests entirely to the Annas.

He himself was going to keep much in the background at all times, but through the half-open door of his office he could see and hear; and he couldn't help thinking, as he sat there watching and observed the effulgence of the beams the old gentleman just arrived turned on the twins, that the first guest appeared to be extraordinarily and undesirably affectionate. He thought he had seen him at the Cosmopolitan, but wasn't sure. He didn't know that the Annas, after their conversation with him there, felt towards him as old friends, and he considered their manner was a little unduly familiar. Perhaps, after all, he thought uneasily, Mrs. Bilton had better do the waiting and the Annas sit with him in the office. The ledger could be written up at the end of the day. Or he could hire somebody....

Mr. Twist felt worried, and pulled at his ear. And why was there only one guest? It was twenty minutes to five; and this time yesterday the road had been choked with cars. He felt very much worried. With every minute this absence of guests grew more and more remarkable. Perhaps he had better, this beings the opening day, go in and welcome the solitary one there was. Perhaps it would be wise to elaborate the idea of the inn for his edification, so that he could hand on what he had heard to those others who so unaccountably hadn't come.

He got up and went into the other room; and just as Anna-Felicitas was reappearing with the teapot followed by Anna-Rose with a tray of cakes, Mr. Ridding, who was sitting up expectantly and giving his tie a little pat of adjustment, perceived bearing down upon him that fellow Teapot Twist.

This was a blow. He hadn't run risks and walked in the afternoon heat to sit and talk to Twist. Mr. Ridding was a friendly and amiable old man, and at any other time would have talked to him with pleasure; but he had made up his mind for the Twinklers as one makes up one's mind for a certain dish and is ravaged by strange fury if it isn't produced. Besides, hang it all, he was going to pay five dollars for his tea, and for that sum he ought to least to have it under the conditions he preferred.

"Glad to meet you, Mr. Twist," he nevertheless said as Mr. Twist introduced himself, his eyes, however, roving over the ministering Annas, — a roving Mr. Twist noticed with fresh misgivings.

It made him sit down firmly at the table and say, "If you don't mind, Mr. —"

"Ridding is my name."

"If you don't mind, Mr. Ridding, I'd like to explain our objects to you."

But he couldn't help wondering what he would do if there were several tables with roving-eyed guests at them, it being clear that there wouldn't be enough of him in such a case to go round.

Mr. Ridding, for his part, couldn't help wondering why the devil Teapot Twist sat down unasked at his table. Five dollars. Come now. For that a man had a right to a table to himself.

But anyhow the Annas wouldn't have stayed talking for at that moment a car stopped in the lane and quite a lot of footsteps were heard coming up the neatly sanded path. Mr. Ridding pricked up his ears, for from the things he had heard being said all the evening before and all that morning in Acapulco, besides most of the night from the lips of that strange old lady with whom by some dreadful mistake he was obliged to sleep, he hadn't supposed there would be exactly a rush.

Four young men came in. Mr. Ridding didn't know them. No class, he thought, looking them over; and was seized with a feeling of sulky vexation suitable to twenty when he saw with what enthusiasm the Twinklers flew to meet them. They behaved, thought Mr. Ridding crossly, as if they were the oldest and dearest friends.

"Who are they?" he asked curtly of Mr. Twist, cutting into the long things he was saying.

"Only the different experts who helped me rebuild the place," said Mr. Twist a little impatiently; he too had pricked up his ears in expectation at the sound of all those feet, and was disappointed.

He continued what Mr. Ridding, watching the group of young people, called sulkily to himself his rigmarole, but continued more abstractedly. He also was watching the Annas and the experts. The young men were evidently in the highest spirits, and were walking round the Annas admiring their get-up and expressing their admiration in laughter and exclamations. One would have thought they had known each other all their lives. The twins were wreathed in smiles. They looked as pleased, Mr. Twist thought, as cats that are being stroked. Almost he could hear them purring. He glanced helplessly across to where Mrs. Bilton sat, as he had told her, bent pen in hand over the ledger. She didn't move. It was true he had told her to sit like that, but hadn't the woman any imagination? What she ought to do now was to bustle forward and take that laughing group in charge.

"As I was telling you—" resumed Mr. Twist, returning with an effort to Mr. Ridding, only to find his eyes fixed on the young people and catch an unmistakably thwarted look in his face.

In a flash Mr. Twist realized what he had come for,—it was solely to see and talk to the twins. He must have noticed them at the Cosmopolitan, and come out just for them. Just for that. "Unprincipled old scoundrel," said Mr. Twist under his breath, his ears flaming. Aloud he said, "As I was telling you—" and went on distractedly with his rigmarole.

Then some more people came in. They had motored, but the noise the experts were making had drowned the sound of their arrival. Mr. Ridding and Mr. Twist, both occupied in glowering at the group in the middle of the room, were made aware of their presence by Anna-Felicitas suddenly dropping the pencil and tablets she had been provided with for writing down orders and taking an uncertain and obviously timid step forward.

They both looked round in the direction of her reluctant step, and saw a man and two women standing on the threshold. Mr. Twist, of course, didn't know them; he hardly knew anybody, even by sight. But Mr. Ridding did. That is, he knew them well by sight and had carefully avoided knowing them any other way, for they were Germans.

Mr. Ridding was one of those who didn't like Germans. He was a man who liked or disliked what his daily paper told him to, and his daily paper was anti-German. For reasons natural to one who disliked Germans and yet at the same time had a thirstily affectionate disposition, he declined to believe the prevailing theory about the Twinklers. Besides, he didn't believe it anyhow. At that age people were truthful, and he had heard them explain they had come from England and had acquired their rolling r's during a sojourn abroad. Why should he doubt? But he refrained from declaring his belief in their innocence of the unpopular nationality, owing to a desire to avoid trouble in that bedroom he couldn't call his but was obliged so humiliatingly to speak of as ours. Except, however, for the Twinklers, for all other persons of whom it was said that they were Germans, naturalized or not, immediate or remote, he had, instructed by his newspaper, what his called a healthy instinctive abhorrence.

"And she's got it too," he thought, much gratified at this bond between them, as he noted Anna-Felicitas's hesitating and reluctant advance to meet the new guests. "There's proof that people are wrong."

But what Anna-Felicitas had got was stage-fright; for here were the first strangers, the first real, proper visitors such as any shop or hotel might have. Mr. Ridding was a friend. So were the experts friends. This was trade coming in,—real business being done. Anna-Felicitas hadn't supposed she would be shy when the long-expected and prepared-for moment arrived, but she was. And it was because the guests seemed so disconcertingly pleased to see her. Even on the threshold the whole three stood smiling broadly at her. She hadn't been prepared for that, and it unnerved her.

"Charming, charming," said the newcomers, advancing towards her and embracing the room and the tables and the Annas in one immense inclusive smile of appreciation.

"Know those?" asked Mr. Ridding, again cutting into Mr. Twist's explanations.

"No," said he.

"Wangelbeckers," said Mr. Ridding briefly.

"Indeed," said Mr. Twist, off whose ignorance the name glanced harmlessly. "Well, as I was telling yous—"

"But this is delicious—this is a conception of genius," said Mr. Wangelbecker all-embracingly, after he had picked up Anna-Felicitas's tablets and restored them to her with a low bow.

"Charming, charming," said Mrs. Wangelbecker, looking round.

"Real cunning," said Miss Wangelbecker, "as they say here." And she laughed at Anna-Felicitas with an air of mutual understanding.

"Will you have tea or coffee?" asked Anna-Felicitas nervously. "Or perhaps you would prefer frothed chocolate. Each of these beverages can be—"

"Delicious, delicious," said Mrs. Wangelbecker, enveloping Anna-Felicitas in her smile.

"The frothed chocolate is very delicious," said Anna-Felicitas with a kind of grave nervousness.

"Ah—charming, charming," said Mrs. Wangelbecker, obstinately appreciative.

"And there's ice-cream as well," said Anna-Felicitas, her eyes on her tablets so as to avoid seeing the Wangelbecker smile. "And—and a great many kinds of cakes—"

"Well, hadn't we better sit down first," said Mr. Wangelbecker genially, "or are all the tables engaged?"

"Oh I *beg* your pardon," said Anna-Felicitas, blushing and moving hastily towards a table laid for three.

"Ah—that's better," said Mr. Wangelbecker, following closely on her heels. "Now we can go into the serious business of ordering what we shall eat comfortably. But before I sit down allow me to present myself. My name is Wangelbecker. An honest German name. And this is my wife. She too had an honest German name before she honoured mine by accepting it—she was a Niedermayer. And this is my daughter, with whom I trust you will soon be friends."

And they all put out their hands to be shaken, and Anna-Felicitas shook them.

"Look at that now," said Mr. Ridding watching.

"As I was telling you—" said Mr. Twist irritably, for really why should Anna II. shake hands right off with strangers? Her business was to wait, not to get shaking hands. He must point out to her very plainly.

"Pleased to meet you Miss von Twinkler," said Mrs. Wangelbecker; and at this Anna-Felicitas was so much startled that she dropped her tablets a second time.

"As they say here," laughed Miss Wangelbecker, again with that air of mutual comprehension.

"But they don't," said Anna Felicitas hurriedly, taking her tablets from the restoring hand of Mr. Wangelbecker and forgetting to thank him.

"What?" said Mrs. Wangelbecker. "When you are both so charming that for once the phrase must be sincere?"

"Miss von Twinkler means she finds it wiser not to use her title," said Mr. Wangelbecker. "Well, perhaps—perhaps. Wiser perhaps from the point of view of convenience. Is that where you will sit, Güstchen? Still, we Germans when we are together can allow ourselves the refreshment of being ourselves, and I hope to be frequently the means of giving you the relief, you and your charming sister, of hearing yourselves addressed correctly. It is a great family, the von Twinklers. A great family. In these sad days we Germans must hang together—"

Anna-Felicitas stood, tablets in hand, looking helplessly from one Wangelbecker to the other. The situation was beyond her.

"But—" she began; then stopped. "Shall I bring you tea or coffee?" she ended by asking again.

"Well now this is amusing," said Mr. Wangelbecker, sitting down comfortably and leaning his elbows on the table. "Isn't it, Güstchen. To see a von Twinkler playing at waiting on us."

"Charming, charming," said his wife.

"It's real sporting," said his daughter, laughing up at Anna-Felicitas, again with comprehension,—with, almost, a wink. "You must let me come and help. I'd look nice in that costume, wouldn't I mother."

"There is also frothed choc—"

"I suppose, now, Mr. Twist—he must be completely sympathy—" interrupted Mr. Wangelbecker confidentially, leaning forward and lowering his voice a little.

Anna-Felicitas gazed at him blankly. Some more people were coming in at the door, and behind them she could see on the path yet more, and Anna-Rose was in the pantry fetching the tea for the experts.

"Would you mind telling me what I am to bring you?" she asked. "Because I'm afraid—"

Mr. Wangelbecker turned his head in the direction she was looking.

"Ah—" he said getting up, "but this is magnificent Güstchen, here are Mrs. Kleinbart and her sister—why, and there come the Diederichs—but splendid, splendid—"

"Say," said Mr. Ridding, turning to Mr. Twist with a congested face, "ever been to Berlin?"

"No," said Mr. Twist, annoyed by a question of such wanton irrelevance flung into the middle of his sentence.

"Well, it's just like this."

"Like this?" repeated Mr. Twist.

"Those there," said Mr. Ridding, jerking his head. "That lot there—see 'em any day in Berlin, or Frankfurt, or any other of their confounded towns."

"I don't follow," said Mr. Twist, very shortly indeed.

"Germans," said Mr. Ridding.

"Germans?"

"All Germans," said Ridding.

"All Germans?"

"Wangelbeckers are Germans," said Mr. Ridding. "Didn't you know?"

"No," said Mr. Twist.

"So are the ones who've just come in."

"Germans?"

"All Germans. So are those behind, just coming in."

"Germans?"

"All Germans."

There was a pause, during which Mr. Twist stared round the room. It was presenting quite a populous appearance. Then he said slowly, "Well I'm damned."

And Mr. Ridding for the first time looked pleased with Mr. Twist. He considered that at last he was talking sense.

"Mr. Twist," he said heartily, "I'm exceedingly glad you're damned. It was what I was sure at the bottom of my heart you would be. Shake hands, sir."

CHAPTER XXXII

That evening depression reigned in The Open Arms.

Mr. Twist paced up and down the tea-room deep in thought that was obviously unpleasant and perplexed; Mrs. Bilton went to bed abruptly, after a short outpour of words to the effect that she had never seen so many Germans at once before, that her psyche was disharmonious to Germans, that they made her go goose-fleshy just as cats in a room made Mr. Bilton go goose-fleshy in the days when he had flesh to go it with, that she hadn't been aware the inn was to be a popular resort and rendezvous for Germans, and that she wished to speak alone with Mr. Twist in the morning; while the twins, feeling the ominousness of this last sentence,—as did Mr. Twist, who started when he heard it,—and overcome by the lassitude that had succeeded the shocks of the afternoon, a lassitude much increased by their having tried to finish up the pailsful of left-over ices and the huge piles of cakes slowly soddening in their own souring cream, went out together on to the moonlit verandah and stood looking up in silence at the stars. There they stood in silence, and thought things about the immense distance and indifference of those bright, cold specks, and how infinitely insignificant after all they, the Twinklers were, and how they would both in any case be dead in a hundred years. And this last reflection afforded them somehow a kind of bleak and draughty comfort.

Thus the first evening, that was to have been so happy, was spent by everybody in silence and apart. Li Koo felt the atmosphere of oppression even in his kitchen, and refrained from song. He put away, after dealing with it cunningly so that it should keep until a more propitious hour, a wonderful drink he had prepared for supper in celebration of the opening day—"Me make li'l celebrity," he had said, squeezing together strange essences and fruits—and he moved softly about so as not to disturb the meditations of the master. Li Koo was perfectly aware of what had gone wrong: it was the unexpected arrival to tea of Germans. Being a member of the least blood-thirsty of the nations, he viewed Germans with peculiar disfavour and understood his master's prolonged walking up and down. Also he had noted through a crack in the door the way these people of blood and death crowded round the white-lily girls; and was not that sufficient in itself to cause his master's numerous and rapid steps?

Numerous indeed that evening were Mr. Twist's steps. He felt he must think, and he could think better walking up and down. Why had all those Germans come? Why, except old Ridding and the experts, had none of the Americans come? It was very strange. And what Germans! So cordial, so exuberant to the twins, so openly gathering them to their bosoms, as though they belonged there. And so cordial too to him, approaching him in spite of his withdrawals, conveying to him somehow, his disagreeable impression had been, that he and they perfectly understood each other. Then Mrs. Bilton; was she going to give trouble? It looked like it. It looked amazingly like it. Was she after all just another edition of his mother, and unable to discriminate between Germans and Germans, between the real thing and mere technicalities like the Twinklers? It is true he hadn't told her the twins were German, but then neither had he told her they weren't. He had been passive. In Mrs. Bilton's presence passivity came instinctively. Anything else involved such extreme and unusual exertion. He had never had the least objection to her discovering their nationality for herself, and indeed had been surprised she hadn't done so long ago, for he felt sure she would quickly begin to love the Annas, and once she loved them she wouldn't mind what their father had happened to be. He had supposed she did love them. How affectionately she had kissed them that very afternoon and wished them luck. Was all that nothing? Was lovableness nothing, and complete innocence, after all in the matter of being born, when weighed against the one fact of the von? What he would do if Mrs. Bilton left him he couldn't imagine. What would happen to The Open Arms and the twins in such a case, his worried brain simply couldn't conceive.

Out of the corner of his eye every time he passed the open door on to the verandah he could see the two Annas standing motionless on its edge, their up-turned faces, as they gazed at the stars, white in the moonlight and very serious. Pathetic children. Pathetic, solitary, alien children. What were they thinking of? He wouldn't mind betting it was their mother.

Mr. Twist's heart gave a kind of tug at him. His sentimental, maternal side heaved to the top. A great impulse to hurry out and put his arms round them seized him, but he frowned and overcame it. He didn't want to go soft now. Nor was this the moment, his nicely brought up soul told him, his soul still echoing with the voice of Clark, to put his arms round them — this, the very first occasion on which Mrs. Bilton had left them alone with him. Whether it would become proper on the very second occasion was one of those questions that would instantly have suggested itself to the Annas themselves, but didn't occur to Mr. Twist. He merely went on to think of another reason against it, which was the chance of Mrs. Bilton's looking out of her window just as he did it. She might, he felt, easily misjudge the situation, and the situation, he felt, was difficult enough already. So he restrained himself; and the Annas continued to consider infinite space and to perceive, again with that feeling of dank and unsatisfactory consolation, that nothing really mattered.

Next day immediately after breakfast Mrs. Bilton followed him into his office and gave notice. She called it formally tendering her resignation. She said that all her life she had been an upholder of straight dealing, as much in herself towards others as in others towards herself—

"Mrs. Bilton—" interrupted Mr. Twist, only it didn't interrupt.

She had also all her life been intensely patriotic, and Mr. Twist, she feared, didn't look at patriotism with quite her single eye—

"Mrs. Bilton—"

As her eye saw it, patriotism was among other things a determination to resist the encroachments of foreigners—

"Mrs. Bilton—"

She had no wish to judge him, but she had still less wish to be mixed up with foreigners, and foreigners for her at that moment meant Germans—

"Mrs. Bilton—"

She regretted, but psychically she would never be able to flourish in a soil so largely composed, as the soil of The Open Arms appeared to be, of that nationality—

"Mrs. Bilton—"

And though it was none of her business, still she must say it did seem to her a pity that Mr. Twist with his well-known and respected American name should be mixed up—

"Mrs. Bilton—"

And though she had no wish to be inquisitive, still she must say it did seem to her peculiar that Mr. Twist should be the guardian of two girls who, it was clear from what she had overheard that afternoon, were German—

Here Mr. Twist raised his voice and shouted. "Mrs. Bilton," he shouted, so loud that she couldn't but stop, "if you'll guarantee to keep quiet for just five minutes—sit down right here at this table and not say one single thing, not one single thing for just five minutes," he said, banging the table, "I'll tell you all about it. Oh yes, I'll accept your resignation at the end of that time if you're still set on leaving, but just for this once it's me that's going to do the talking."

And this must be imagined as said so loud that only capital letters would properly represent the noise Mr. Twist made.

Mrs. Bilton did sit down, her face flushed by the knowledge of how good her intentions had been when she took the post, and how deceitful—she was forced to think it—Mr. Twist's were when he offered it. She was prepared, however, to give him a hearing. It was only fair. But Mr. Twist had to burst into capitals several times before he had done, so difficult was it for Mrs. Bilton, even when she had agreed, even when she herself wished, not to say anything.

It wasn't five minutes but twenty before Mrs. Bilton came out of the office again. She went straight into the garden, where the Annas, aware of the interview going on with Mr. Twist, had been lingering anxiously, unable at so crucial a moment to settle to anything, and with solemnity kissed them. Her eyes were very bright. Her face, ordinarily colourless as parchment, was red. Positively she kissed them without saying a single word; and they kissed her back with such enthusiasm, with a relief that made them hug her so tight and cling to her so close, that the brightness in her eyes brimmed over and she had to get out her handkerchief and wipe it away.

"Gurls," said Mrs. Bilton, "I had a shock yesterday, but I'm through with it. You're motherless. I'm daughterless. We'll weld."

And with this unusual brevity did Mrs. Bilton sum up the situation.

She was much moved. Her heart was touched; and once that happened nothing could exceed her capacity for sticking through what she called thick and thin to her guns. For years Mr. Bilton had occupied the position of the guns; now it would be these poor orphans. No Germans could frighten her away, once she knew their story; no harsh judgments and misconceptions of her patriotic friends. Mr. Twist had told her everything, from the beginning on the *St. Luke*, harking back to Uncle Arthur and the attitude of England, describing what he knew of their mother and her death, not even concealing the part his own mother had played or that he wasn't their guardian at all. He made the most of Mrs. Bilton's silence; and as she listened her heart melted within her, and the immense store of grit which was her peculiar pride came to the top and once and for all overwhelmed her prejudices. But she couldn't think, and at last she burst out and told Mr. Twist she couldn't think, why he hadn't imparted all this to her long ago.

"Ah," murmured Mr. Twist, bowing his head as a reed in the wind before the outburst of her released volubility.

Hope once more filled The Open Arms, and the Twist party looked forward to the afternoon with renewed cheerfulness. It had just happened so the first day, that only Germans came. It was just accident. Mr. Twist, with the very large part of him that wasn't his head, found himself feeling like this too and declining to take any notice of his intelligence, which continued to try to worry him.

Yet the hope they all felt was not realized, and the second afternoon was almost exactly like the first. Germans came and clustered round the Annas, and made friendly though cautious advances to Mr. Twist. The ones who had been there the first day came again and brought others with them worse than themselves, and they seemed more at home than ever, and the air was full of rolling r's—among them, Mr. Twist was unable to deny, being the r's of his blessed Annas. But theirs were such little r's, he told himself. They rolled, it is true, but with how sweet a rolling. While as for these other people—confound it all, the place might really have been, from the sounds that were filling it, a *Conditorei* Unter den Linden.

All his doubts and anxieties flocked back on him as time passed and no Americans appeared. Americans. How precious. How clean, and straight, and admirable. Actually he had sometimes, he remembered, thought they weren't. What an aberration. Actually he had been, he remembered, impatient with them when first he came back from France. What folly. Americans. The very word was refreshing, was like clear water on a thirsty day. One American, even one, coming in that afternoon would have seemed to Mr. Twist a godsend, a purifier, an emollient—like some blessed unction dropped from above.

But none appeared; not even Mr. Ridding.

At six o'clock it was quite dark, and obviously too late to go on hoping. The days in California end abruptly. The sun goes down, and close on its heels comes night. In the tea-room the charmingly shaded lights had been turned on some time, and Mr. Twist, watching from the partly open door of his office, waited impatiently for the guests to begin to thin out. But they didn't. They took no notice of the signals of lateness, the lights turned on, the stars outside growing bright in the surrounding blackness.

Mr. Twist watched angrily. He had been driven into his office by the disconcerting and incomprehensible overtures of Mr. Wangelbecker, and had sat there watching in growing exasperation ever since. When six struck and nobody showed the least sign of going away he could bear it no longer, and touched the little muffled electric bell that connected him to Mrs. Bilton in what Anna-Felicitas called a mystical union—Anna II. was really excessively tactless; she had said this to Mrs. Bilton in his presence, and then enlarged on unions, mystical and otherwise, with an embarrassing abundance of imagery—by buzzing gently against her knee from the leg of the desk.

She laid down her pen, as though she had just finished adding up a column, and went to him.

"Now don't talk," said Mr. Twist, putting up an irritable hand directly she came in.

Mrs. Bilton looked at him in much surprise. "Talk, Mr. Twist?" she repeated. "Why now, as though—"

"Don't *talk* I say, Mrs. Bilton, but listen. Listen now. I can't stand seeing those children in there. It sheer makes my gorge rise. I want you to fetch them in here—now don't talk—you and me'll do the confounded waiting—no, no, don't talk—they're to stay quiet in here till the last of those Germans have gone. Just go and fetch them, please Mrs. Bilton. No, no, we'll talk afterwards. I'll stay here till they come." And he urged her out into the tea-room again.

The guests had finished their tea long ago, but still sat on, for they were very comfortable. Obviously they were thoroughly enjoying themselves, and all were growing, as time passed, more manifestly at home. They were now having a kind of supper of ices and fruit-salads. Five dollars, thought the sensible Germans, was after all a great deal to pay for afternoon tea, however good the cause might be and however important one's own ulterior motives; and since one had in any case to pay, one should eat what one could. So they kept the Annas very busy. There seemed to be no end, thought the Annas as they ran hither and thither, to what a German will hold.

Mrs. Bilton waylaid the heated and harried Anna-Rose as she was carrying a tray of ices to a party she felt she had been carrying ices to innumerable times already. The little curls beneath her cap clung damply to her forehead. Her face was flushed and distressed. What with having to carry so many trays, and remember so many orders, and try at the same time to escape from the orderers and their questions and admiration, she was in a condition not very far from tears.

Mrs. Bilton took the tray out of her hands, and told her Mr. Twist wanted to speak to her; and Anna-Rose was in such a general bewilderment that she felt quite scared, and thought he must be going to scold her. She went towards the office reluctantly. If Mr. Twist were to be severe, she was sure she wouldn't be able not to cry. She made her way very slowly to the office, and Mrs. Bilton looked round the room for the other one. There was no sign of her. Perhaps, thought Mrs. Bilton, she was fetching something in the kitchen, and would appear in a minute; and seeing a group over by the entrance door, for whom the tray she held was evidently destined, gesticulating to her, she felt she had better keep them quiet first and then go and look for Anna-Felicitas.

Mrs. Bilton set her teeth and plunged into her strange new duties. Never would she have dreamed it possible that she should have to carry trays to Germans. If Mr. Bilton could see her now he would certainly turn in his grave. Well, she was a woman of grit, of adhesiveness to her guns; if Mr. Bilton did see her and did turn in his grave, let him; he would, she dared say, be more comfortable on his other side after all these years.

For the next few minutes she hurried hither and thither, and waited single-handed. She seemed to be swallowed up in activity. No wonder that child had looked so hot and bewildered. Mr. Twist didn't come and help, as he had promised, and nowhere was there any sign of Anna-Felicitas; and the guests not only wanted things to eat, they wanted to talk,—talk and ask questions. Well, she would wait on them, but she wouldn't talk. She turned a dry, parchment-like face to their conversational blandishments, and responded only by adding up their bills. Wonderful are the workings of patriotism. For the first time in her life, Mrs. Bilton was grumbled at for not talking.

CHAPTER XXXIII

In the office Anna-Rose found Mr. Twist walking up and down.

"See here," he said, turning on her when she came in, "I'm about tired of looking on at all this twittering round that lot in there. You're through with that for to-day, and maybe for to-morrow and the day after as well."

He waved his arm at the deep chair that had been provided for his business meditations. "You'll sit down in that chair now," he said severely, "and stay put."

Anna-Rose looked at him with a quivering lip. She went rather unsteadily to the chair and tumbled into it. "I don't know if you're angry or being kind," she said tremulously, "but whichever it is I—I wish you wouldn't. I—I wish you'd manage to be something that isn't either." And, as she had feared, she began to cry.

"Anna-Rose," said Mr. Twist, staring down at her in concern mixed with irritation—out there all those Germans, in here the weeping child; what a day he was having—"for heaven's sake don't do that."

"I know," sobbed Anna-Rose. "I don't want to. It's awful being so natu—natu—naturally liquid."

"But what's the matter?" asked Mr. Twist helplessly.

"Nothing," sobbed Anna-Rose.

He stood over her in silence for a minute, his hands in his pockets. If he took them out he was afraid he might start stroking her, and she seemed to him to be exactly between the ages when such a form of comfort would be legitimate. If she were younger ... but she was a great girl now; if she were older ... ah, if she were older, Mr. Twist could imagine....

"You're overtired," he said aloofly. "That's what you are."

"No," sobbed Anna-Rose.

"And the Germans have been too much for you."

"They haven't," sobbed Anna-Rose, her pride up at the suggestion that anybody could ever be that.

"But they're not going to get the chance again," said Mr. Twist, setting his teeth as much as they would set, which wasn't, owing to his natural kindliness, anything particular. "Mrs. Bilton and me—" Then he remembered Anna-Felicitas. "Why doesn't she come?" he asked.

"Who?" choked Anna-Rose.

"The other one. Anna II. Columbus."

"I haven't seen her for ages," sobbed Anna-Rose, who had been much upset by Anna-Felicitas's prolonged disappearance and had suspected her, though she couldn't understand it after last night's finishings up, of secret unworthy conduct in a corner with ice-cream.

Mr. Twist went to the door quickly and looked through. "I can't see her either," he said. "Confound them—what have they done to her? Worn her out too, I daresay. I shouldn't wonder if she'd crawled off somewhere and were crying too."

"Anna-F.—doesn't crawl," sobbed Anna-Rose, "and she—doesn't cry but—I wish you'd find—her."

"Well, will you stay where you are while I'm away, then?" he said, looking at her from the door uncertainly.

And she seemed so extra small over there in the enormous chair, and somehow so extra motherless as she obediently gurgled and choked a promise not to move, that he found himself unable to resist going back to her for a minute in order to pat her head. "There, there," said Mr. Twist, very gently patting her head, his heart yearning over her; and it yearned the more that, the minute he patted, her sobs got worse; and also the more because of the feel of her dear little head.

"You little bit of blessedness," murmured Mr. Twist before he knew what he was saying; at which her sobs grew louder than ever,—grew, indeed, almost into small howls, so long was it since anybody had said things like that to her. It was her mother who used to say things like that; things almost exactly like that.

"Hush," said Mr. Twist in much distress, and with one anxious eye on the half-open door, for Anna-Rose's sobs were threatening to outdo the noise of teacups and ice-cream plates, "hush, hush—here's a clean handkerchief— you just wipe up your eyes while I fetch Anna II. She'll worry, you know, if she sees you like this,—hush now, hush—there, there—and I expect she's being miserable enough already, hiding away in some corner. You wouldn't like to make her more miserable, would you—"

And he pressed the handkerchief into Anna-Rose's hands, and feeling much flurried went away to search for the other one who was somewhere, he was sure, in a state of equal distress.

He hadn't however to search. He found her immediately. As he came out of the door of his office into the tea-room he saw her come into the tea-room from the door of the verandah, and proceed across it towards the pantry. Why the verandah? wondered Mr. Twist. He hurried to intercept her. Anyhow she wasn't either about to cry or getting over having done it. He saw that at once with relief. Nor was she, it would seem, in any sort of distress. On the contrary, Anna-Felicitas looked particularly smug. He saw that once too, with surprise,—why smug? wondered Mr. Twist. She had a pleased look of complete satisfaction on her face. She was oblivious, he noticed, as she passed between the tables, of the guests who tried in vain to attract her attention and detain her with orders. She wasn't at all hot, as Anna-Rose had been, nor rattled, nor in any way discomposed; she was just smug. And also she was unusually, extraordinarily pretty. How dared they all stare up at her like that as she passed? And try to stop her. And want to talk to her. And Wangelbecker actually laying his hand—no, his paw; in his annoyance Mr. Twist wouldn't admit that the object at the end of Mr. Wangelbecker's arm was anything but a paw—on her wrist to get her to listen to some confounded order or other. She took no notice of that either, but walked on towards the pantry. Placidly. Steadily. Obvious. Smug.

"You're to come into the office," said Mr. Twist when he reached her.

She turned her head and considered him with abstracted eyes. Then she appeared to remember him. "Oh, it's you," she said amiably.

"Yes. It's me all right. And you're to come into the office."

"I can't. I'm busy."

"Now Anna II.," said Mr. Twist, walking beside her towards the pantry since she didn't stop but continued steadily on her way, "that's trifling with the facts. You've been in the garden. I saw you come in. Perhaps you'll tell me the exact line of business you've been engaged in."

"Waiting," said Anna-Felicitas placidly.

"Waiting? In the garden? Where it's pitch dark, and there's nobody to wait on?"

They had reached the pantry, and Anna-Felicitas gave an order to Li Koo through the serving window before answering; the order was tea and hot cinnamon toast for one.

"He's having his tea on the verandah," she said, picking out the most delicious of the little cakes from the trays standing ready, and carefully arranging them on a dish. "It isn't pitch dark at all there. There's floods of light coming through the windows. He won't come in."

"And why pray won't he come in?" asked Mr. Twist.

"Because he doesn't like Germans."

"And who pray is he?"

"I don't know."

"Well I do," burst out Mr. Twist. "It's old Ridding, of course. His name is Ridding. The old man who was here yesterday. Now listen: I won't have—"

But Anna-Felicitas was laughing, and her eyes had disappeared into two funny little screwed-up eyelashy slits.

Mr. Twist stopped abruptly and glared at her. These Twinklers. That one in there shaken with sobs, this one in here shaken with what she would no doubt call quite the contrary. His conviction became suddenly final that the office was the place for both the Annas. He and Mrs. Bilton would do the waiting.

"I'll take this," he said, laying hold of the dish of cakes. "I'll send Mrs. Bilton for the tea. Go into the office, Anna-Felicitas. Your sister is there and wants you badly. I don't know," he added, as Li Koo pushed the tea-tray through the serving window, "how it strikes you about laughter, but it strikes me as sheer silly to laugh except at something."

"Well, I was," said Anna-Felicitas, unscrewing her eyes and with gentle firmness taking the plate of cakes from him and putting it on the tray. "I was laughing at your swift conviction that the man out there is Mr. Ridding. I don't know who he is but I know heaps of people he isn't, and one of the principal ones is Mr. Ridding."

"I'm going to wait on him," said Mr. Twist, taking the tray.

"It would be most unsuitable," said Anna-Felicitas, taking it too.

"Let go," said Mr. Twist, pulling.

"Is this to be an unseemly wrangle?" inquired Anna-Felicitas mildly; and her eyes began to screw up again.

"If you'll oblige me by going into the office," he said, having got the tray, for Anna-Felicitas was never one to struggle, "Mrs. Bilton and me will do the rest of the waiting for to-day."

He went out grasping the tray, and made for the verandah. His appearance in this new rôle was greeted by the Germans with subdued applause—subdued, because they felt Mr. Twist wasn't quite as cordial to them as they had supposed he would be, and they were accordingly being a little more cautious in their methods with him than they had been at the beginning of the afternoon. He took no notice of them, except that his ears turned red when he knocked against a chair and the tray nearly fell out of his hands and they all cried out *Houp là*. Damn them, thought Mr. Twist. *Houp là* indeed.

In the farthest corner of the otherwise empty and very chilly verandah, sitting alone and staring out at the stars, was a man. He was a young man. He was also an attractive young man, with a thin brown face and very bright blue twinkling eyes. The light from the window behind him shone on him as he turned his head when he heard the swing doors open, and Mr. Twist saw these things distinctly and at once. He also saw how the young man's face fell on his, Mr. Twist's, appearance with the tray, and he also saw with some surprise how before he had reached him it suddenly cleared again. And the young man got up too, just as Mr. Twist arrived at the table—got up with some little difficulty, for he had to lean hard on a thick stick, but yet obviously with *empressement*.

"You've forgotten the sugar," said Anna-Felicitas's gentle voice behind Mr. Twist as he was putting down the tray; and there she was, sure enough, looking smugger than ever.

"This is Mr. Twist," said Anna-Felicitas with an amiable gesture. "That I was telling you about," she explained to the young man.

"When?" asked Mr. Twist, surprised.

"Before," said Anna-Felicitas. "We were talking for some time before I went in to order the tea, weren't we?" she said to the young man, angelically smiling at him.

"Rather," he said; and since he didn't on this introduction remark to Mr. Twist that he was pleased to meet him, it was plain he couldn't be an American. Therefore he must be English. Unless, suddenly suspected Mr. Twist who had Germans badly on his nerves that day and was ready to suspect anything, he was German cleverly got up for evil purposes to appear English. But the young man dispersed these suspicions by saying that he was over from England on six months' leave, and that his name was Elliott.

"Like us," said Anna-Felicitas.

The young man looked at her with what would have been a greater interest than ever if a greater interest had been possible, only it wasn't.

"What, are you an Elliott too?" he asked eagerly.

Anna-Felicitas shook her head. "On the contrary," she said, "I'm a Twinkler. And so is my sister. What I meant was, you're like us about coming from England. We've done that. Only our leave is for ever and ever. Or the duration of the war."

Mr. Twist waved her aside. "Anna-Felicitas," he said, "your sister is waiting for you in the office and wants you badly. I'll see to Mr. Elliott."

"Why not bring your sister here?" said the young man, who, being in the navy, was fertile in resourcefulness. And he smiled at Anna-Felicitas, who smiled back; indeed, they did nothing but smile at each other.

"I think that's a brilliant idea," she said; and turned to Mr. Twist. "You go," she said gently, thereby proving herself, the young man considered, at least his equal in resourcefulness. "It's much more likely," she continued, as Mr. Twist gazed at her without moving, "that she'll come for you than for me. My sister," she explained to the young man, "is older than I am."

"Then certainly I should say Mr. Twist is more likely—"

"But only about twenty minutes older."

"What? A twin? I say, how extraordinarily jolly. Two of you?"

"Anna-Felicitas," interrupted Mr. Twist, "you will go to your sister immediately. She needs you. She's upset. I don't wish to draw Mr. Elliott behind the scenes of family life, but as nothing seems to get you into the office you force me to tell you that she is very, much upset indeed, and is crying."

"Crying?" echoed Anna-Felicitas. "Christopher?" And she turned and departed in such haste that the young man, who luckily was alert as well as resourceful, had only just time to lean over and grab at a chair in her way and pull it aside, and so avert a deplorable catastrophe.

"I hope it's nothing serious?" he inquired of Mr. Twist.

"Oh no. Children will cry."

"Children?"

Mr. Twist sat down at the table and lit a cigarette. "Tell me about England," he said. "You've been wounded, I see."

"Leg," said the young man, still standing leaning on his stick and looking after Anna-Felicitas.

"But that didn't get you six months' leave."

"Lungs," said the young man, looking down impatiently at Mr. Twist.

Then the swing doors swung to, and he sat down and poured out his tea.

He had been in the battle of Jutland, and was rescued after hours in the water. For months he was struggling to recover, but finally tuberculosis had developed and he was sent to California, to his sister who had married an American and lived in the neighbourhood of Acapulco. This Mr. Twist extracted out of him by diligent questioning. He had to question very diligently. What the young man wanted to talk about was Anna-Felicitas; but every time he tried to, Mr. Twist headed him off.

And she didn't come back. He waited and waited, and drank and drank. When the teapot was empty he started on the hot water. Also he ate all the cakes, more and more deliberately, eking them out at last with slowly smoked cigarettes. He heard all about France and Mr. Twist's activities there; he had time to listen to the whole story of the ambulance from start to finish; and still she didn't come back. In vain he tried at least to get Mr. Twist off those distant fields, nearer home—to the point, in fact, where the Twinklers were. Mr. Twist wouldn't budge. He stuck firmly. And the swing doors remained shut. And the cakes were all eaten. And there was nothing for it at last but to go.

So after half-an-hour of solid sitting he began slowly to get up, still spreading out the moments, with one eye on the swing doors. It was both late and cold. The Germans had departed, and Li Koo had lit the usual evening wood fire in the big fireplace. It blazed most beautifully, and the young man looked at it through the window and hesitated.

"How jolly," he said.

"Firelight is very pleasant," agreed Mr. Twist, who had got up too.

"I oughtn't to have stayed so long out here," said the young man with a little shiver.

"I was thinking it was unwise," said Mr. Twist.

"Perhaps I'd better go in and warm myself a bit before leaving."

"I should say your best plan is to get back quickly to your sister and have a hot bath before dinner," said Mr. Twist.

"Yes. But I think I might just go in there and have a cup of hot coffee first."

"There is no hot coffee at this hour," said Mr. Twist, looking at his watch. "We close at half-past six, and it is now ten minutes after."

"Then there seems nothing for it but to pay my bill and go," said the young man, with an air of cheerful adaptation to what couldn't be helped. "I'll just nip in there and do that."

"Luckily there's no need for you to nip anywhere," said Mr. Twist, "for surely that's a type of movement unsuited to your sick leg. You can pay me right here."

And he took the young man's five dollars, and went with him as far as the green gate, and would have helped him into the waiting car, seeing his leg wasn't as other legs and Mr. Twist was, after all, humane, but the chauffeur was there to do that; so he just watched from the gate till the car had actually started, and then went back to the house.

He went back slowly, perturbed and anxious, his eyes on the ground. This second day had been worse than the first. And besides the continued and remarkable absence of Americans and the continued and remarkable presence of Germans, there was a slipperiness suddenly developed in the Annas. He felt insecure; as though he didn't understand, and hadn't got hold. They seemed to him very like eels. And this Elliott—what did he think *he* was after, anyway?

For the second time that afternoon Mr. Twist set his teeth. He defied Elliott. He defied the Germans. He would see this thing successful, this Open Arms business, or his name wasn't Twist. And he stuck out his jaw— or would have stuck it out if he hadn't been prevented by the amiable weakness of that feature. But spiritually and morally, when he got back into the house he was all jaw.

CHAPTER XXXIV

That night he determined he would go into Acapulco next morning and drop in at his bank and at his lawyer's and other places, and see if he could pick up anything that would explain why Americans wouldn't come and have tea at The Open Arms. He even thought he might look up old Ridding. He didn't sleep. He lay all night thinking.

The evening had been spent *tête-à-tête* with Anna-Felicitas. Anna-Rose was in bed, sleeping off her tears; Mrs. Bilton had another headache, and disappeared early; so he was left with Anna-Felicitas, who slouched about abstractedly eating up the remains of ice-cream. She didn't talk, except once to remark a little pensively that her inside was dreadfully full of cold stuff, and that she knew now what it must feel like to be a mausoleum; but, eyeing her sideways as he sat before the fire, Mr. Twist could see that she was still smug. He didn't talk either. He felt he had nothing at present to say to Anna-Felicitas that would serve a useful purpose, and was, besides, reluctant to hear any counter-observations she might make. Watchfulness was what was required. Silent watchfulness. And wariness. And firmness. In fact all the things that were most foreign to his nature, thought Mr. Twist, resentful and fatigued.

Next morning he had a cup of coffee in his room, brought by Li Koo, and then drove himself into Acapulco in his Ford without seeing the others. It was another of the perfect days which he was now beginning to take as a matter of course, so many had there been since his arrival. People talked of the wet days and of their desolate abundance once they started, but there had been as yet no sign of them. The mornings succeeded each other, radiant and calm. November was merging into December in placid loveliness. "Oh yes," said Mr. Twist to himself sardonically, as he drove down the sun-flecked lane in the gracious light, and crickets chirped at him, and warm scents drifted across his face, and the flowers in the grass, standing so bright and unruffled that they seemed almost as profoundly pleased as Anna-Felicitas, nodded at him, and everything was obviously perfectly contented and happy, "Oh yes—I daresay." And he repeated this remark several times as he looked round him,—he couldn't but look, it was all so beautiful. These things hadn't to deal with Twinklers. No wonder they could be calm and bright. So could he, if—

He turned a corner in the lane and saw some way down it two figures, a man and a girl, sitting in the grass by the wayside. Lovers, of course. "Oh yes—I daresay," said Mr. Twist again, grimly. They hadn't to deal with Twinklers either. No wonder they could sit happily in the grass. So could he, if—

At the noise of the approaching car, with the smile of the last thing they had been saying still on their faces, the two turned their heads, and it was that man Elliott and Anna-Felicitas.

"Hello," called out Mr. Twist, putting on the brakes so hard that the Ford skidded sideways along the road towards them.

"Hello," said the young man cheerfully, waving his stick.

"Hello," said Anna-Felicitas mildly, watching his sidelong approach with complacent interest.

She had no hat on, and had evidently escaped from Mrs. Bilton just as she was. Escaped, however, was far too violent a word Mr. Twist felt; sauntered from Mrs. Bilton better described her effect of natural and comfortable arrival at the place where she was.

"I didn't know you were here," said Mr. Twist addressing her when the car had stopped. He felt it was a lame remark. He had torrents of things he wanted to say, and this was all that came out.

Anna-Felicitas considered it placidly for a moment, and came to the conclusion that it wasn't worth answering, so she didn't.

"Going into the town?" inquired Elliott pleasantly.

"Yes. I'll give you a lift."

"No thanks. I've just come from there."

"I see. Then *you'd* better come with me," said Mr. Twist to Anna-Felicitas.

"I'm afraid I can't. I'm rather busy this morning."

"Really," said Mr. Twist, in a voice of concentrated sarcasm. But it had no effect on Anna-Felicitas. She continued to contemplate him with perfect goodwill.

He hesitated a moment. What could he do? Nothing, that he could see, before the young man; nothing that wouldn't make him ridiculous. He felt a fool already. He oughtn't to have pulled up. He ought to have just waved to them and gone on his way, and afterwards in the seclusion of his office issued very plain directions to Anna-Felicitas as to her future conduct.

Sitting by the roadside like that! Openly; before everybody; with a young man she had never seen twenty-four hours ago.

He jammed in the gear and let the clutch out with such a jerk that the car leaped forward. Elliott waved his stick again. Mr. Twist responded by the briefest touch of his cap, and whirred down the road out of sight.

"Does he mind your sitting here?" asked Elliott.

"It would be very unreasonable," said Anna-Felicitas gently. "One has to sit somewhere."

And he laughed with delight at this answer as he laughed with delight at everything she said, and he told her for the twentieth time that she was the most wonderful person he had ever met, and she settled down to listen again, after the interruption caused by Mr. Twist, with a ready ear and the utmost complacency to these agreeable statements, and began to wonder whether perhaps after all she mightn't at last be about to fall in love.

In the new interest of this possibility she turned her head to look at him, and he told her tumultuously—for being a sailor-man he went straight ahead on great waves when it came to love-making—that her eyes were as if pansies had married stars.

She turned her head away again at this, for though it sounded lovely it made her feel a little shy and unprovided with an answer; and then he said, again tumultuously, that her ear was the most perfect thing ever stuck on a girl's cheek, and would she mind turning her face to him so that he might see if she had another just like it on the other side.

She blushed at this, because she couldn't remember whether she had washed it lately or not—one so easily forgot one's ears; there were so many different things to wash—and he told her that when she blushed it was like the first wild rose of the first summer morning of the world.

At this Anna-Felicitas was quite overcome, and subsided into a condition of blissful, quiescent waiting for whatever might come next. Fancy her face reminding him of all those nice things. She had seen it every day for years and years in the looking-glass, and not noticed anything particular about it. It had seemed to her just a face. Something you saw out of, and ate with, and had to clean whatever else you didn't when you were late for breakfast, because there it was and couldn't be hidden,—an object remote indeed from pansies, and stars, and beautiful things like that.

She would have liked to explain this to the young man, and point out that she feared his imagination ran ahead of the facts and that perhaps when his leg was well again he would see things more as they were, but to her surprise when she turned to him to tell him this she found she was obliged to look away at once again. She couldn't look at him. Fancy that now, thought Anna-Felicitas, attentively gazing at her toes. And he had such dear eyes; and such a dear, eager sort of face. All the more, then, she reasoned, should her own eyes have dwelt with pleasure on him. But they couldn't. "Dear me," she murmured, watching her toes as carefully as if they might at any moment go away and leave her there.

"I know," said Elliott. "You think I'm talking fearful flowery stuff. I'd have said Dear me at myself three years ago if I had ever caught myself thinking in terms of stars and roses. But it's all the beastly blood and muck of the war that does it,—sends one back with a rush to things like that. Makes one shameless. Why, I'd talk to you about God now without turning a hair. Nothing would have induced me so much as to mention seriously that I'd even heard of him three years ago. Why, I write poetry now. We all write poetry. And nobody would mind now being seen saying their prayers. Why, if I were back at school and my mother came to see me I'd hug her before everybody in the middle of the street. Do you realize what a tremendous change that means, you little girl who's never had brothers? You extraordinary adorable little lovely thing?"

And off he was again.

"When I was small," said Anna-Felicitas after a while, still watching her feet, "I had a governess who urged me to consider, before I said anything, whether it were the sort of thing I would like to say in the hearing of my parents. Would you like to say what you're saying to me in the hearing of your parents?"

"Hate to," said Elliott promptly.

"Well, then," said Anna-Felicitas, gentle but disappointed. She rather wished now she hadn't mentioned it.

"I'd take you out of earshot," said Elliott.

She was much relieved. She had done what she felt might perhaps be regarded by Aunt Alice as her duty as a lady, and could now give herself up with a calm conscience to hearing whatever else he might have to say.

And he had an incredible amount to say, and all of it of the most highly gratifying nature. On the whole, looking at it all round and taking one thing with another, Anna-Felicitas came to the conclusion that this was the most agreeable and profitable morning she had ever spent. She sat there for hours, and they all flew. People passed in cars and saw her, and it didn't disturb her in the least. She perfectly remembered she ought to be helping Anna-Rose pick and arrange the flowers for the tea-tables, and she didn't mind. She knew Anna-Rose would be astonished and angry at her absence, and it left her unmoved. By midday she was hopelessly compromised in the eyes of Acapulco, for the people who had motored through the lane told the people who hadn't what they had seen. Once a great car passed with a small widow in it, who looked astonished when she saw the pair but had gone almost before Elliott could call out and wave to her.

"That's my sister," he said. "You and she will love each other."

"Shall we?" said Anna-Felicitas, much pleased by this suggestion of continuity in their relations; and remarked that she looked as if she hadn't got a husband.

"She hasn't. Poor little thing. Rotten luck. Rotten. I hate people to die now. It seems so infernally unnatural of them, when they're not in the fighting. He's only been dead a month. And poor old Dellogg was such a decent chap. She isn't going anywhere yet, or I'd bring her up to tea this afternoon. But it doesn't matter. I'll take you to her."

"Shall you?" said Anna-Felicitas, again much pleased. Dellogg. The name swam through her mind and swam out again. She was too busy enjoying herself to remark it and its coincidences now.

"Of course. It's the first thing one does."

"What first thing?"

"To take the divine girl to see one's relations. Once one has found her. Once one has had"—his voice fell to a whisper—"the God-given luck to find her." And he laid his hand very gently on hers, which were clasped together in her lap.

This was a situation to which Anna-Felicitas wasn't accustomed, and she didn't know what to do with it. She looked down at the hand lying on hers, and considered it without moving. Elliott was quite silent now, and she knew he was watching her face. Ought she, perhaps, to be going? Was this, perhaps, one of the moments in life when the truly judicious went? But what a pity to go just when everything was so pleasant. Still, it must be nearly lunch-time. What would Aunt Alice do in a similar situation? Go home to lunch, she was sure. Yet what was lunch when one was rapidly arriving, as she was sure now that she was, at the condition of being in love? She must be, or she wouldn't like his hand on hers. And she did like it.

She looked down at it, and found that she wanted to stroke it. But would Aunt Alice stroke it? No; Anna-Felicitas felt fairly clear about that.

Aunt Alice wouldn't stroke it; she would take it up, and shake it, and say good-bye, and walk off home to lunch like a lady. Well, perhaps she ought to do that. Christopher would probably think so too. But what a pity.... Still, behaviour was behaviour; ladies were ladies.

She drew out her right hand with this polite intention, and instead— Anna-Felicitas never knew how it happened—she did nothing of the sort, but quite the contrary: she put it softly on the top of his.

CHAPTER XXXV

Meanwhile Mr. Twist had driven on towards Acapulco in a state of painful indecision. Should he or shouldn't he take a turning he knew of a couple of miles farther that led up an unused and practically undrivable track back by the west side to The Open Arms, and instruct Mrs. Bilton to proceed at once down the lane and salvage Anna-Felicitas? Should he or shouldn't he? For the first mile he decided he would; then, as his anger cooled, he began to think that after all he needn't worry much. The Annas were lucidly too young for serious philandering, and even if that Elliott didn't realize this, owing to Anna-Felicitas's great length, he couldn't do much before he, Mr. Twist, was back again along the lane. In this he underestimated the enterprise of the British Navy, but it served to calm him; so that when he did reach the turning he had made up his mind to continue on his way to Acapulco.

There he spent some perplexing and harassing hours.

At the bank his reception was distinctly chilly. He wasn't used, since his teapot had been on the market, to anything but warmth when he went into a bank. On this occasion even the clerks were cold; and when after difficulty—actual difficulty—he succeeded in seeing the manager, he couldn't but perceive his unusual reserve. He then remembered what he had put down to mere accident at the time, that as he drove up Main Street half an hour before, all the people he knew had been looking the other way.

From the bank, where he picked up nothing in the way of explanation of the American avoidance of The Open Arms, the manager going dumb at its mere mention, he went to the solicitors who had arranged the sale of the inn, and again in the street people he knew looked the other way. The solicitor, it appeared, wouldn't be back till the afternoon, and the clerk, an elderly person hitherto subservient, was curiously short about it.

By this time Mr. Twist was thoroughly uneasy, and he determined to ask the first acquaintance he met what the matter was. But he couldn't find anybody. Every one, his architect, his various experts—those genial and frolicsome young men—were either engaged or away on business somewhere else. He set his teeth, and drove to the Cosmopolitan to seek out old Ridding—it wasn't a place he drove to willingly after his recent undignified departure, but he was determined to get to the bottom of this thing—and walking into the parlour was instantly aware of a hush falling upon it, a holding of the breath.

In the distance he saw old Ridding,—distinctly; and distinctly he saw that old Ridding saw him. He was sitting at the far end of the great parlour, facing the entrance, by the side of something vast and black heaped up in the adjacent chair. He had the look on his pink and naturally pleasant face of one who has abandoned hope. On seeing Mr. Twist a ray of interest lit him up, and he half rose. The formless mass in the next chair which Mr. Twist had taken for inanimate matter, probably cushions and wraps, and now perceived was one of the higher mammals, put out a hand and said something,—at least, it opened that part of its face which is called a mouth but which to Mr. Twist in the heated and abnormal condition of his brain seemed like the snap-to of some great bag,—and at that moment a group of people crossed the hall in front of old Ridding, and when the path was again clear the chair that had contained him was empty. He had disappeared. Completely. Only the higher mammal was left, watching Mr. Twist with heavy eyes like two smouldering coals.

He couldn't face those eyes. He did try to, and hesitated while he tried, and then he found he couldn't; so he swerved away to the right, and went out quickly by the side door.

There was now one other person left who would perhaps clear him up as to the meaning of all this, and he was the lawyer he had gone to about the guardianship. True he had been angry with him at the time, but that was chiefly because he had been angry with himself. At bottom he had carried away an impression of friendliness. To this man he would now go as a last resource before turning back home, and once more he raced up Main Street in his Ford, producing by these repeated appearances an effect of agitation and restlessness that wasn't lost on the beholders.

The lawyer was in his office, and disengaged. After his morning's experience Mr. Twist was quite surprised and much relieved by being admitted at once. He was received neither coldly nor warmly, but with unmistakable interest.

"I've come to consult you," said Mr. Twist.

The lawyer nodded. He hadn't supposed he had come not to consult him, but he was used to patience with clients, and he well knew their preference in conversation for the self-evident.

"I want a straight answer to a straight question," said Mr. Twist, his great spectacles glaring anxiously at the lawyer who again nodded.

"Go on," he said, as Mr. Twist paused.

"What I want to know is," burst out Mr. Twist, "what the hell—"

The lawyer put up a hand. "One moment, Mr. Twist," he said. "Sorry to interrupt—"

And he got up quickly, and went to a door in the partition between his office and his clerks' room.

"You may go out to lunch now," he said, opening it a crack.

He then shut it, and came back to his seat at the table.

"Yes, Mr. Twist?" he said, settling down again. "You were inquiring what the hell—?"

"Well, I was about to," said Mr. Twist, suddenly soothed, "but you're so calm—"

"Of course I'm calm. I'm a quietly married man."

"I don't see what that's got to do with it."

"Everything. For some dispositions, everything. Mine is one. Yours is another."

"Well, I guess I've not come here to talk about marriage. What I want to know is why—"

"Quite so," said the lawyer, as he stopped. "And I can tell you. It's because your inn is suspected of being run in the interests of the German Government."

A deep silence fell upon the room. The lawyer watched Mr. Twist with a detached and highly intelligent interest. Mr. Twist stared at the lawyer, his kind, lavish lips fallen apart. Anger had left him. This blow excluded anger. There was only room in him for blank astonishment.

"You know about my teapot?" he said at last.

"Try me again, Mr. Twist."

"It's on every American breakfast table."

"Including my own."

"They wouldn't use it if they thought—"

"My dear sir, they're not going to," said the lawyer. "They're proposing, among other little plans for conveying the general sentiment to your notice, to boycott the teapot. It is to be put on an unofficial black list. It is to be banished from the hotels."

Mr. Twist's stare became frozen. The teapot boycotted? The teapot his mother and sister depended on and The Open Arms depended on, and all his happiness, and the twins? He saw the rumour surging over America in great swift waves, that the proceeds of the Twist Non-Trickler were used for Germany. He saw—but what didn't he see in that moment of submerged horror? Then he seemed to come to the surface again and resume reason with a gasp. "Why?" he asked.

"Why they're wanting to boycott the teapot?"

"No. Why do they think the inn—"

"The Miss Twinklers are German."

"Half."

"The half that matters—begging my absent wife's pardon. I know all about that, you see. You started me off thinking them over by that ward notion of yours. It didn't take me long. It was pretty transparent. So transparent that my opinion of the intelligence of my fellow-townsfolk has considerably lowered. But we live in unbalanced times. I guess it's women at the bottom of this. Women got on to it first, and the others caught the idea as they'd catch scarlet fever. It's a kind of scarlet fever, this spy scare that's about. Mind you, I admit the germs are certainly present among us." And the lawyer smiled. He thought he saw he had made a little joke in that last remark.

Mr. Twist was not in the condition to see jokes, and didn't smile. "Do you mean to say those children—" he began.

"They're not regarded as children by any one except you."

"Well, if they're not," said Mr. Twist, remembering the grass by the wayside in the lane and what he had so recently met in it, "I guess I'd best be making tracks. But I know better. And so would you if you'd seen them on the boat. Why, twelve was putting their age too high on that boat."

"No doubt. No doubt. Then all I can say is they've matured pretty considerably since. Now do you really want me to tell you what is being believed?"

"Of course. It's what I've come for."

"You mayn't find it precisely exhilarating, Mr. Twist."

"Go ahead."

"What Acapulco says—and Los Angeles, I'm told, too, and probably by this time the whole coast—is that you threw over your widowed mother, of whom you're the only son, and came off here with two German girls who got hold of you on the boat—now, Mr. Twist, don't interrupt—on the boat crossing from England, that England had turned them out as undesirable aliens—quite so, Mr. Twist, but let me finish—that they're in the pay of the German Government—no doubt, no doubt, Mr. Twist—and that you're their cat's-paw. It is known that the inn each afternoon has been crowded with Germans, among them Germans already suspected, I can't say how rightly or how wrongly, of spying, and that these people are so familiar with the Miss von Twinklers as to warrant the belief in a complete secret understanding."

For a moment Mr. Twist continued both his silence and his stare. Then he took off his spectacles and wiped them. His hand shook. The lawyer was startled. Was there going to be emotion? One never knew with that sort of lips. "You're not—" he began.

Then he saw that Mr. Twist was trying not to laugh.

"I'm glad you take it that way," he said, relieved but surprised.

"It's so darned funny," said Mr. Twist, endeavouring to compose his features. "To anybody who knows those twins it's so darned funny. Cat's-paw. Yes—rather feel that myself. Cat's-paw. That does seem a bit of a bull's-eye—" And for a second or two his features flatly refused to compose.

The lawyer watched him. "Yes," he said. "Yes. But the effect of these beliefs may be awkward."

"Oh, damned," agreed Mr. Twist, going solemn again.

And there came over him in a flood the clear perception of what it would mean,—the sheer disaster of it, the horrible situation those helpless Annas would be in. What a limitless fool he must have been in his conduct of the whole thing. His absorption in the material side of it had done the trick. He hadn't been clever enough, not imaginative enough, nor, failing that, worldly enough to work the other side properly. When he found there was no Dellogg he ought to have insisted on seeing Mrs. Dellogg, intrusion or no intrusion, and handing over the twins; and then gone away and left them. A woman was what was wanted. Fool that he was to suppose that he, a man, an unmarried man, could get them into anything but a scrape. But he was so fond of them. He just couldn't leave them. And now here they all were, in this ridiculous and terrible situation.

"There are two things you can do," said the lawyer.

"Two?" said Mr. Twist, looking at him with anxious eyes. "For the life of me I can't see even one. Except running amoke in slander actions—"

"Tut, tut," said the lawyer, waving that aside. "No. There are two courses to pursue. And they're not alternative, but simultaneous. You shut down the inn—at once, to-morrow—that's Saturday. Close on Saturday, and give notice you don't re-open—now pray let me finish—close the inn as an inn, and use it simply as a private residence. Then, as quick as may be, marry those girls."

"Marry what girls?"

"The Miss von Twinklers."

Mr. Twist stared at him. "Marry them?" he said helplessly. "Marry them who to?"

"You for one."

Mr. Twist stared at him in silence. Then he said, "You've said that to me before."

"Yep. And I'll say it again. I'll go on saying it till you've done it."

"'Well, if that's all you've got to offer as a suggestion for a way out—"

But Mr. Twist wasn't angry this time; he was too much battered by events; he hadn't the spirits to be angry.

"You've—got to—marry—one—of—those—girls," said the lawyer, at each word smiting the table with his open palm. "Turn her into an American. Get her out of this being a German business. And be able at the same time to protect the one who'll be your sister in-law. Why, even if you didn't want to, which is sheer nonsense, for of course any man would want to—I know what I'm talking about because I've seen them—it's your plain duty, having got them into this mess."

"But—marry which?" asked Mr. Twist, with increased helplessness and yet a manifest profound anxiety for further advice.

For the first time the lawyer showed impatience "Oh—either or both," he said. "For God's sake don't be such a—"

He pulled up short.

"I didn't quite mean that," he resumed, again calm. "The end of that sentence was, as no doubt you guess, fool. I withdraw it, and will substitute something milder. Have you any objection to ninny?"

No, Mr. Twist didn't mind ninny, or any other word the lawyer might choose, he was in such a condition of mental groping about. He took out his handkerchief and wiped away the beads on his forehead and round his mouth.

"I'm thirty-five," he said, looking terribly worried.

Propose to an Anna? The lawyer may have seen them, but he hadn't heard them; and the probable nature of their comments if Mr. Twist proposed to them—to one, he meant of course, but both would comment, the one he proposed to and the one he didn't—caused his imagination to reel. He hadn't much imagination; he knew that now, after his conduct of this whole affair, but all there was of it reeled.

"I'm thirty-five," he said helplessly.

"Pooh," said the lawyer, indicating the negligibleness of this by a movement of his shoulder.

"They're seventeen," said Mr. Twist.

"Pooh," said the lawyer again, again indicating negligibleness. "My wife was—"

"I know. You told me that last time. Oh, I know all *that*" said Mr. Twist with sudden passion. "But these are children. I tell you they're *children*—"

"Pooh," said the lawyer a third time, a third time indicating negligibleness.

Then he got up and held out his hand. "Well, I've told you," he said. "You wanted to know, and I've told you. And I'll tell you one thing more, Mr. Twist. Whichever of those girls takes you, you'll have the sweetest, prettiest wife of any man in the world except one, and that's the man who has the luck to get the other one. Why, sweetest and prettiest are poor words. She'll be the most delectable, the most—"

Mr. Twist rose from his chair in such haste that he pushed the table crooked. His ears flamed.

"See here," he said very loud. "I won't have you talk familiarly like that about my wife."

CHAPTER XXXVI

Wife. The word had a remarkable effect on him. It churned him all up. His thoughts were a chaotic jumble, and his driving on the way home matched them. He had at least three narrow shaves at cross streets before he got out of the town and for an entire mile afterwards he was on the wrong side of the road. During this period, deep as he was in confused thought, he couldn't but vaguely notice the anger on the faces of the other drivers and the variety and fury of their gesticulations, and it roused a dim wonder in him.

Wife. How arid existence had been for him up to then in regard to the affections, how knobbly the sort of kisses he had received in Clark. They weren't kisses; they were disapproving pecks. Always disapproving. Always as if he hadn't done enough, or been enough, or was suspected of not going to do or be enough.

His wife. Mr. Twist dreadfully longed to kiss somebody,—somebody kind and soft, who would let herself be adored. She needn't even love him,—he knew he wasn't the sort of man to set passion alight; she need only be kind, and a little fond of him, and let him love her, and be his very own.

His own little wife. How sweet. How almost painfully sweet. Yes. But the Annas....

When he thought of the Annas, Mr. Twist went damp. He might propose—indeed, everything pointed to his simply having got to—but wouldn't they very quickly dispose? And then what? That lawyer seemed to think all he had to do was to marry them right away; not them, of course,— one; but they were so very plural in his mind. Funny man, thought Mr. Twist; funny man,—yet otherwise so sagacious. It is true he need only propose to one of them, for which he thanked God, but he could imagine what that one, and what the other one too, who would be sure to be somewhere quite near would ... no, he couldn't imagine; he preferred not to imagine.

Mr. Twist's dampness increased, and a passing car got his mud-guard. It was a big car which crackled with language as it whizzed on its way, and Mr. Twist, slewed by the impact half across the road, then perceived on which side he had been driving.

The lane up to the inn was in its middle-day emptiness and somnolence. Where Anna-Felicitas and Elliott had been sitting cool and shaded when he passed before, there was only the pressed-down grass and crushed flowers in a glare of sun. She had gone home long ago of course. She said she was going to be very busy. Secretly he wished she hadn't gone home, and that little Christopher too might for a bit be somewhere else, so that when he arrived he wouldn't immediately have to face everybody at once. He wanted to think; he wanted to have time to think; time before four o'clock came, and with four o'clock, if he hadn't come to any conclusion about shutting up the inn—and how could he if nobody gave him time to think?—those accursed, swarming Germans. It was they who had done all this. Mr. Twist blazed into sudden fury. They and their blasted war....

At the gate stood Anna-Rose. Her face looked quite pale in the green shade of the tunnelled-out syringa bushes. She as peering out down the lane watching him approach. This was awful, thought Mr. Twist. At the very gate one of them. Confronted at once. No time, not a minute's time given him to think.

"Oh," cried out Anna-Rose the instant he pulled up, for she had waved to him to stop when he tried to drive straight on round to the stable, "she isn't with you?"

"Who isn't?" asked Mr. Twist.

Anna-Rose became paler than ever. "She has been kidnapped," she said.

"How's that?" said Mr. Twist, staring at her from the car.

"Kidnapped," repeated Anna-Rose, with wide-open horror-stricken eyes; for from her nursery she carried with her at the bottom of her mind, half-forgotten but ready to fly up to the top at any moment of panic, an impression that the chief activities and recreations of all those Americans who weren't really good were two: they lynched, and they kidnapped. They lynched you if they didn't like you enough, and if they liked you too much they kidnapped you. Anna-Felicitas, exquisite and unsuspecting, had been kidnapped. Some American's concupiscent eye had alighted on her, observed her beauty, and marked her down. No other explanation was possible of a whole morning's absence from duties of one so conscientious and painstaking as Anna-Felicitas. She never shirked; that is, she never had been base enough to shirk alone. If there was any shirking to be done they had always done it together. As the hours passed and she didn't appear, Anna-Rose had tried to persuade herself that she must have motored into Acapulco with Mr. Twist, strange and unnatural and reprehensible and ignoble as such arch shirking would have been; and now that the car had come back empty except for Mr. Twist she was convinced the worst had happened—her beautiful, her precious Columbus had been kidnapped.

"Kidnapped," she said again, wringing her hands.

Mr. Twist was horror-struck too, for he thought she was announcing the kidnapping of Mrs. Bilton. Somehow he didn't think of Anna-Felicitas; he had seen her too recently. But that Mrs. Bilton should be kidnapped seemed to him to touch the lowest depths of American criminal enterprise and depravity. At the same time though he recoiled before this fresh blow a thought did fan through his mind with a wonderful effect of coolness and silence,—"Then they'll gag her," he said.

"What?" cried Anna-Rose, as though a whip had lashed her. "Gag her?" And pulling open the gate and running out to him as one possessed she cried again, "Gag Columbus?"

"Oh that's it, is it," said Mr. Twist, with relief but also with disappointment, "Well, if it's that way I can tell you—"

He stopped; there was no need to tell her; for round the bend of the lane, walking bare-headed in the chequered light and shade as leisurely as if such things as tours of absence didn't exist, or a distracted household, or an anguished Christopher, with indeed, a complete, an extraordinary serenity, advanced Anna-Felicitas.

Always placid, her placidity at this moment had a shining quality. Still smug, she was now of a glorified smugness. If one could imagine a lily turned into a god, or a young god turned into a lily and walking down the middle of a sun-flecked Californian lane, it wouldn't be far out, thought Mr. Twist, as an image of the advancing Twinkler. The god would be so young that he was still a boy, and he wouldn't be worrying much about anything in the past or in the future, and he'd just be coming along like that with the corners of his mouth a little turned up, and his fair hair a little ruffled, and his charming young face full of a sober and abstracted radiance.

"Not much kidnapping there, I guess," said Mr. Twist with a jerk of his thumb. "And you take it from me, Anna I.," he added quickly, leaning over towards her, determined to get off to the garage before he found himself faced by both twins together, "that when next your imagination gets the jumps the best thing you can do is to hold on to it hard till it settles down again, instead of wasting your time and ruining your constitution going pale."

And he started the Ford with a bound, and got away round the corner into the yard.

Here, in the yard, was peace; at least for the moment. The only living thing in it was a cat the twins had acquired, through the services of one of the experts, as an indispensable object in a really homey home. The first thing this cat had done had been to eat the canary, which gave the twins much unacknowledged relief. It was, they thought secretly, quite a good plan to have one's pets inside each other,—it kept them so quiet. She now sat unmoved in the middle of the yard, carefully cleaning her whiskers while Mr. Twist did some difficult fancy driving in order to get into the stable without inconveniencing her.

Admirable picture of peace, thought Mr. Twist with a sigh of envy.

He might have got out and picked her up, but he was glad to manoeuvre about, reversing and making intricate figures in the dust, because it kept him longer away from the luncheon-table. The cat took no notice of him, but continued to deal with her whiskers even when his front wheel was within two inches of her tail, for though she hadn't been long at The Open Arms she had already sized up Mr. Twist and was aware that he wouldn't hurt a fly.

Thanks to her he had a lot of trouble getting the Ford into the stable, all of which he liked because of that luncheon-table; and having got it in he still lingered fiddling about with it, examining its engine and wiping its bonnet; and then when he couldn't do that any longer he went out and lingered in the yard, looking down at the cat with his hands in his pockets. "I must think," he kept on saying to himself.

"Lunchee," said Li Koo, putting his head out of the kitchen window.

"All right," said Mr. Twist.

He stooped down as though to examine the cat's ear. The cat, who didn't like her ears touched but was prepared to humour him, got out of it by lying down on her back and showing him her beautiful white stomach. She was a black cat, with a particularly beautiful white stomach, and she had discovered that nobody could see it without wanting to stroke it. Whenever she found herself in a situation that threatened to become disagreeable she just lay down and showed her stomach. Human beings in similar predicaments can only show their tact.

"Nice pussy—nice, nice pussy," said Mr. Twist aloud, stroking this irresistible object slowly, and forgetting her ear as she had intended he should.

"Lunchee get cold," said Li Koo, again putting his head out of the kitchen window. "Mis' Bilton say, Come in."

"All right," said Mr. Twist.

He straightened himself and looked round the yard. A rake that should have been propped up against the tool-shed with some other gardening tools had fallen down. He crossed over and picked it up and stood it up carefully again.

Li Koo watched him impassively from the window.

"Mis' Bilton come out," he said; and there she was in the yard door.

"Mr. Twist," she called shrilly, "if you don't come in right away and have your food before it gets all mushed up with cold I guess you'll be sorry."

"All right—coming," he called back very loud and cheerfully, striding towards her as one strides who knows there is nothing for it now but courage. "All right, Mrs. Bilton—sorry if I've kept you waiting. You shouldn't have bothered about me—"

And saying things like this in a loud voice, for to hear himself being loud made him feel more supported, he strode into the house, through the house, and out on to the verandah.

They always lunched on the verandah. The golden coloured awning was down, and the place was full of a golden shade. Beyond it blazed the garden. Beneath it was the flower-adorned table set as usual ready for four, and he went out to it, strung up to finding the Annas at the table, Anna-Felicitas in her usual seat with her back to the garden, her little fair head outlined against the glowing light as he had seen it every day since they had lived in the inn, Anna-Rose opposite, probably volubly and passionately addressing her.

And there was no one.

"Why—" he said, stopping short.

"Yes. It's real silly of them not to come and eat before everything is spoilt," said Mrs. Bilton bustling up, who had stayed behind to give an order to Li Koo. And she went to the edge of the verandah and shaded her eyes and called, "Gurls! Gurls! I guess you can do all that talking better after lunch."

He then saw that down at the bottom of the garden, in the most private place as regards being overheard, partly concealed by some arum lilies that grew immensely there like splendid weeds, stood the twins facing each other.

"Better leave them alone," he said quickly. "They'll come when they're ready. There's nothing like getting through with one's talking right away,

Mrs. Bilton. Besides," he went on still more quickly for she plainly didn't agree with him and was preparing to sally out into the sun and fetch them in, "you and I don't often get a chance of a quiet chat together—"

And this, combined with the resolute way he was holding her chair ready for her, brought Mrs. Bilton back under the awning again.

She was flattered. Mr. Twist had not yet spoken to her in quite that tone. He had always been the gentleman, but never yet the eager gentleman. Now he was unmistakably both.

She came back and sat down, and so with a sigh of thankfulness immediately did he, for here was an unexpected respite,—while Mrs. Bilton talked he could think. Fortunately she never noticed if one wasn't listening. For the first time since he had known her he gave himself up willingly to the great broad stream that at once started flowing over him, on this occasion with something of the comfort of warm water, and he was very glad indeed that anyhow that day she wasn't gagged.

While he ate, he kept on furtively looking down the garden at the two figures facing each other by the arum lilies. Whenever Mrs. Bilton remembered them and wanted to call them in, as she did at the different stages, of the meal,—at the salad, at the pudding—he stopped her. She became more and more pleased by his evident determination to lunch alone with her, for after all one remains female to the end, and her conversation took on a gradual tinge of Mr. Bilton's views about second marriages. They had been liberal views; for Mr. Bilton, she said, had had no post-mortem pettiness about him, but they were lost on Mr. Twist, whose thoughts were so painfully preoccupied by first marriage.

The conclusions he came to during that trying meal while Mrs. Bilton talked, were that he would propose first to Anna-Rose, she being the eldest and such a course being accordingly natural, and, if she refused, proceed at once to propose to Anna-Felicitas. But before proceeding to Anna-Felicitas, a course he regarded with peculiar misgiving, he would very earnestly explain to Anna-Rose the seriousness of the situation and the necessity, the urgency, the sanity of her marrying him. These proposals would be kept on the cool level of strict business. Every trace of the affection with which he was so overflowing would be sternly excluded. For instance, he wasn't going to let himself remember the feel of Christopher's little head the afternoon before when he patted it to comfort her. Such remembrances would be bound to bring a warmth into his remarks which wouldn't be fair. The situation demanded the most scrupulous fairness and delicacy in its treatment, the most careful avoidance of taking any advantage of it. But how difficult, thought Mr. Twist, his hand shaking as he poured himself out a glass of iced water, how difficult when he loved the Annas so inconveniently much.

Mrs. Bilton observed the shaking of his hand, and felt more female than ever.

Still, there it was, this situation forced upon them all by the war. Nobody could help it, and it had to be faced with calmness, steadfastness and tact. Calmness, steadfastness and tact, repeated Mr. Twist, raising the water to his mouth and spilling some of it.

Mrs. Bilton observed this too, and felt still more female.

Marriage was the quickest, and really the only, way out of it. He saw that now. The lawyer had been quite right. And marriage, he would explain to the Annas, would be a mere formal ceremony which after the war they— he meant, of course, she—could easily in that land of facile and honourable divorce get rid of. Meanwhile, he would point out, they—she, of course; bother these twins—would be safely American, and he would undertake never to intrude love on them—her—unless by some wonderful chance, it was wanted. Some wonderful chance ... Mr. Twist's spectacles suddenly went dim, and he gulped down more water.

Yes. That was the line to take: the austere line of self-mortification for the Twinkler good. One Twinkler would be his wife—again at the dear word he had to gulp down water—and one his sister-in-law. They would just have to agree to this plan. The position was too serious for shilly-shallying. Yes. That was the line to take; and by the time he had got to the coffee it was perfectly clear and plain to him.

But he felt dreadfully damp. He longed for a liqueur, for anything that would support him....

"Is there any brandy in the house?" he suddenly flung across the web of Mrs. Bilton's words.

"Brandy, Mr. Twist?" she repeated, at this feeling altogether female, for what an unusual thing for him to ask for,—"You're not sick?"

"With my coffee," murmured Mr. Twist, his mouth very slack, his head drooping. "It's nice...."

"I'll go and see," said Mrs. Bilton, getting up briskly and going away rattling a bunch of keys.

At once he looked down the garden. Anna-Felicitas was in the act of putting her arm round Anna-Rose's shoulder, and Anna-Rose was passionately disengaging herself. Yes. There was trouble there. He knew there would be.

He gulped down more water.

Anna-Felicitas couldn't expect to go off like that for a whole morning and give Anna-Rose a horrible fright without hearing about it. Besides, the expression on her face wanted explaining,—a lot of explaining. Mr. Twist didn't like to think so, but Anna-Felicitas's recent conduct seemed to him almost artful. It seemed to him older than her years. It seemed to justify the lawyer's scepticism when he described the twins to him as children. That young man Elliott—

But here Mr. Twist started and lost his thread of thought, for looking once more down the garden he saw that Anna-Felicitas was coming towards the verandah, and that she was alone. Anna-Rose had vanished. Why had he bothered about brandy, and let Mrs. Bilton go? He had counted, somehow, on beginning with Anna-Rose....

He seized a cigarette and lit it. He tried vainly to keep his hand steady. Before the cigarette was fairly plight there was Anna-Felicitas, walking in beneath the awning.

"I'm glad you're alone," she said, "for I want to speak to you."

And Mr. Twist felt that his hour had come.

CHAPTER XXXVII

"Hadn't you better have lunch first?" he asked, though he knew from the look on her face that she wouldn't. It was a very remarkable look. It was as though an angel, dwelling in perfect bliss, had unaccountably got its feet wet. Not more troubled than that; a little troubled, but not more than that.

"No thank you," she said politely. "But if you've finished yours, do you mind coming into the office? Because otherwise Mrs. Bilton—"

"She's fetching me some brandy," said Mr. Twist.

"I didn't know you drank," said Anna-Felicitas, even at this moment interested. "But do you mind having it afterwards? Because otherwise Mrs. Bilton—"

"I guess the idea was to have it first," said Mr. Twist.

She was however already making for the tea-room, proceeding towards it without hurry, and with a single-mindedness that would certainly get her there.

He could only follow.

In the office she said, "Do you mind shutting the door?"

"Not at all," said Mr. Twist; but he did mind. His hour had come, and he wasn't liking it. He wanted to begin with Anna-Rose. He wanted to get things clear with her first before dealing with this one. There was less of Anna-Rose. And her dear little head yesterday when he patted it.... And she needed comforting.... Anna-Rose cried, and let herself be comforted.... And it was so sweet to Mr. Twist to comfort....

"Christopher—" began Anna-Felicitas, directly he had shut the door.

"I know. She's mad with you. What can you expect, Anna II.?" he interrupted in a very matter-of-fact voice, leaning against a bookcase. Even a bookcase was better than nothing to lean against.

"Christopher is being unreasonable," said Anna-Felicitas, her voice softer and gentler than he had yet heard it.

Then she stopped, and considered him a moment with much of the look of one who on a rather cold day considers the sea before diving in—with, that is, a slight but temporary reluctance to proceed.

"Won't you sit down?" said Mr. Twist.

"Perhaps I'd better," she said, disposing herself in the big chair. "It's very strange, but my legs feel funny. You wouldn't think being in love would make one want to sit down."

"I beg your pardon?" said Mr. Twist.

"I have fallen in love," said Anna-Felicitas, looking up at him with a kind of pensive radiance. "I did it this morning."

Mr. Twist stared at her. "I beg your—what did you say?" he asked.

She said, still with that air as she regarded him of pensive radiance, of not seeing him but something beyond him that was very beautiful to her and satisfactory, "I've fallen in love, and I can't tell you how pleased I am because I've always been afraid I was going to find it a difficult thing to do. But it wasn't. Quite the contrary."

Then, as he only staged at her, she said, "He's coming round this afternoon on the new footing, and I wanted to prepare your and Christopher's minds in good time so that you shouldn't be surprised."

And having said this she lapsed into what was apparently, judging from her expression, a silent contemplation of her bliss.

"But you're too young," burst out Mr. Twist.

"Too young?" repeated Anna-Felicitas, coming out of her contemplation for a moment to smile at him. "We don't think so."

Well. This beat everything.

Mr. Twist could only stare down at her.

Conflicting emotions raged in him. He couldn't tell for a moment what they were, they were so violent and so varied. How dared Elliott. How dared a person they had none of them heard of that time yesterday come making love to a girl he had never seen before. And in such a hurry. So suddenly. So instantly. Here had he himself been with the twins constantly for weeks, and wouldn't have dreamed of making love to them. They had been sacred to him. And it wasn't as if he hadn't wanted to hug them often and often, but he had restrained himself as a gentleman should from the highest motives of delicacy, and consideration, and respect, and propriety, besides a great doubt as to whether they wouldn't very energetically mind. And then comes along this blundering Britisher, and straight away tumbles right in where Mr. Twist had feared to tread, and within twenty-four hours had persuaded Anna-Felicitas to think she was in love. New footing indeed. There hadn't been an old footing yet. And who was this Elliott? And how was Mr. Twist going to be able to find out if he were a proper person to be allowed to pay his addresses to one so precious as a Twinkler twin?

Anger, jealousy, anxiety, sense of responsibility and mortification, all tumbled about furiously together inside Mr. Twist as he leaned against the bookcase and gazed down at Anna-Felicitas, who for her part was gazing beatifically into space; but through the anger, and the jealousy, and the anxiety, and the sense of responsibility and mortification one great thought was struggling, and it finally pushed every other aside and got out to the top of the welter: here, in the chair before him, he beheld his sister-in-law. So much at least was cleared up.

He crossed to the bureau and dragged his office-stool over next to her and sat down. "So that's it, is it?" he said, trying to speak very calmly, but his face pulled all sorts of ways, as it had so often been since the arrival in his life of the twins.

"Yes," she said, coming out of her contemplation. "It's love at last."

"I don't know about at last. Whichever way you look at it, Anna II., that don't seem to hit it off as a word. What I meant was, it's Elliott."

"Yes," said Anna-Felicitas. "Which is the same thing. I believe," she added, "I now have to allude to him as John."

Mr. Twist made another effort to speak calmly. "You don't," he said, "think it at all unusual or undesirable that you should be calling a man John to-day of whom you'd never heard yesterday."

"I think it's wonderful," said Anna-Felicitas beaming.

"It doesn't strike you in any way as imprudent to be so hasty. It doesn't strike you as foolish."

"On the contrary," said Anna-Felicitas. "I can't help thinking I've been very clever. I shouldn't have thought it of myself. You see, I'm not *naturally* quick." And she beamed with what she evidently regarded as a pardonable pride.

"It doesn't strike you as even a little—well, a little improper."

"On the contrary," said Anna-Felicitas. "Aunt Alice told us that the one man one could never be improper about, even if one tried, was one's husband."

"Husband?" Mr. Twist winced. He loved, as we have seen, the word wife, but then that was different.

"It's not time yet to talk of husbands," he said, full of a flaming unreasonableness and jealousy and the sore feeling that he who had been toiling so long and so devotedly in the heat of the Twinkler sun had had a most unfair march stolen on him by this eleventh-hour stranger.

He flamed with unreasonableness. Yet he knew this was the solution of half his problem, — and of much the worst half, for it was after all Anna-Felicitas who had produced the uncomfortable feeling of slipperiness, of eels; Anna-Rose had been quite good, sitting in a chair crying and just so sweetly needing comfort. But now that the solution was presented to him he was full of fears. For on what now could he base his proposal to Anna-Rose? Elliott would be the legitimate protector of both the Twinklers. Mr. Twist, who had been so much perturbed by the idea of having to propose to one or other twin, was miserably upset by the realization that now he needn't propose to either. Elliott had cut the ground from under his feet. He had indeed — what was the expression he used the evening before? — yes, nipped in. There was now no necessity for Anna-Rose to marry him, and Mr. Twist had an icy and forlorn feeling that on no other basis except necessity would she. He was thirty-five. It was all very well for Elliott to get proposing to people of seventeen; he couldn't be more than twenty-five. And it wasn't only age. Mr. Twist hadn't shaved before looking-glasses for nothing, and he was very distinctly aware that Elliott was extremely attractive.

"It's not time yet to talk of husbands," he therefore hotly and jealously said.

"On the contrary," said Anna-Felicitas gently, "it's not only time but war-time. The war, I have observed, is making people be quick and sudden about all sorts of things."

"You haven't observed it. That's Elliott said that."

"He may have," said Anna-Felicitas. "He said so many things—"

And again she lapsed into contemplation; into, thought Mr. Twist as he gazed jealously at her profile, an ineffable, ruminating, reminiscent smugness.

"See here, Anna II.," he said, finding it impossibly painful to wait while she contemplated, "suppose you don't at this particular crisis fall into quite so many ecstatic meditations. There isn't as much time as you seem to think."

"No—and there's Christopher," said Anna-Felicitas, giving herself a shake, and with that slightly troubled look coming into her face again as of having, in spite of being an angel in glory, somehow got her feet wet.

"Precisely," said Mr. Twist, getting up and walking about the room. "There's Christopher. Now Christopher, I should say, would be pretty well heart-broken over this."

"But that's so unreasonable," said Anna-Felicitas with gentle deprecation.

"You're all she has got, and she'll be under the impression—the remarkably vivid impression—that she's losing you."

"But *that's* so unreasonable. She isn't losing me. It's sheer gain. Without the least effort or bother on her part she's acquiring a brother-in-law."

"Oh, I know what Christopher feels," said Mr. Twist, going up and down the room quickly. "I know right enough, because I feel it all myself."

"But *that's* so unreasonable," said Anna-Felicitas earnestly. "Why should two of you be feeling things that aren't?"

"She has always regarded herself as responsible for you, and I shouldn't be surprised if she were terribly shocked at your conduct."

"But there has to *be* conduct," said Anna-Felicitas, still very gentle, but looking as though her feet were getting wetter. "I don't see how anybody is ever to fall in love unless there's been some conduct first."

"Oh, don't argue—don't argue. You can't expect Anna-Rose not to mind your wanting to marry a perfect stranger, a man she hasn't even seen."

"But everybody you marry started by being a perfect stranger and somebody you hadn't ever seen," said Anna-Felicitas.

"Oh Lord, if only you wouldn't *argue!*" exclaimed Mr. Twist. "And as for your aunt in England, what's she going to say to this twenty-four-hours, quick-lunch sort of engagement? She'll be terribly upset. And Anna-Rose knows that, and is I expect nigh worried crazy."

"But what," asked Anna-Felicitas, "have aunts to do with love?"

Then she said very earnestly, her face a little flushed, her eyes troubled, "Christopher said all that you're saying now, and a lot more, down in the garden before I came to you, and I said what I've been saying to you, and a lot more, but she wouldn't listen. And when I found she wouldn't listen I tried to comfort her, but she wouldn't be comforted. And then I came to you; for besides wanting to tell you what I've done I wanted to ask you to comfort Christopher."

Mr. Twist paused a moment in his walk. "Yes," he said, staring at the carpet. "Yes. I can very well imagine she needs it. But I don't suppose anything I would say—"

"Christopher is very fond of you," said Anna-Felicitas gently.

"Oh yes. You're both very fond of me," said Mr. Twist, pulling his mouth into a crooked and unhappy smile.

"We love you," said Anna-Felicitas simply.

Mr. Twist looked at her, and a mist came over his spectacles. "You dear children," he said, "you dear, dear children—"

"I don't know about children—" began Anna-Felicitas; but was interrupted by a knock at the door.

"It's only the brandy," said Mr. Twist, seeing her face assume the expression he had learned to associate with the approach of Mrs. Bilton. "Take it away, please Mrs. Bilton," he called out, "and put it on the—"

Mrs. Bilton however, didn't take anything away, but opened the door an inch instead. "There's someone wants to speak to you, Mr. Twist," she said in a loud whisper, thrusting in a card. "He says he just must. I found him on the verandah when I took your brandy out, and as I'm not the woman to leave a stranger alone with good brandy I brought him in with me, and he's right here back of me in the tea-room."

"It's John," remarked Anna-Felicitas placidly. "Come early."

"I say—" said a voice behind Mrs. Bilton.

"Yes," nodded Anna-Felicitas, getting up out of the deep chair. "That's John."

"I say—may I come in? I've got something important—"

Mr. Twist looked at Anna-Felicitas. "Wouldn't you rather—?" he began.

"I don't mind John," she said softly, her face flooded with a most beautiful light.

Mr. Twist opened the door and went out. "Come in," he said. "Mrs. Bilton, may I present Mr. Elliott to you—Commander Elliott of the British Navy."

"Pleased to meet you, Commander Elliott," said Mrs. Bilton. "Mr. Twist, your brandy is on the verandah. Shall I bring it to you in here?"

"No thank you, Mrs. Bilton. I'll go out there presently. Perhaps you wouldn't mind waiting for me there—I don't suppose Mr. Elliott will want to keep me long. Come in, Mr. Elliott."

And having disposed of Mrs. Bilton, who was in a particularly willing and obedient and female mood, he motioned Elliott into the office.

There stood Anna-Felicitas.

Elliott stopped dead.

"This isn't fair," he said, his eyes twinkling and dancing.

"What isn't?" inquired Anna-Felicitas gently, beaming at him.

"Your being here. I've got to talk business. Look here, sir," he said, turning to Mr. Twist, "could *you* talk business with her there?"

"Not if she argued," said Mr. Twist.

"Argued! I wouldn't mind her arguing. It's just her being there. I've got to talk business," he said, turning to Anna-Felicitas,—"business about marrying you. And how can I with you standing there looking like—well, like that?"

"I don't know," said Anna-Felicitas placidly, not moving.

"But you'll interrupt—just your being there will interrupt. I shall see you out of the corner of my eye, and it'll be impossible not to—I mean I know I'll want to—I mean, Anna-Felicitas my dear, it isn't done. I've got to explain all sorts of things to your guardian—"

"He isn't my guardian," corrected the accurate Anna-Felicitas gently. "He only very nearly once was." "Well, anyhow I've got to explain a lot of things that'll take some time, and it isn't so much explain as persuade—for I expect," he said, turning to Mr. Twist, "this strikes you as a bit sudden, sir?"

"It would strike anybody," said Mr. Twist trying to be stern but finding it difficult, for Elliott was so disarmingly engaging and so disarmingly in love. The radiance on Anna-Felicitas's face might have been almost a reflection caught from his. Mr. Twist had never seen two people look so happy. He had never, of course, before been present at the first wonderful dawning of love. The whole room seemed to glow with the surprise of it.

"There. You see?" said Elliott, again appealing to Anna-Felicitas, who stood smiling beatifically at him without moving. "I've got to explain that it isn't after all as mad as it seems, and that I'm a fearfully decent chap and can give you lots to eat, and that I've got a jolly little sister here who's respectable and well-known besides, and I'm going to produce references to back up these assertions, and proofs that I'm perfectly sound in health except for my silly foot, which isn't health but just foot and which you don't seem to mind anyhow, and how—I ask you *how*, Anna-Felicitas my dear, am I to do any of this with you standing there looking like—well, like that?"

"I don't know," said Anna-Felicitas again, still not moving.

"Anna-Felicitas, my dear," he said, "won't you go?"

"No, John," said Anna-Felicitas gently.

His eyes twinkled and danced more than ever. He took a step towards her, then checked himself and looked round beseechingly at Mr. Twist.

"*Somebody's* got to go," he said.

"Yes," said Mr. Twist. "And I guess it's me."

CHAPTER XXXVIII

He went straight in search of Anna-Rose.

He was going to propose to her. He couldn't bear it. He couldn't bear the idea of his previous twins, his blessed little Twinklers, both going out of his life at the same time, and he couldn't bear, after what he had just seen in the office, the loneliness of being left outside love.

All his life he had stood on the door-mat outside the shut door of love. He had had no love; neither at home, where they talked so much about it and there wasn't any, nor, because of his home and its inhibitions got so thoroughly into his blood, anywhere else. He had never tried to marry,—again because of his home and his mother and the whole only-son-of-a-widow business. He would try now. He would risk it. It was awful to risk it, but it was more awful not to. He adored Anna-Rose. How nearly the afternoon before, when she sat crying in his chair, had he taken her in his arms! Why, he would have taken her into them then and there, while she was in that state, while she was in the need of comfort, and never let her go out of them again, if it hadn't been that he had got the idea so firmly fixed in his head that she was a child. Fool that he was. Elliott had dispelled that idea for him. It wasn't children who looked as Anna-Felicitas had looked just now in the office. Anna-Rose, it is true, seemed younger than Anna-Felicitas, but that was because she was little and easily cried. He loved her for being little. He loved her because she easily cried. He yearned and hungered to comfort, to pet to take care of. He was, as has been pointed out, a born mother.

Avoiding the verandah and Mrs. Bilton, Mr. Twist filled with recklessness, hurried upstairs and knocked at Anna-Rose's door. No answer. He listened. Dead silence. He opened it a slit and peeped in. Emptiness. Down he went again and made for the kitchen, because Li Koo, who always knew everything, might know where she was. Li Koo did. He jerked his head towards the window, and Mr. Twist hurried to it and looked out. There in the middle of the yard was the cat, exactly where he had left her an hour before, and kneeling beside her stroking her stomach was Anna-Rose.

She had her back to the house and her face was hidden. The sun streamed down on her bare head and on the pale gold rings of hair that frisked round her neck. She didn't hear him till he was close to her, so much absorbed was she apparently in the cat; and when she did she didn't look up, but bent her head lower than before and stroked more assiduously.

"Anna-Rose," said Mr. Twist.

"Yes."

"Come and talk to me."

"I'm thinking."

"Don't think. Come and talk to me, little—little dear one."

She bent her head lower still. "I'm thinking," she said again.

"Come and tell me what you're thinking."

"I'm thinking about cats."

"About cats?" said Mr. Twist, uncertainly.

"Yes," said Anna-Rose, stroking the cat's stomach faster and carefully keeping her face hidden from him. "About how wise and wonderful they are."

"Well then if that's all, you can go on with that presently and come and talk to me now."

"You see," said Anna-Rose, not heeding this, "they're invariably twins, and more than twins, for they're often fours and sometimes sixes, but still they sit in the sun quietly all their lives and don't mind a bit what their— what their twins do—"

"Ah," said Mr. Twist. "Now I'm getting there."

"They don't mind a bit about anything. They just clean their whiskers and they purr. Perhaps it's that that comforts them. Perhaps if I—if I had whiskers and a—and a purr—"

The cat leaped suddenly to her feet and shook herself violently. Something hot and wet had fallen on her beautiful stomach.

Anna-Rose made a little sound strangers might have taken for a laugh as she put out her arms and caught her again, but it was a sound so wretched, so piteous in the attempt to hide away from him, that Mr. Twist's heart stood still. "Oh, don't go," she said, catching at the cat and hugging her tight, "I can't let *you* go—" And she buried her face in her fur, so that Mr. Twist still couldn't see it.

"Now that's enough about the cat," he said, speaking very firmly. "You're coming with me." And he stooped and picked her up, cat and all, and set her on her feet.

Then he saw her face.

"Good God, Anna-Rose!" he exclaimed.

"I did try not to show you," she said; and she added, taking shelter behind her pride and looking at him as defiantly as she could out of eyes almost closed up, "but you mustn't suppose just because I happen to—to seem as if I'd been crying that I—that I'm minding anything."

"Oh no," said Mr. Twist, who at sight of her face had straightway forgotten about himself and his longings and his proposals, and only knew that he must comfort Christopher. "Oh no," he said, looking at her aghast, "I'm not supposing we're minding anything, either of us."

He took her by the arm. Comfort Christopher; that's what he had got to do. Get rid as quickly as possible of that look of agony—yes, it was downright agony—on her face.

He thought he guessed what she was thinking and feeling; he thought— he was pretty sure—she was thinking and feeling that her beloved Columbus had gone from her, and gone to a stranger, in a day, in a few hours, to a stranger she had never even seen, never even heard of; that her Columbus had had secrets from her, had been doing things behind her back; that she had had perfect faith and trust in her twin, and now was tasting the dreadful desolation of betrayal; and he also guessed that she must be sick with fears,—for he knew how responsible she felt, how seriously she took the charge of her beautiful twin—sick with fear about this unknown man, sick with the feeling of helplessness, of looking on while Columbus rushed into what might well be, for all any one knew, a deadly mess-up of her happiness.

Well, he could reason her out of most of this, he felt. Certainly he could reassure her about Elliott, who did inspire one with confidence, who did seem, anyhow outwardly, a very fitting mate for Anna-Felicitas. But he was aghast at the agony on her face. All that he guessed she was thinking and feeling didn't justify it. It was unreasonable to suffer so violently on account of what was, after all, a natural happening. But however unreasonable it was, she was suffering.

He took her by the arm. "You come right along with me," he said; and led her out of the yard, away from Li Koo and the kitchen window, towards the eucalyptus grove behind the house. "You come right along with me," he repeated, holding her firmly for she was very wobbly on her feet, "and we'll tell each other all about the things we're not minding. Do you remember when the *St. Luke* left Liverpool? You thought I thought you were minding things then, and were very angry with me. We've made friends since, haven't we, and we aren't going to mind anything ever again except each other."

But he hardly knew what he was saying, so great was his concern and distress.

Anna-Rose went blindly. She stumbled along, helped by him, clutching the cat. She couldn't see out of her swollen eyes. Her foot caught in a root, and the cat, who had for some minutes past been thoroughly uneasy, became panic-stricken and struggled out of her arms, and fled into the wood. She tried to stop it, but it would go. For some reason this broke down her self-control. The warm cat clutched to her breast had at least been something living to hold on to. Now the very cat had gone. Her pride collapsed, and she tumbled against Mr. Twist's arm and just sobbed.

If ever a man felt like a mother it was Mr. Twist at that moment. He promptly sat her down on the grass. "There now—there, there now," he said, whipping out his handkerchief and anxiously mopping up her face. "This is what I did on the *St. Luke*—do you remember?—there now—that time you told me about your mother—it looks like being my permanent job—there, there now—don't now—you'll have no little eyes left soon if you go on like this—"

"Oh but—oh but—Co-Columbus—"

"Yes, yes I know all about Columbus. Don't you worry about her. She's all right. She's all right in the office at this moment, and we're all right out here if only you knew it, if only you wouldn't cry such quantities. It beats me where it all comes from, and you so little—there, there now—"

"Oh but—oh but Columbus—"

"Yes, yes, I know—you're worrying yourself sick because you think you're responsible for her to your aunt and uncle, but you won't be, you know, once she's married—there, there now—"

"Oh but—oh but—"

"Now don't—now please—yes, yes, I know—he's a stranger, and you haven't seen him yet, but everybody was a stranger once," said Mr. Twist, quoting Anna-Felicitas's own argument, the one that had especially irritated him half-an-hour before, "and he's real good—I'm sure of it. And you'll be sure too the minute you see him. That's to say, if you're able to see anything or anybody for the next week out of your unfortunate stuck-together little eyes."

"Oh but—oh but—you don't—you haven't—"

"Yes, yes, I have. Now turn your face so that I can wipe the other side properly. There now, I caught an enormous tear. I got him just in time before he trickled into your ear. Lord, how sore your poor little eyes are. Don't it even cheer you to think you're going to be a sister-in-law, Anna-Rose?"

"Oh but you don't—you haven't—" she sobbed, her face not a whit less agonized for all his reassurances.

"Well, I know I wish I were going to be a brother-in-law," said Mr. Twist, worried by his inability to reassure, as he tenderly and carefully dabbed about the corners of her eyes and her soaked eyelashes. "My, shouldn't I think well of myself."

Then his hand shook.

"I wish I were going to be Anna-Felicitas's brother-in-law," he said, suddenly impelled, perhaps by this failure to get rid of the misery in her face, to hurl himself on his fate. "Not *yours*—get your mind quite clear about that,—but Anna-Felicitas's." And his hand shook so much that he had to leave off drying. For this was a proposal. If only Anna-Rose would see it, this was a proposal.

Anna-Rose, however, saw nothing. Even in normal times she wasn't good at relationships, and had never yet understood the that-man's-father-was-my-father's-son one; now she simply didn't hear. She was sitting with her hands limply in her lap, and sobbing in a curious sort of anguish.

He couldn't help being struck by it. There was more in this than he had grasped. Again he forgot himself and his proposal. Again he was overwhelmed by the sole desire to help and comfort.

He put his hand on the two hands lying with such an air of being forgotten on her lap. "What is it?" he asked gently. "Little dear one, tell me. It's clear I'm not dead on to it yet."

"Oh—Columbus—"

She seemed to writhe in her misery.

"Well yes, yes Columbus. We know all about that."

Anna-Rose turned her quivering face to him. "Oh, you haven't seen— you don't see—it's only me that's seen—"

"Seen what? What haven't I seen? Ah, don't cry—don't cry like that—"

"Oh, I've lost her—lost her—"

"Lost her? Because she's marrying?"

"Lost her—lost her—" sobbed Anna-Rose.

"Come now," remonstrated Mr. Twist. "Come now. That's just flat contrary to the facts. You've lost nothing, and you've gained a brother."

"Oh,—lost her—lost her," sobbed Anna-Rose.

"Come, come now," said Mr. Twist helplessly.

"Oh," she sobbed, looking at him out of her piteous eyes, "has nobody thought of it but me? Columbus hasn't. I—I know she hasn't from what— from what—she said. She's too—too happy to think. But—haven't you thought—haven't you seen—that she'll be English now—really English— and go away from me to England with him—and I—I can't go to England— because I'm still—I'm still—an alien enemy—and so I've lost her—lost her—lost my own twin—"

And Anna-Rose dropped her head on to her knees and sobbed in an abandonment of agony.

Mr. Twist sat without saying or doing anything at all. He hadn't thought of this; nor, he was sure, had Anna-Felicitas. And it was true. Now he understood Anna-Rose's face and the despair of it. He sat looking at her, overwhelmed by the realization of her misfortune. For a moment he was blinded by it, and didn't see what it would mean for him. Then he did see. He almost leaped, so sudden was the vision, and so luminous.

"Anna-Rose," he said, his voice trembling, "I want to put my arm round you. That's because I love you. And if you'll let me do that I could tell you of a way there is out of this for you. But I can't tell you so well unless—unless you let me put my arm round you first...."

He waited trembling. She only sobbed. He couldn't even be sure she was listening. So he put his arm round her to try. At least she didn't resist. So he drew her closer. She didn't resist that either. He couldn't even be sure she knew about it. So he put his other arm round her too, and though he couldn't be sure, he thought—he hardly dared think, but it did seem as if—she nestled.

Happiness, such as in his lonely, loveless life he had never imagined, flooded Mr. Twist. He looked down at her face, which was now so close to his, and saw that her eyes were shut. Great sobs went on shaking her little body, and her tears, now that he wasn't wiping them, were rolling down her cheeks unchecked.

He held her closer to him, close to his heart where she belonged, and again he had that sensation, that wonderful sensation, of nestling.

"Little Blessed, the way out is so simple," he whispered. "Little Blessed, don't you see?"

But whether Anna-Rose saw seemed very doubtful. There was only that feeling, as to which he was no doubt mistaken, of nestling to go on. Her eyes, anyhow, remained shut, and her body continued to heave with sobs.

He bent his head lower. His voice shook. "It's so, so simple," he whispered. "All you've got to do is to marry me."

And as she made an odd little movement in his arms he held her tighter and began to talk very fast.

"No, no," he said, "don't answer anything yet. Just listen. Just let me tell you first. I want to tell you to start with how terribly I love you. But that doesn't mean you've got to love me—you needn't if you don't want to—if you can't—if you'd rather not I'm eighteen years older than you, and I know what I'm like to look at—no, don't say anything yet—just listen quiet first—but if you married me you'd be an American right away, don't you see? Just as Anna-Felicitas is going to be English. And I always intended going back to England as soon as may be, and if you married me what is to prevent your coming too? Coming to England? With Anna-Felicitas and her husband. Anna-Rose—little Blessed—think of it—all of us together. There won't be any aliens in that quartette, I guess, and the day you marry me you'll be done with being German for good and all. And don't you get supposing it matters about your not loving me, because, you see, I love you so much, I adore you so terribly, that anyhow there'll be more than enough love to go round, and you needn't ever worry about contributing any if you don't feel like it—"

Mr. Twist broke off abruptly. "What say?" he said, for Anna-Rose was making definite efforts to speak. She was also making definite and unmistakable movements, and this time there could be no doubt about it; she was coming closer.

"What say?" said Mr. Twist breathlessly, bending his head.

"But I do," whispered Anna-Rose.

"Do what?" said Mr. Twist, again breathlessly.

She turned her face up to his. On it was the same look he had lately seen on Anna-Felicitas's, shining through in spite of the disfiguration of her tears.

"But—*of course* I do," whispered Anna-Rose, an extraordinary smile, an awe-struck sort of smile, coming into her face at the greatness of her happiness, at the wonder of it.

"What? Do what?" said Mr. Twist, still more breathlessly.

"I—always did," whispered Anna-Rose.

"*What* did you always did?" gasped Mr. Twist, hardly able to believe it, and yet—and yet—there on her little face, on her little transfigured face, shone the same look.

"Oh—*love* you," sighed Anna-Rose, nestling as close as she could get.

It was Mr. Twist himself who got on a ladder at five minutes past four that afternoon and pasted a strip of white paper obliquely across the sign of The Open Arms with the word.

SHUT

on it in big letters. Li Koo held the foot of the ladder. Mr. Twist had only remembered the imminence of four o'clock and the German inrush a few minutes before the hour, because of his being so happy; and when he did he flew to charcoal and paper. He got the strip on only just in time. A car drove up as he came down the ladder.

"What?" exclaimed the principal male occupant of the car, pointing, thwarted and astonished, to the sign.

"Shut," said Mr. Twist.

"Shut?"

"Shut."